ETERNAL PUPPY™

Groundbreaking Veterinary Advances
to Enrich Your Senior Dog's Life

By Janice Willard DVM

A KENNEL CLUB BOOK®

Dedication

To my mother Alice Mildred Schreiber, who always
believed, always encouraged and always
supported my dreams.

EDITORIAL

Andrew DePrisco	*Editor-in-Chief*
Peter Bauer	*Managing Editor*
Amy Deputato	*Senior Editor*
Jonathan Nigro	*Editor*
Matt Strubel	*Assistant Editor*

ART

Sherise Buhagiar	*Graphic Layout*
Bill Jonas	*Book Design*
Joanne Muzyka	*Digital Graphics*

Photography by
Donnie Gilpin
with additional
photographs by Mary
Bloom, Sherri Regalbuto,
Miles J. Willard and
Michael D. Miller.

Copyright © 2008

Kennel Club Books®

A Division of BowTie, Inc.
40 Broad Street • Freehold, NJ • 07728 • USA

Library of Congress Cataloging-in-Publication Data

Willard, Janice.
  Eternal puppy / by Janice Willard; with foreword by Marty Becker.
    p. cm.
  Includes index.
  ISBN-13: 978-1-59378-675-5
  ISBN-10: 1-59378-675-1
  1. Dogs. 2. Dogs–Aging. 3. Dogs–Health. 4. Dogs–Diseases. 5.
Veterinary geriatrics. I. Title.
  SF427.W56 2007
636.7'08930438--dc22

                                        2007022725

Printed and bound in the United States of America
10 9 8 7 6 5 4 3 2 1

Contents

Acknowledgments

"Let the beauty we love be what we do
There are a thousand ways to kneel and kiss the ground."

—Jelaluddin Rumi

When embarking on the journey of writing my first book, my driving force and constant companions have been my love for animals and my desire for learning and communicating ways to improve our understanding and care for them.

Those who learn from and care for animals are special people. When I asked others for guidance, I was never at a lack for the assistance of those who answered my questions, directed me to useful research, offered suggestions, corrected my incorrect assumptions, read and critiqued portions of my manuscript and always gave me the benefit of their wisdom. And what they have done to help was never really to help only me, but rather their help was given so that through me, they could additionally help animals and the people who care for them.

My heartfelt thanks go to Mark Epstein DVM, ABVP (C/F), Franklin McMillan DVM, DACVIM, Lawrence Myers DVM, PhD, Gary Bryan DVM, DACVO, Phil Roudebush DVM, DACVIM, Marty Becker DVM, Steve Austad PhD, Donna Holmes PhD, James Evermann PhD, Robin Downing DVM, CVA, DAAPM, Nancy E. Willard MS, JD, George M. Strain PhD, Ellison Bentley DVM, DACVO, Denis Marcellin-Little DEDV, DACVS, James L. Cook DVM, PhD, DACVS, Shawn Delaney DVM, DACVN, Dorothy Laflamme DVM, DACVN, Steve Hanson DVM, DAVBT, Linda Aronson DVM, Greg Ogilvie DVM, DACVIM, J.Veronika Kiklevich DVM, Jan Bellows DVM ACVD, Sandra Coon DVM, William Fortney DVM, Narda Robinson DO, DVM, Janet Steiss DVM, PhD, Sophia Yin DVM, MS, Melissa Bain DVM, DACVB, Pria Nippak PhD, Gary Landsberg DVM, DACVB, John Ciribassi DVM, DACVB, E. Kathryn Meyer VMD, Joseph Araujo PhD, Myrna Milani DVM, Mary Lee Nitche PhD, Fred Metzger DVM, Diplomate ABVP, and my colleagues in the American Veterinary Society for Animal Behavior.

My thanks also go to the gifted team at Kennel Club Books for nurturing me along the way, particularly Amy Deputato for her professionalism, Peter Bauer for minding the details and Andrew DePrisco, the passionate force behind this book who guided me with humor, patience and really good questions.

With love and gratitude, I also wish to thank my friends and my family, both four-legged and two legged, for their encouragement and support, particularly my siblings Nancy and David, my children Ethan and Robin and particularly my husband Eric for holding down the fort, being chief library go-fer and helping me keep my sanity.

And lastly I wish to thank my dogs who have taught me, brought me joy and live on, eternally, in my heart.

Foreword

by Marty Becker DVM

Like humans, our canine friends are living healthier, longer lives, thanks to dedicated veterinarians and researchers like Dr. Janice Willard and her many consultants. Having written countless articles with Dr. Willard and having admired her research, writing and convictions, I am honored to introduce her to you. She's a dedicated, passionate veterinarian and pet lover whose first book, Eternal Puppy, may add years to your dog's life and life to his years.

Veterinarians and their clients, concerned loving dog owners like you, are learning more and more about maintaining the wellness of senior pets. Our goal is optimal health. This is an exciting field of research, and the rewards of our hard work and proactive care will add to the quality of our dogs' lives for generations to come. Likewise, Eternal Puppy is a book whose time has come. The information contained in this volume promises to improve every dog owner's knowledge and understanding of "the canine condition." This book is a perfect blend of science and soul.

As a child growing up on a farm in southern Idaho, I remember having many dogs around the property, rugged dogs that grew up and grew old. Not much thought was given to their "senior wellness," and most suffered the ravages of old age with no relief. But now, as dogs have made the transition from the field and farm to our homes and hearts, we regard them as members of our families. We care for them the way we care for every family member. We work hard to prevent problems, treat conditions with the latest high-tech medicines and therapies, alleviate pain and provide assistance in the form of ramps, padded beddings, special diets, etc.

No dog can live forever, but every dog can live well until his last days. This book is a celebration of the love and life of dogs, infused with the author's very personal touch. On every page the reader is reminded how our bond with our dogs enriches our own lives and deepens our desires as pet owners to do what is right for them every day.

Recently I lost a pal of mine, a 14-year-old terrier named Scooter. She lived a great life with me and my family, and this book is a testament to her and to all dogs who don't just survive but thrive in their double digits!

Introduction

"A dog is like an eternal Peter Pan, a child who never grows old and who there-fore is always available to love and be loved."

—Aaron Katcher

I was nine years old when Smokey, a gray Miniature Poodle puppy, came to live with us. An awkward kid who had problems in school, I found love and received unconditional acceptance from Smokey, even when I doubted myself. She became my best buddy. She tolerated my dressing her up in costumes like a living doll, and she taught me how to train dogs with little bits of cheese long before positive-reinforcement training was a term heard anywhere but in research laboratories. With her quick intelligence and my imagination, Smokey soon learned an impressive string of tricks.

Smokey was still in my home when I matured into a teen and started dating. (Guys had to the pass the "Smokey Test"—get along with my dog or your first date was your last date.) She lived with my mom when I left to go to a nearby college. Wherever my life took me, I would come home to find Smokey always there with my mom, smiling, wiggling, happy to see me.

Smokey aged gracefully into a senior citizen. Her eyes became cloudy and her step slower, but her enthusiasm for chasing balls was still undiminished. She died at 17 years of age, not of disease but as the result of an accident, slipping on the steps to the back yard. She lived a full, rich life to her very last day, and she lives on in my heart.

It is a bold and wonderful thing we do to love another living being. Of course, you can't stay young forever...no one can, including our dogs. How we wish we could stop the clock and keep them always with us. But time marches forward for us all, and even faster for dogs than for people. Loving dogs, even as we know they will leave us, is perhaps the most hopeful and human thing we can do.

Although his body ages faster than your own does, your dog will be a puppy, young at heart, until the day he dies. That is one of the endearing things about dogs—like Peter Pan, they grow old but never completely grow up, our eternal puppies.

Your dog will be your eternal puppy in another way as well: he always will need you to care for him and make the best decisions for him. Our dogs live in the moment; they don't project into the future to understand the consequences of their actions or to make sensible healthcare decisions and life choices. They eat what they like when they are hungry, with no thought to what is nutritionally best for them. They can't understand that a particular vaccination will reduce their risk of disease or that a certain medication will make them feel better. Dogs live wonderfully, deliciously, joyfully in the moment, and it is up to us to consider and care for their futures. Loving them, caring for them and living with them enriches us in immeasurable ways. How empty our lives would be without our dogs to care for and to love. In return for all that, it is up to us to take the best care of them that we can.

What this book hopes to do is give you the tools to make the choices that will keep your eternal puppy young at heart, helping him through life changes, guiding him over medical humps and supporting him along the pathway of his life. That your dog will age is a given; we can't change that. But it turns out that the expression of aging and the toll it takes on our mortal bodies is somewhat elastic—we all come to the same end, but with the right care and decisions, we have some influence on the health of our dogs as they age and can stretch the amount of time it takes to get there. And while we can't stop the clock and we can't stop the inevitable effects of time, we can make the most of the time we have with our dogs by keeping them, our eternal puppies, as healthy, happy, vigorous and engaged in life as is possible. This book will teach you how.

Your Forever Young Dog

It's About Time

And a Whole Lot More

When is a dog old? It turns out that this is not really an easy question to answer. The simple answer is, "It depends." There are a number of factors that can exert some influence, and this chapter will discuss some of those factors.

WHAT IS AGING?

One way to conceptualize aging is that living beings have two types of age: chronological and biological. Chronological age is essentially how much time has passed since a person or animal was born. Biological age (or senescence), by contrast, is associated with the appearance of specific age-related changes that are seen in adulthood. These are irreversible and progressive changes that occur in aging bodies (of both humans and animals), changes that can lead to certain kinds of disease, disability and even death. While we can see some of these changes on the outside, those changes are reflective of a number of important changes on the inside.

The chronological age at which age-related changes in adulthood become apparent depends on three main factors: the amount of time that has passed since birth, genetic makeup and environmental influences. Although not all of the genetic factors involved in the appearance of age-related changes have yet been identified, medical studies performed on animals from worms to humans have found that only about 20–25 percent of variability of longevity within a species seems to be determined by genetic factors. This means, then, that 75–80 percent of the variability that determines your dog's lifespan is governed by the way he lives.

HOW OLD IS YOUR DOG IN HUMAN YEARS?

	YOUNG ADULT	ADULT	SENIOR	GERIATRIC
Dog's Age	**0-20 lbs**	**20-50 lbs**	**50-90 lbs**	**90+ lbs**
1	7	7	8	9
2	13	14	16	18
3	20	21	24	26
4	26	27	31	34
5	33	34	38	41
6	40	42	45	49
7	44	47	50	56
8	48	51	55	64
9	52	56	61	71
10	56	60	66	78
11	60	65	72	86
12	64	69	77	93
13	68	74	82	101
14	72	78	88	108
15	76	83	93	115
16	80	87	99	123
17	84	92	104	131
18	88	96	109	139
19	92	101	115	
20	96	105	120	

Chart used with permission from Fred Metzger DVM, Diplomate ABVP (canine/feline), Metzger Animal Hospital, State College, PA 16801

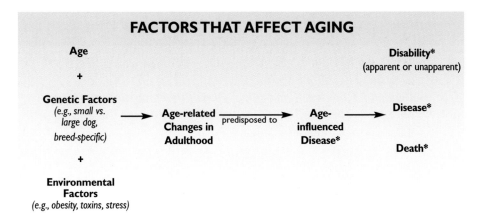

FACTORS THAT AFFECT AGING

* indicates places where pet owners have some ability to control rate of changes or influence wellfare.

Something else that is of interest to both dog owners and scientific researchers is the observation that, in general, small dogs age (that is, experience the onset and progression of age-related changes) more slowly than big dogs do (see chart). This relationship between size and aging rate is also seen in some strains of experimental mice. There are a number of environmental factors that also appear to influence the rate of aging. For example, studies have shown that the amount of food a dog eats and the resulting body condition (ratio of amount of fat to lean body weight) are associated with as much as a two-year difference in the average number of years that genetically similar dogs will live. In essence, fat dogs age more quickly. Of course, environmental influences on aging are of particular interest to us because we can exert some control over them. While we can't stop the clock and we can't change our dog's genetic makeup, we can care for our dog in ways that maximize his ability to live as long and healthy a life as possible.

However, from a practical standpoint, these variables make it tough to identify "middle age" and the onset of "old age" in an individual dog based solely on his chronological age. Age-related changes are gradual, and the rates of onset for various age-related changes are variable. It is common to use seven as the average age at which dogs should start to be considered "seniors," but this is only an average. The factors affecting aging—genetics, size, environmental influences—must be taken into account, as well as how these factors affect each dog individually.

CHANGES IN ADULTHOOD

- *Metabolic rate decreases:* Metabolic rate is the way that a body uses fuel for energy production.
- *Immune competence and cell-mediated immunity decrease:* Both of these are parts of the immune system and how the body fights disease organisms and cancer.
- *Increase in autoantibodies and autoimmune diseases:* Generally the immune system of an individual recognizes the cells of that body as "self" and doesn't attack them. In autoimmune diseases, the body's immune system starts to attack its own cells.
- Increase in the percentage of body weight represented by fat (fat-to-lean ratio). Also, the distribution of fat changes.
- *Muscle, bone and cartilage mass decrease:* Bones become less solid, there is less muscle mass and the cartilage gets thinner.
- Skin becomes thickened, darker and less elastic.
- Footpads become dryer and thicker and nails more brittle.
- Lungs lose elasticity and lung secretions become more thickened.
- *Vital capacity of the lungs is diminished:* The vital capacity is the amount of air that can be expelled from the lungs after breathing in as deeply as possible (basically a measurement of how much air the lungs can take in).
- *Cough reflex and expiratory capacity decrease:* The expiratory capacity is the amount of air that can be breathed out of the lungs.
- Urinary incontinence can develop.
- Changes in sensory system, hearing loss, sclerosis of lenses, proprioceptive deficits.
- Cardiovascular changes, including loss of elasticity of veins and arteries.

AGE-RELATED CHANGES IN ADULTHOOD

While aging in and of itself is not a disease, there are a number of conditions that appear as a result of the passage of time, genetic factors and environmental factors. No one knows for certain why all of these conditions occur. Some may be results of healthy, programmed (in the genetic code) cellular death. Some may result from the cumulative effects of toxic metabolic by-products (toxic free radicals). Some are probably results of the cumulative effects of environmental factors and toxins. How much and to what extent each of these causes affects aging is a subject of active research and debate. Whatever their causes, age-related changes are progressive and irreversible.

AGE-INFLUENCED DISEASES

Dorland's Medical Dictionary defines disease as "any deviation from or interruption of the normal structure or function of any body part, organ or system that is manifested by a characteristic set of symptoms and signs." Another way to conceptualize it is "dis-ease." When we are at ease, we are comfortable and well. Disease, then, is an absence or reduction of ease (the state of physical and mental wellness).

Although age-related changes are inevitable, they don't necessarily always reflect a state of disease or disability. They do, however, predispose to diseases. Here is an example: an age-related change is increased autoantibodies (antibodies against self) and autoimmune disease. Thyroiditis is an autoimmune disease of the thyroid gland. The incidence of thyroiditis in dogs increases with age and leads to hypothyroidism (insufficient thyroid hormone). This means that the age-related change, increased autoimmunity, predisposes to the age-influenced disease of hypothyroidism. Left untreated, hypothyroidism can cause considerable disability, additional disease conditions and even death.

Here is another example: decreased immune competence and cell-mediated immunity are natural age-related changes. One action of the immune system is to do surveillance for and remove cancerous cells, so a reduction in immune system competence can reduce this protective mechanism. In addition, the more times a cell divides, the greater its potential for mutations due to DNA copy/editing mistakes, and thus the more likely it is to become malignantly transformed. The older the animal, the more often the cells that replicate have copied themselves. Another time-related factor is that cumulative environmental factors (example, low-level environmental toxins) that accrue over the years also contribute to increased cancer risk.

So, while cancer itself is not caused by age, there are age-related changes that increase the tendency to get cancer; if you look at the statistics, you will see an increase in cancer with increased age.

THE SNOWBALL EFFECT

Age-related changes leading to age-influenced diseases and disability can snowball. For example, it is normal for a dog's cartilage to become thinner and more brittle with age. Lack of exercise can make this worse by reducing the turnover of joint fluid that nourishes the cartilage. Obesity also can make this worse through the production of pro-inflammatory cellular products. At some point, irreversible damage can occur to the cartilage, causing an inflammatory response, which is a disease state. From there, the process continues to snowball—the inflammation further damages the cartilage, worsening the disease, while the pain of the inflammation reduces activity and creates disability. It's easy to see how the snowball becomes an avalanche.

Of course, we want to prevent these problems from developing in the first place or keep them to a minimum. By doing so, we can prevent the avalanches of pain, disability and suffering.

We can't do anything about the passage of time or our dog's genetics, but we can influence some of the environmental factors and perhaps delay the onset of age-related changes. We can also influence the environmental factors that contribute to the age-influenced changes' becoming age-influenced diseases. If age-related diseases occur, we can prevent or reduce the amount of disability and the additional disease conditions that can result.

Most importantly, we need to avoid the "Oh, he is just old and slowing down" misconception. Probably the biggest threat to our aging dog's well-being is our tendency to dismiss the signs of aging and not see the age-influenced disabilities and diseases as preventable, treatable or manageable. We need to be able to recognize when our dog's signs are the results of a preventable or treatable age-influenced disease rather than just normal age-related changes. Is your dog just slowing down, or is he hypothyroid? Is he in pain from arthritis? Is he suffering from cognitive dysfunction? Is he bored or not getting enough exercise? Is he obese? Because these are things we can do something about.

We can't, for example, prevent autoimmune diseases, so we likely can't prevent thyroiditis and hypothyroidism. But we can prevent the disability caused by hypothyroidism by simply giving thyroid hormone. What we instead need to be thinking is: "Yes, he is old, but what else could be causing him to slow down? Is there something we could be doing to help him live in ease rather than with disease?" What we really don't want is to be doing nothing for a dog who is suffering from a disease or disability when we could be helping.

Nothing will stop the eventual death of our pet. What is important is how he lives. We don't want our aging dog to spend the last five years of his life as a couch potato or in pain because we mistook disability and disease for normal aging and failed to act when we could have helped.

HOW CAN WE HELP?

Is it easier to put out a smoldering match or a raging forest fire? This question illustrates why this book discusses beginning proactive care in our dog's middle-age years, rather than just beginning

THE ROLE OF THE DOG OWNER

There are many things that will be discussed and described in this book that you can do to help your dog lead a good life as he ages. Some of them include:

- Proper weight control
- Exercise
- Good nutrition
- Cognitive stimulation
- Coat maintenance and grooming
- Dental care
- Comfortable environment
- Regular veterinary exams and proper medical intervention
- Love and attention

Some of these things may slow the onset of age-related changes and will help manage the disability that often accompanies age-influenced diseases.

in their geriatric years. The sooner you start, the better you can prevent the changes that occur with age from causing disease, disability and suffering. No matter when we start, there is a lot we can do to help keep our dogs healthy as they age. Every little bit helps. Ideally you should be as well informed as possible so that you can work as a team with your veterinarian to keep your aging dog from experiencing unnecessary suffering.

The Role of the Veterinarian

The role of the veterinarian is to guide you in your preventative-care tactics and to intervene where good living practices leave off. In addition to diagnosing problems in your dog, your vet will help you identify and manage age-influenced disabilities and diseases in your dog. No matter what we do and no matter how diligent our prevention and management practices, some diseases will still occur. For example, all of the nutrition and exercise in the world won't prevent the debilitating effects of hypothyroidism if your dog's thyroid gland is not making enough thyroid hormone. Giving thyroid medication, on the other hand, will.

Preventative medicine is more effective—and kinder to your dog—than waiting until something has progressed to a point where it is difficult to treat. Ideally you want to catch a problem when it is still barely detectable. However, a complication in your ability to do so is the slow onset of many of the age-influenced diseases. Because you see your dog every day, infinitesimal changes can be difficult for you to notice. Unless you do a reality check from time to time, you could be living on a cloud of optimism while your dog is living in misery. That reality check is a regular physical exam by someone specifically trained to look for problems (i.e., your veterinarian).

PREPARING FOR THE INEVITABLE

Age-related changes are inevitable. We cannot stop them, only slow them by trying to control those environmental influences that we understand and can affect. The changes still will come, and eventually age-influenced diseases will follow. An old adage tells us, "If you want to dance the dance, then you have to pay the piper."

The cost of living life includes the onset of age-related changes along with the need for increased awareness so that you are able to recognize these changes and treat the problems that can, and likely will, accompany them.

As age-related changes start to take hold, your dog's need for veterinary medicine increases to maintain his level of health and comfort. However, proactive medicine is generally more cost-effective than reactive medicine, so moving to a twice-a-year wellness exam system has the potential of being financially as well as medically effective. Also cost-effective is increasing your index of suspicion so that you notice early disease signs and start monitoring and treating them as needed before they become a medical avalanche.

Another aspect of good care for your dog is recognizing and preparing for the fact that the financial burden will increase as your dog's age increases. It is very sad to have a treatable problem occur in an old dog and not have the resources to deal with it. Depending on your financial management style, you might consider some advanced planning, such as having pet insurance or a savings account for your pet's medical needs.

What does ideal aging look like? It is worthwhile to examine our own thoughts and philosophies about this. I think the ideal would be to have as long a period of healthy, active life as possible with a short period of disability or rapid decline to mortality.

In summary, your best approach is to do everything you can to keep your dog healthy, engage in routine preventative medicine, intervene early when a problem occurs and have a financial plan to cover the things that can't be prevented. The approach that is the most cost-effective is also, it turns out, the approach that is the most beneficial to your dog's welfare. Time will still win in the long run, but love and knowledge can make that passage of time as rich and painless as possible.

2 Proactive Care

A Stitch in Time

"A stitch in time saves nine" is something my mother used to say, an old adage warning you to mend that tiny hole in your favorite sweater before it becomes a huge hole requiring a lot more stitches—or even becoming beyond repair. Similarly, checking the pressure of your car's tires is a lot less expensive and significantly less of a hassle than having a blowout while you're driving. As a blown-out tire can cause an accident, this is an important safety precaution as well. Keeping up requires a lot less effort and money than catching up. It only makes good sense. Fail to check the oil, and you may need to get a whole new engine for your lawnmower, Land Cruiser or private jet. Fail to replace some loose roof shingles, and soon you'll be replacing the whole roof after the next big storm blows through. Checking the battery in your smoke detector can save your house and even the lives of your family and beloved pets. A stitch in time truly does save nine, and we do it all the time. The same holds true in medicine. If you wait to treat a condition until it has progressed to something more serious, it is harder to treat, it causes more pain and suffering and it can cause irreparable damage. Remember, it is easier to blow out a candle than a forest fire. It is always easier to treat disease earlier in the disease process rather than later.

Early detection and early intervention can make a huge difference in the life and well-being of your aging dog. Older dogs do not have the same reserves or ability to recover that they had when they were younger. And your dog cannot make his healthcare

Eternal Puppy

choices for himself—you have to be the one to make the benefits of preventative medicine available to him.

One important aspect of proactive medicine is seeing the doctor frequently enough that developing problems can be caught early in the disease process. Another aspect is that you are less likely to find those problems early on unless you specifically look for them. What this means, practically speaking, is that you will need to shift from your annual veterinary visit to a more frequent exam schedule specifically designed to look for problems that are often seen in older dogs.

A recent task force of the American Animal Hospital Association (AAHA) recommended a twice-annual senior pet wellness program. This recommendation makes good common sense. Because our dogs age faster than we do, changing to a schedule of twice a year is like checking the tire pressure, oil and batteries on an older car. For a dog to be examined by a veterinarian only once a year is roughly equivalent to a person's seeing a doctor only once every seven years. You can understand that if you saw a doctor only once every seven years, the potential for any early detection and intervention would be lost. Significant damage, from what may have been treatable problems initially, may have already occurred, and now you would be playing catch-up. Proactive, preventative medicine is more effective and more cost-effective, too.

The other obvious but too-often overlooked principle is this: you are more likely to find things if you are looking for them. Our nervous systems are flooded every minute with a barrage of thoughts and sensory stimuli. We spend most of our lives tuning things out and learning just to focus on those things that we think really matter at the time. As a result, many important things, like the early signs of illness in our dogs, can go unnoticed because we are not tuned into them. By specifically focusing on health problems more commonly seen in aging dogs, learning to recognize and taking the time to look for them, you are more likely to find them early in the disease process, when treatment is more effective.

As part of the health-maintenance exam, the veterinarian will take a complete and comprehensive history, asking you what you are noticing with your dog. This is because almost every disease

A Case For Proactive Medicine

Kidney disease is a leading killer of dogs. Properly functioning kidneys are necessary for life, and these organs have no reparative capability. Kidney functions include filtering many of the waste products of metabolism out of the blood, salvaging and returning necessary minerals to the blood, maintaining water balance and producing hormones that regulate red-blood-cell production, blood pressure and calcium metabolism.

Kidneys can stop working acutely from a severe medical condition or poisoning (such as antifreeze poisoning), but they also can be damaged slowly and insidiously from a daily onslaught of conditions that affect them. Many things can cause low-level chronic damage to the kidneys, from certain common drugs to low-grade urinary-tract infections, and the results of this damage can accumulate.

Just by looking at your dog, there is no way for you to determine that chronic kidney damage is occurring until there is already significant damage. (This is different from acute kidney disease, where signs of illness develop rapidly and are obvious). Because the kidneys are so essential and yet can't regenerate, mammals are born with more kidney tissue than they need, essentially a functional reserve. But as that reserve is chipped away by insidious damage, eventually the body gets to the point where the kidneys are not able to keep up with the demand. By the time 66% of the kidney function is gone, the animal is having troubles with fluid balance, will be thirsty and drinking more and will urinate more. By the time 75% of kidney function is gone, the animal is not able to filter out metabolic wastes, and overt illness from the build-up of wastes is present.

Obviously dog owners want to try to recognize and slow the development of chronic kidney disease before it gets to this point. Since there are no external signs until the kidneys are severely affected, this is a place where proactive medicine can be of great benefit. At regular veterinary visits, tests can be run to screen for conditions that could harm the kidneys (like low-grade bladder or kidney infections), review medications being used and test for changes in kidney function. New tests for early changes in kidney function currently are being developed. Research is progressing and improving our ability to find and fight the causes of kidney damage.

process will first be seen as behavioral changes. Those changes may be subtle, but when recalling the dog's day-to-day or week-to-week activities, you become more aware of behavioral changes that you hadn't really thought significant. Observations as simple as your dog's asking to go out more frequently or your needing to fill the water bowl three times a day instead of once can be important clues about a developing health problem.

There is no more powerful tool than having a trained veterinary clinician lay his hands on your pet and give him a comprehensive physical exam. After his trained eyes and hands have examined the dog, your vet then probes more deeply. This means that your veterinarian will use some of the available diagnostic procedures to investigate more thoroughly what is going on in your pet. For example, you can't see the effects of kidney disease on an animal from the outside until the disease has progressed beyond a point where treatment is very effective. But blood tests can look for early changes in kidney function and urine tests can look for low-grade infections that have the potential of damaging kidneys. Testing procedures allow veterinarians to give more in-depth examinations.

What this all boils down to is that you will want to change to a twice-annual health-maintenance exam system for your dog, starting around his seventh year of age (sooner for giant breeds, as they age faster).

WHY A SENIOR-CARE PROGRAM?

Why start by seven years of age? While a senior wellness program is beneficial whenever it is initiated in a senior dog, it is a good idea to start a senior-care program when your dog has reached his middle-aged years. It may be hard, when looking at a seven- or eight-year-old dog, to consider that he is in need of a senior-care program. After all, the dog may not be showing many signs of age yet and may still seem vigorous and energetic. However, this is the optimal time to get started for the following reasons:

Establishing baselines. As your dog enters his senior years, laboratory testing will become more important for monitoring changes in his health. When looking at the results of a physical exam and laboratory data in a dog who has an illness, it is helpful for the

SENIOR-CARE GUIDELINES

The American Animal Hospital Association (AAHA), established in 1933, is an organization that comprises more than 33,000 veterinary-care providers who treat companion animals. It is well known among veterinarians for its high standards for hospitals and pet healthcare.

In 2005 the AAHA released its *Senior-Care Guidelines for Dogs and Cats* to assist veterinary practitioners in enhancing their care of senior dogs and cats. The guidelines recommend more extensive laboratory testing beginning in middle age to establish baseline values and twice-yearly examinations and testing once a pet reaches his senior years to promote the early detection of disease. The guidelines were developed by a task force of seven expert veterinarians in a wide variety of specialty fields, from evidence-based research whenever possible and from a consensus of expert opinions, to develop care guidelines that help veterinary practice teams provide optimal care for aging pets.

Not all practices offer a senior wellness program such as the one developed by the AAHA. If your practice does not, it wouldn't hurt to mention it to your veterinarian and ask what your vet thinks about this program. Based upon experience and preferences, your veterinary practice may have come up with its own standard practices for its hospital.

veterinarian and for you to know what the normal values were for the dog before the illness began. With age-related physical changes, again it helps to know what the starting point was. For example, the profile of a specific blood constituent measured over time gives more information than look-ing at that constituent at just one point in time. Ideally it is best to estab-lish baselines prior to the seventh year.

Identifying and starting treatment for subclinical problems. A subclinical problem is one that we can't observe outwardly yet. But these diseases can still be causing problems even if we see no signs. Studies have shown that a number of age-related illnesses, such as hypothyroidism and "silent" bladder infections, can be present in dogs who don't yet appear ill. These diseases can nevertheless be taking a slow but insidious toll on your dog.

Starting proactive disease-prevention programs. Of course, you and your vet have been engaging in proactive preventative medical treatments ever since your puppy got his first vaccination. But now your focus will have changed to those diseases more typically associated with the mature and aging dog.

Having weight and body-condition scoring monitored. Gradual changes are harder to recognize than rapid changes. As your dog gets into his middle years, his metabolic changes may make it easier for him to gain weight. But because these changes are gradual, your dog's weight gain may not be easily noticeable to you. Keeping your dog at his ideal weight is an important element in keeping him healthy.

Many veterinary practices already have instituted programs of increased management and surveillance for senior-dog healthcare. All you need to do is to ask your vet about it or agree to be included in your vet's program. The program can be tailored to your individual needs. The twice-a-year physical exams are the most important part of the program, but the amount of testing needed can vary. Once you have established baselines, you and your veterinarian can develop a plan based on your veterinarian's experience, an assessment of risk for your dog based on individual factors, your expectations and your budget. The objective of veterinary medicine is to help families, not bankrupt them. Good proactive care doesn't have to be expensive to be good medicine. The degree to which you follow the guidelines set forth by the AAHA can be flexible depending on need. What to do if your veterinary practice does not offer a senior-care program? There are several things that I can suggest:

First, there is a great medical benefit in going to a practice where you know the veterinarians and staff and where you and your dog are known. Familiarity is an important, yet often overlooked, component of medicine. If the veterinarian and staff know your family and your dog, you are more comfortable talking with them and you feel respected. It's a wonderful feeling knowing that your veterinarian and his people care about you and your dog—this is an invaluable component of a successful veterinarian-client-patient relationship.

Assuming you are happy with your veterinarian and his practice, request that they help you institute a senior wellness plan for your pet. Your veterinarian may have been considering adding this to his practice

VETERINARY SPECIALISTS

Paralleling human medicine, some veterinarians complete additional training after veterinary school in specific specialties, such as neurology, cardiology, behavior and nutrition. After completing extensive training and a difficult and comprehensive board exam, they become board certified in their specialty.

Veterinary specialists complement the kind of care your dog can get from his primary-care veterinarian. Because they have focused their training on one field, specialists usually have more advanced diagnostic and therapeutic options than a general practice does. Specialists also have the advantage of seeing unusual conditions more frequently. For example, a general practice may see an animal with a certain uncommon disease type only several times a year, while at a specialty practice they may see a number of animals with that disease type several times a week, giving them additional experience. The ideal situation is to have your general practice veterinarian referring to and working in conjunction with a specialist veterinarian when conditions warrant this.

and just wasn't sure if there was a desire in the clientele. By opening a door of communication, you may help other pets, too.

If you are patronizing a veterinary practice with which you are presently dissatisfied, look for a new one that offers specific senior-care services. If you are moving to a new community and shopping for a new veterinary practice, don't just select the one that is closest to your house. Instead, shop around and see what services each one provides and how progressive the practices are. The presence of a quality senior wellness program could be an important factor in deciding which practice to patronize. But be sure to visit the practice and pay close attention to how it makes you feel—do the people there really seem to love animals and treat both their clients and patients with kindness and respect? If you do not feel comfortable at a practice, you will not feel comfortable volunteering information or asking questions in the exam room—both essential aspects of good healthcare. Go with your head as well as your heart: consider the type of services offered as well as how welcome the practice makes you feel.

CHANGES IN VACCINATION SCHEDULES

It used to be that getting vaccinations for your adult dog was a simple process—you got a reminder card once a year and then went to your veterinarian for an exam and vaccination booster shots. Those were the days. In recent years, advances in vaccination technology and some concerns about risks from overvaccinating have caused a revamping of our concepts of how to handle vaccinations. Yes, some vaccinations are now being given less frequently; however, this does not mean that you should bring your dog to the veterinarian less often. Vaccination is not the same as examination, and the most powerful medical tool we have available to us today is a physical examination by a trained veterinary professional. Vaccinations cover only a small number of diseases of concern. Even if your dog is not due for a vaccination because of a longer vaccination interval, regular veterinary exams (annually for adult dogs or twice annually for senior dogs) are still your best tool for keeping your dog healthy.

Because of recent changes in vaccination technology and risk assessment, it is better to tailor the vaccination schedule into a protocol for your specific dog rather than to follow a one-size-fits-all approach. A plan that details which vaccinations and at what frequency they should be given is best when individually tailored to your dog, his age, his activities and his level of risk.

Why so complicated? Why can't we just follow a simple plan?

Variability of Disease Organisms

Some disease organisms produce a very lasting immunity when the immune system encounters them. Some disease organisms, such as canine leptospirosis, do not produce a lasting immune response. Some disease organisms are capable of changing, which means that the immune responses developed to previous incarnations of the diseases no longer protect against the current strains. And, in the arms race between animals and disease organisms, new viruses and bacteria are always probing our defenses. Before 1976, for example, no one needed to vaccinate dogs against canine parvovirus, because it had never been seen. But within two years of its first appearance, the virus had spread worldwide. Canine influenza is an emerging virus, and the potential disease spread and level of protection from vaccinations developed against it have yet to be determined.

Note that in humans there are diseases that we will get only once and then have a lifelong immunity against, such as chicken pox or measles, whereas colds and influenza come back time and time again. This variation among organisms is also seen in how frequently a person will get certain vaccinations. The tetanus vaccine is given infrequently because the vaccine produces a very long-lasting immunity, while the influenza virus vaccine is one that you need to get each year. The reason why the influenza vaccine needs to be given so frequently is twofold. First, the vaccine doesn't produce a lasting immunity; second, the virus mutates and changes, so immunity to last year's influenza variant may not help protect you against this year's version.

Changes in Vaccination Technology

We are improving our ability to develop vaccinations. With the new technologies, there is not only variability in the disease organisms against which you must vaccinate, but also variability in the immunity that the different vaccines can generate. So a vaccination from one company against a specific organism may not produce the same level of immunity as a different vaccination against the same organism. In addition, changes are being made in the way that vaccines are formulated. An adjuvant is a substance that is added to a vaccine to stimulate a stronger immune response. In some cases, there have been concerns about the adjuvants used, which may be more of a concern than the vaccines themselves. Some companies have switched to different adjuvants or have eliminated them entirely.

Changes in Your Dog's Risk

Stress and illness can reduce immune function, which may make an animal more susceptible to infection and can reduce the effectiveness of the immune protection from a vaccination. Changes in the environment can also alter the risk. For example, if you are going on a road trip and want to bring your dog along, or if you are moving to a new area, he will be exposed to many different organisms that his immune system has not seen before. So when the risk changes, so too should your vaccination protocol. Boosting your dog's immunity before you travel is a good plan.

In addition, the immune system of an older dog is not as competent as that of a younger dog. Ideally you should make sure that the younger dogs and middle-aged dogs with whom your dog comes into contact have been adequately vaccinated, because this reduces their likelihood of shedding disease organisms into the environment. (Likewise, if you are breeding dogs, your pregnant bitches should be kept well vaccinated, as this reduces the potential for them to pass diseases to their puppies.) Unfortunately, while you can appropriately care for the dogs in your own household, there is nothing you can do about the neighbors' dogs. Again, this is a change in risk that you should discuss with your veterinarian.

There are also genetic factors to consider. Certain breeds, such as herding breeds and some breeds of smaller dog, are more prone to adverse reactions to vaccines; this needs to be considered when deciding on the vaccination protocol and vaccinations used.

What the Future Holds

An individual's antibody level is not the only factor in determining that individual's immune response. Other physiologic factors also determine how well the individual can utilize his antibodies, and these all come together to create the total immune response. Testing for the antibodies gives us another piece of the puzzle about the immune status of the dog.

Currently, the most accurate way to assess immune status is to have the blood antibody titers (levels of immune competence measured in the bloodstream) against specific organisms determined and to revaccinate before the immune components drop below a protective level. While this is the most accurate method, the technology has not yet developed to make it readily available and feasible for most pet owners. You will notice that even in human medicine, checking for effective titers is not often done. If I were to step on a rusty nail, my doctor would be more likely to see how long ago my last tetanus shot was and revaccinate if needed rather than to check my antibody titers.

It is hoped that in the future, instead of vaccinating on a specific time schedule, your veterinarian can draw your dog's blood at set time intervals to run a convenient and accurate testing procedure, which would identify your dog's current immune status and determine which vaccines are needed. However, until this technology is in place and widely available, developing a plan with your veterinarian based on your dog's individual risk is your best option.

LISTENING TO YOUR INTUITION

Many of us are not good at listening to the "still, small" voice of our intuition. Everything in our culture and training has taught us to listen instead to the logical, rational, verbal part of our consciousness. We are trained to look for evidence, for reasons, to be practical, to make sense. The voice of intuition is often drowned out by our seemingly superior logical intellect, which roars like a drill sergeant on a bullhorn. And we are so busy, with many worries to distract us from listening to our inner voice.

Many diseases come on like gangbusters and present dog owners with plenty of evidence that something is wrong. No one can miss a dog with diarrhea, for example. But some diseases come on slowly and subtly.

We connect with our pets on an emotional level and often it is with the emotional, nonverbal, intuitive part of your brain that a developing problem with your pet will first be noticed. You can't quite put your finger on it, but you just feel that something is amiss.

Your dog has no words with which to communicate with you, so it is with the nonverbal, intuitive part of your brain that he has to first communicate. Once your intuition has been alerted, then the logical portion of your brain can start looking for evidence. But there is no more sensitive observer than your intuition.

Sometimes the logical part of your mind will not find concrete evidence to corroborate the concern coming from your intuition. The rational, verbal, doubtful part of your mind will try to drown out the small voice of intuition. Listen to your intuition. If it tells you that something is wrong with your dog, then something is likely wrong, even if you can't see it yet.

Many a veterinarian has been presented with a patient whose concerned owner says, "I don't know what it is, Doc, but something is wrong with Missy." That is where the systematic examination that veterinarians are trained to do starts as the vet looks for what it is

TAKE YOUR DOG TO THE VET NOW!

Just because you are using a semi-annual health management schedule does not mean that everything that can happen medically in your dog will be caught at those visits. Some life-threatening conditions can develop very quickly and need rapid intervention to save your dog's life. These are the signs that you should not ignore; you need to get your dog to a veterinarian right away if you see any of the following:

- Rapid swelling in the abdomen (especially in deep-chested dogs predisposed to bloat)
- Bleeding from any body orifice
- Bloody or black, tarry stool (both indicate gastrointestinal bleeding, but from different locations)
- Lethargy
- Labored breathing
- Seizure, fainting or collapse
- Eye injury (no matter how mild it appears)
- Straining to urinate or defecate
- Any wound or laceration that is open and bleeding
- Any animal bite
- Thermal stress, either too hot or too cold (even if the animal appears to have recovered, the situation on the inside could be different)
- Trauma, such as being hit by a car (even if your dog seems fine, again the situation on the inside could be different)
- Allergic reactions, like swelling of the face or hives
- Sudden changes in behavior, like unusual withdrawal or out-of-character aggressiveness

that triggered the owner's intuition. And the veterinarian might find something significant.

But what if you take your dog to the vet and he finds nothing abnormal? Should you be embarrassed that you went to the veterinarian? Of course not. Some disease processes can take a while to develop to the point where a vet can measure them. Plus, the results of any veterinary examination give valuable information.

Here is an example: let's say that you bring Missy to the vet, feeling that something is wrong. The vet does a thorough examination, draws blood and does laboratory tests and finds nothing dangerously out of kilter.

Let's say that one blood element (we'll call it X) that was measured has a normal value ranging from 2.0 to 5.0, and Missy's measurement was a 3.5. "Looks OK," the vet will say, "right in the normal range."

Although you take Missy home, she still doesn't seem right, but there's nothing specific you can hang your hat on. Two weeks later you go back to the vet and again do the tests. This time, blood constituent X is 5.0. Is this of concern now? You betcha! In two short weeks the blood factor has gotten significantly higher and is now on the edge of the normal range, which could indicate a rapid trend toward an active disease condition. At this point, the veterinarian can now focus on the body system that this test measures and look more closely to see whether something serious is developing.

Now let's look at how we would interpret the data if you only came in for the second visit. It is not uncommon to find blood values that are at the high end of the normal range or even in the low elevated range and not get very excited about them. A 5.0 on the first measurement might not trigger active concern in a doctor, but seeing the rapid upward trend will. Listening to your intuition provided valuable information.

An older dog does not have the reserves of a younger dog. Intervening medically in the early stages of a disease will always give you a better shot of combating the disease, and earlier is always better.

Your dog is dependent on you to give him the care he needs. He can't make a veterinary appointment and take himself to the clinic when he feels something is amiss. He can't talk to you and tell you what is wrong. He needs you to pay attention to his behavior and the outward evidence and also to the voice of your intuition. Of course, you don't want to be calling the veterinarian every time your dog sneezes. But if something seems wrong to you, have it checked out.

Remember that irreparable hole in your favorite sweater: you need to be the advocate for your dog and make sure that he gets the proactive healthcare that he needs. By providing that stitch in time, you can be the one who saves your dog's life, maybe extending it by nine months or nine years!

3 Information

Finding Reliable Sources

"There's a sucker born every minute."

—Attributed to P. T. Barnum
(Case in point about misinformation—there is question as to
whether or not Barnum actually was the source of this famous
quote that is attributed to him.)

Our pets are dependent on us. They do not read or have opposable thumbs, nor can they choose what food to buy at the store or when to go out or where to go. We have assumed the responsibility for their care. And that means that, when we gather information that will play a role in how we manage their lives and care for them, it is necessary for us to use our brains, our common sense and, yes, our skepticism, to make sure that we are not making decisions on their health based on bad or biased information. There are so many ways for people to get information these days; while this can be extremely helpful, we also must remember to be careful about what we believe.

How important is getting the correct information? Consider the Mars Polar Lander. This expensive state-of-the-art exploratory spacecraft crashed while attempting to land on the surface of Mars on December 3, 1999, likely because it got the wrong information, causing it to shut off its descent engines before it had safely reached the surface of the planet.

THE INTERNET

We live in the information age, and there has never been a time like this in which we've been able to learn so much, so easily, about so many things. Unfortunately, while information abounds on the

Internet, it doesn't mean that what is found there is always good information. There are no "cyberspace truth monitors" on the Internet—no person, company or government agency making sure that what is on a website or discussed on a message board is accurate and unbiased information. And "truth" itself is a slippery concept because what is commonly accepted as true may simply be what is accepted at the moment, given the available information and biases. Remember, at one time a commonly accepted "truth" was that the world was flat.

The Internet has become a place for marketing, merchandising, entertaining, propagandizing and proselytizing. In the information age it has become even more critical that we are able to determine what is believable. Determining the credibility of online information is complicated by the fact that everyone, from trustworthy non-biased information providers to "snake-oil salesmen," is using the same techniques to create websites that look highly credible.

In 2002 *Consumer Reports* launched a Credibility Campaign to improve the trustworthiness of all websites. As part of this campaign, they established guidelines that call for easy-to-find disclosures of site identity, site ownership, policies on advertising, sponsorships, customer service and privacy. These guidelines also oblige site administrators to quickly and prominently correct wrong information. But when they did a study of how people assess credibility, they found that people did not look at these features. In fact, the study provided indications that are of significant concern.

The *Consumer Reports* data showed that the average consumer paid far more attention to the superficial aspects of a site, such as visual cues, than to its content. They found that participants seemed to make their credibility-based decisions about the people or organization behind the site based upon the site's overall visual appeal instead of more rigorous evaluation strategies.

Another recent study assessed the ability of people to determine the credibility of websites in the context of concerns related to "phishing," which refers to online schemes designed to trick people into providing financial information for the purpose of identity theft. The participants in the study were shown 20 websites, only 7 of which were legitimate, and asked to determine which were the legitimate sites. The participants knew that some of the sites presented to them were fake sites. The researchers found that almost all of the participants were easily fooled.

There was, however, one participant in this study who was highly successful in determining which sites were the legitimate ones. His strategy was not based on an analysis of "what was on" the site, but rather "how he got to" the site. This is a very important finding. It is easy for someone to produce a site that is credible in appearance, but it is much harder for someone to create a site that professionals and search engines will link to.

In the following information literacy guidelines, there will be a strong focus on effective strategies to get to credible sites:

How important is it that the information/site be credible? Information searches vary in importance and thus vary in the need to pay attention to credibility. Consider the importance of determining the credibility of a site that provides health information as compared with one that gives information about a new movie.

How controversial is the issue? The degree of controversy over the subject for which you are searching is related to the likelihood of finding sites with potential bias. For example, there is likely less potential for bias on a website that lists the features of different models of cars when compared with a website that discusses feeding raw-food diets to dogs (a topic on which people tend to have very strong opinions for or against).

How did you get to the website? If you get to a website by following a link on a website that already has credibility, such as a veterinary school's public education site, it is more likely that this website is also credible. Websites found through search engines will vary in quality and credibility. It is highly unlikely that a link to a website in an email message from a stranger will lead to a credible site.

Who provided the information? Has a university, government agency, well-respected organization or individual with expertise provided the information? This is a good start, but note that even institutions, agencies, organizations and individuals have the potential for bias. Government agencies may provide information to support the policies of the political party currently in power. The material on a university's site may come from a researcher who has been funded by a company with direct financial interest in the results of the research. Reputable scientists and research journals report the sources of their research funding so that potential biases can be considered.

The source of funding is a dicey problem for those engaging in veterinary research. While there are many funding sources available in human medicine, this is not as much the case in veterinary medicine. And so primary funding for veterinary research frequently comes from companies. While that introduces the potential for bias, in reality there is no one else providing the funds for this necessary research, so looking to see that the results were reported in respected scientific journals with high standards for experimental methods and peer reviews is also a way to determine credibility.

As an example, several highly significant studies discussed in this book were conducted with industry involvement. However, these research studies were reported in reputable journals and at scientific meetings and have been cited by other researchers. So while you might find these studies discussed on company websites, you can also look to see where else the research has been reported. You may also find the results of significant research studies presented on the websites of companies with competing products to the one that funded the research, another credibility measure.

Is there independent evidence of the expertise and credibility of the source? A good technique is to type the site name in quotes (without using http://) into a search engine. By doing so, you can determine who links to the site. Assess the possible motivations and biases of the people or organizations behind the sites that link to this information.

Is there evidence of bias? Does the material appear to be presented for the purpose of providing information, or is the site an advocacy site designed to persuade people to agree with a certain position? Does the entity presenting the information have anything to gain by convincing people to agree with the facts or opinions set forth? The material presented by an advocacy site is likely to be more biased. Is there any evidence of self-serving, such as sources of funding, seeking participants in advocating a cause or selling of products or services? This does not mean the information is inaccurate, but it is necessary to be more careful in an evaluation. As long as you are fully aware of what the biases are, you can consider them in your evaluation of the information presented.

Although there is an automatic bias in information provided by a company that sells products, many of these companies are to be commended for providing excellent resources for pet owners on their websites, some even referring to research conducted by competing companies. On the other hand, many organizations will present information with a bias towards their underlying philosophy. Provided you recognize the potential for bias, you can find some good material on these sites. Look for companies or organizations with good track records, with reputable research programs, who have been around for a long time, who supply more than one product and who have a wide view. Avoid websites of companies or organizations with controversial products or extreme viewpoints; likewise, avoid companies, organizations or people that act as if they have all the answers.

Is the information fact-based or opinion-based? Fact-based information is likely to be more credible than opinion-based information, but you have to investigate the source of the facts. Just because something is repeated frequently on the Internet doesn't make it true. Urban legends, myths and old wives' tales proliferate like weeds on the Internet. An alarming bit of misinformation can take on a life of its own, spread by well-meaning people who send it along to their friends as a way of kindly warning—not knowing that the information was disproved years ago. Look very carefully at material presented in alarmist language warning of dire consequences. Also check urban legend watchdog websites to see if the piece of information you are reading has been discussed on these sites.

Does your veterinarian and others have opinions? Ask for the opinions of others, including your veterinarian. What do they think of the information and the source?

Does the information feel right? Evaluate the information itself. Is it logical? Is it consistent with what you already believe is true? Does it "feel" right?

WHAT CONSTITUTES GOOD "EVIDENCE"?

When we make decisions about how to care for our aging dog, these decisions are based on our past experience and what we are currently learning. New information is always being added to our database, and we

EXAMPLES OF REPUTABLE ONLINE SOURCES*

VETERINARY COLLEGE PUBLIC EDUCATION SITES

The nation's 27 veterinary colleges are excellent sources of top pet care advice. One example is Washington State University College of Veterinary Medicine's Pet Health Topics:

www.vetmed.wsu.edu/cliented

REPUTABLE VETERINARY ORGANIZATIONS

American Veterinary Medical Association

www.avma.org

American Animal Hospital Association

www.aahanet.org

VETERINARY SPECIALTY COLLEGES

In order to become a board-certified veterinary specialist, a veterinarian needs to take additional training in the form of a residency and pass a rigorous exam administered by the specialty college. Many specialty colleges maintain websites that tell you how to find members and also offer good pet-care information. An example is the American College of Veterinary Internal Medicine:

www.acvim.org

VETERINARY SPECIALTY ASSOCIATIONS

A veterinary association is a group of veterinarians who are interested in a specific facet of medicine and often get additional training in this area. Veterinary specialty associations usually include members who are board-certified in that field as well as others who may have extensive training but chose not to pursue certification. Websites of such organizations have information for members as well as a public education component. An example is the American Veterinary Society of Animal Behavior:

www.avsabonline.org

OTHER ANIMAL-RELATED SCIENTIFIC ORGANIZATIONS

Example: Animal Behavior Society

www.animalbehavior.org

HUMANE DOG TRAINING ASSOCIATIONS

Example: Association of Pet Dog Trainers

www.apdt.com

HUMANE ORGANIZATIONS

Humane Society of the United States

www.hsus.org

American Humane Association

www.americanhumane.org

American Society for the Prevention of Cruelty to Animals

www.aspca.org

The Delta Society

www.deltasociety.org

VETERINARY INFORMATION NETWORK (PUBLIC INFORMATION WEBSITE)

www.veterinarypartner.com

ANGEL CARE CANCER CENTER AT CALIFORNIA VETERINARY SPECIALISTS

An example of a private practice with an excellent resource website:

www.cvangelcare.com

ASPCA ANIMAL POISON CONTROL CENTER

www.aspca.org—click on "Poison Control" link

*Note that inclusion in this list does not mean that I endorse everything on these websites, nor is this a complete listing of good pet information sites.

need to be able to assess the validity of the information with which we are presented. Part of caring for your eternal puppy is to be a life-long learner and also to be a critical thinker when it comes to evaluating the information presented to you.

It is often thought that science has all the answers, but this is a misconception. Science does not have all the answers; science has the questions. Science asks questions, looks for evidence and draws conclusions based on the evidence seen at the time. The validity of the conclusion is dependent on how good the evidence was and the point in time when you asked the question. Science is a forward-moving process. With new evidence, you might throw out the previous conclusion and form a new one. Plus, a conclusion can only be as good as the evidence that formed it. Opinion and bias dilute the quality of evidence and the validity of conclusions.

When you read that there is evidence that something works, you need to stop and ask yourself what really is meant by "evidence." Different kinds of testing can result in different levels of reliability. Examples include (from least reliable to most reliable):

• Observations or testimonials (personal experiences)
• Case reports
• Case series
• Retrospective studies
• Prospective experimental or clinical trials

Observations or testimonials: Recently I was curious about a substance used by organic sheep farmers for parasite control. Many farmers seemed to use it, but the purported mechanism didn't make sense to me. I asked organic farmers if there was any scientific evidence that it actually did what it was supposed to do. "Sure," they told me, "we have been using it and our sheep have very low internal worm counts." They then suggested a number of websites to me. All of the sites that they mentioned were those of companies selling the compound. And they all had a great number of wonderful testimonials that sounded just like the farmers that I talked to: "We use it and our sheep have low parasite counts." But nowhere could I find any comparisons; there was no information on the parasite counts when not using the compound versus when using the compound. Many factors can influence parasite loads, including good management and pasture rotation, also practiced by these farmers. There was nothing to say that this compound was even contributing to the low parasite levels. After a long search, I did find one old research report that did a comparison study and found no effect when using this compound. The compound is still being sold, but until I see better evidence, I'm not buying it.

Observations and testimonials have the lowest level of reliability because they don't rule out the possibility that something else is having the primary effect. However, personal experiences and observation are good for suggesting that something *may* be having a beneficial effect and indicating a direction for additional research. Most good scientific discoveries started out with an observation.

Case reports and case series: Case reports are written reports by a veterinarian or doctor about a case or series of similar cases in which all observations are documented, from the clinical findings to the outcomes. These are often reports of previously unseen disorders, disorders that have been seen but under different circumstances and disorders that have an uncommon occurrence. Case reports are useful for clinicians to see what others have seen and to point to a direction for treatment or further research.

Retrospective studies: Retrospective studies are an "after the fact" analysis of what might have produced the effect you have seen. For example, if you see a difference between two populations (such as comparing dogs that had a specific illness to similar dogs that didn't get the illness) you can look in the past at what has been recorded or reported to see if you can statistically identify what factors were associated with the differences. These are very useful for directing a researcher's attention to something that he might not have noticed before all the data were grouped and examined.

Prospective experimental or clinical trials: In a prospective experiment, you do something and then look for the effect. The more controls you apply, the more valid your results, because you are eliminating other variables that could be having an effect. For example, you take two groups of college students, have one group stay up all night and study and have the other group study until 11:00 p.m. and then get a good night's sleep. Give both groups the same test the next morning and compare the scores. In this case you would be looking at the effect of sleep on test scores. Your results will be more valid if you randomize which student goes into which experimental group and you can hold everything else constant (for example, if both groups had similar scores going into the experiment and got the same total number of hours studying).

The gold standard is a double- or triple-blinded research study. In this case there are control groups (subjects that are given a placebo) as well as experimental groups (subjects that are given the substance being studied). Everything else is held constant between the two groups and neither the test subjects nor the researcher know which groups the subjects are in (this is why it is called "blinded") until all testing is done.

The best experimental studies of any kind are those published in peer-reviewed journals. This means that in order for the study to be published, other researchers in the field must evaluate the research paper, and the experimental methods and conclusions are held to a high standard. There is a great deal more reliability in an experimental finding that had proper controls and was published in a peer-reviewed journal.

When you hear about research in which something was discovered or evidence that "proves" something was found, it is always important to examine how the people reporting this came to that conclusion. A company that is just providing testimonials about its own products may not be giving evidence that will stand up well to further testing. If it is a major study that was initially reported in a respected journal like *Nature* or the *New England Journal of Medicine,* it is a lot more likely that further testing will show the conclusions to be sound.

Conclusions are only as good as the evidence that generated them. As new discoveries are made, new evidence may cause us to reject older conclusions in favor of newer ones. This too is part of the scientific method.

Portions of this chapter were adapted from *Cyber-Safe Kids, Cyber-Savvy Teens: Helping Young People Learn to Use the Internet Safely and Responsibly* by Nancy E. Willard.

Common Medical Considerations in Aging Dogs

4 Perceptions

Sensory Changes in Older Dogs

I have a little shadow that goes in and out with me
And what can be the use of him is more than I can see....
One morning, very early, before the sun was up,
I rose and found the shining dew on every buttercup;
But my lazy little shadow, like an arrant sleepyhead,
Had stayed at home behind me and was fast asleep in bed.

In Robert Louis Stevenson's charming poem, a child delights in noticing that his shadow goes everywhere with him. He even sees it jump before him as he jumps into his bed. Then one day it seems that the shadow has become lazy and forgotten all about following our young narrator around. Of course the shadow is not really lazy, as our child protagonist concludes.

You may notice that your dog has stopped jumping up and greeting you at the door or stopped coming when you call and, like the child in this poem, you conclude that your canine companion is simply lazy—or old. However, like the incorrect assumption of the child in the poem, there might be an essential ingredient missing—just like the shadow needs sunlight to form, your dog needs to hear that you are home to come and greet you. In other words, your dog may have changed how he reacts to you because he can no longer hear you or see you as well (or at all).

The first thing to consider, if your dog changes a previously consistent behavior, is that his health needs to be examined by his veterinarian. We know that the first sign of illness in an older dog

Eternal Puppy

is often a change in behavior like drinking more water or needing to go outside more often. Not every behavior change is due to a medical problem although sometimes it is. Don't accept every behavioral change as normal—be on top of your dog's day-to-day activity. I don't want to say, "Run to the vet every other day," but you have to know when immediate veterinary help will make a significant difference. You're reading this book so that you can make the best educated guess and therefore be a responsible dog owner. Other chapters in this book will describe some of the subtle behavior changes that could be indicative of illness in older dogs. However, a behavioral change also can be an indication that a dog's senses have begun to deteriorate.

HEARING

Hearing impairment is, unfortunately, fairly common in older dogs. It is possible that any mammal that lives long enough will experience hearing loss.

Here is how a person or a dog is able to perceive sound: sound waves enter the ear and move the tympanic membrane (ear drum), which in turn moves a complex structure made of tiny bones (ossicles) called the malleus, incus and stapes in the middle ear. This in turn stimulates nerve cells located in the cochlea, a structure containing sensory nerve cells in the inner ear. The nerve impulses from the cochlea travel to the brain, where they are recognized and understood. So there are three major areas in which disruption can occur and result in hearing loss: a failure to conduct the sound waves through the mechanical structures of the ear due to damage of these structures; loss of nerve cells in the cochlea (neurogenic) and failure of the brain to recognize and understand the incoming signals.

Causes of Hearing Loss

Most frequently, the hearing loss in aging dogs is of the neurogenic category—loss of nerve cell receptors in the inner ear. This age-related hearing loss, called presbycusis, is progressive and cannot be prevented or reversed. A hearing aid cannot help this form of deafness for long, since it is caused by progressive nerve damage.

Hearing aids are only sound amplifiers and can't help if there are no receptors left to detect the amplified sound. (It is also hard to get a dog to be cooperative with the use of this expensive device.)

Other causes of hearing loss can be prevented. For instances, gundogs and other hunting dogs who are exposed to sudden loud noises can lose their hearing, as can dogs who suffer from recurrent ear infections. Both types of hearing loss can be prevented: the first by not exposing dogs to loud sudden noises (like on a shooting range), and the second by consistently and completely treating ear infections.

Chronic ear infections can be a result of systemic illnesses such as allergies or hypothyroidism, so if your dog is getting ear infections with regularity, a more thorough work-up may be in order. Chronic infections can lead to calcification and a narrowing of the ear canal in addition to the muffling of sound caused by build-up of crud (infective material and exudates) in the ear canal. The calcification is painful and in time can lead to the need for a total or partial ear-canal resection. Depending on the degree of damage, the hearing loss from infections can be reversible.

You should also be careful not to be too aggressive or too frequent in cleaning the ears of your dog, as this can cause inflammation and make ear-infection problems worse. Other sporadic causes of hearing loss can be from some drugs and rare anesthesia reactions.

Signs of Hearing Loss

There is not a lot of research on the prevalence of presbycusis in dogs. We also don't know enough to state a typical age of onset, and there are so many variables that we may never be able to determine this with great accuracy. A "guesstimate" is that it will probably become noticeable in the fourth quarter of a dog's expected lifespan.

It may seem to you that your dog "lost his hearing overnight," when in reality the hearing loss has likely been progressive and just passed a threshold where it is now noticeable. Your dog may engage in some behaviors that can be misinterpreted to be cognitive dysfunction or senility. For example, your dog may wake abruptly in the night with a loud hullabaloo of barking, as though he suddenly heard an intruder. Or you may be talking to your dog but he is gazing around with a strange look on his face because he can't locate the sound. Or he may be startled if you touch him when he's sleeping because he didn't hear you approach. He might even jump up and snap due to being startled.

Some dog owners are convinced that a dog with hearing loss can actually hear them and is just ignoring them. This is because, while the dog doesn't respond to the owner's calls, he does come running when he "hears" the can opener or the car keys jangling. It helps you to know that with the hearing loss observed in canine presbycusis, the sound frequencies are not all lost in an even fashion. It is possible that your dog might not easily hear the sound frequency of your voice but is still able to hear another frequency well, such as the grinding of the can opener or you clapping your hands.

Helping Your Dog

What can you do to help? First of all, recognize that the loss of hearing can occur before we notice it and give your dog the benefit of the doubt when his behavior changes (such as not coming when you call). Second, be aware that once this process has begun, your dog is at risk from threats he can no longer hear, like an approaching car or a collapsing chair. This means that you will need to become more proactive about your dog's safety and not assume that he can take care of himself. As the hearing impairment progresses, your old-timer will have difficulty hearing your voice or locating sounds. For example, if you go walking and let your dog off leash in a wooded area, your dog could get lost and not be able to follow your voice back to you. If you know that your dog has hearing loss and might not be able to hear your voice, he should not be allowed to go unleashed in unfenced outdoor locations.

An additional threat to a middle-aged or old dog who is losing his ability to hear is that his owner might not notice the hearing loss and thus continue to do the same outdoor activities with the dog, not realizing that the dog is now unable to hear his voice at a distance. In my part of the country, it is very common for dog owners to enjoy the outdoors with their dogs on weekends, doing things like going to the lake or hiking in the woods. While dog and owner may have been sharing pleasurable activities like this for years, the owner may not realize that his dog can no longer hear well enough to find his way back after going off to follow an interesting scent. Having your dog get lost in the woods (and potentially losing him permanently) is not a good way to discover that your dog can no longer hear your voice. A way to deal with this potential problem is to put a bell on your older dog if you are going on an outdoor jaunt so that you can hear the bell and locate him if he gets out of your sight. You also must recognize that as the years increase, your dog's ability to hear you will decrease, and keep him leashed when outdoors if you are unsure that he can hear you.

Another useful strategy to use at home is to train your dog to hand signals. Hand signals are a good way to communicate requests (such as sit, down and stay) to a deaf dog. In addition, training to respond to a whistle may help some dogs because they may continue to be able to hear the frequency range of the whistle even after they have lost the ability to hear the frequency range of your voice.

If your dog is waking up disoriented at night, barking "intruder alert" at burglars who aren't there, this may be happening in a moment of disorientation between sleep and waking. Humans experiencing hearing loss can develop tinnitus, a subjective sound that no one else can hear. We don't know if dogs also experience this, but it could explain some of the unusual behaviors seen in dogs developing deafness. To help, placing a small night light near your dog's sleeping area might assist him in orienting to where he is and what is happening around him.

You can also help by running interference for your dog and recognizing that he may not hear you or others approaching when he is resting. Be gentle and careful about waking him. Also be cautious of letting young children (or other pets) play around the dog when he is resting, as they may accidentally stumble over him, startling him awake. This precaution prevents injuries to all parties, human and canine.

Although they do require some adaptation, dogs don't suffer when affected by age-related hearing loss. It is not painful and, for the most part, they adjust to the gradual changes with little difficulty. Their quality of life can be as good as ever. And with a little understanding and common sense, few changes will be needed on your part.

VISION

As you gaze into the eyes of your eternal puppy, you will notice that his eyes are not as clear and reflective as they were in his youth. The eyes of older dogs take on a cloudy appearance that you can see if you look closely. At first it seems that a dog may be getting cataracts, yet he appears to still be able to see as well as before. At other times, it may seem as though a dog has lost his sight overnight. And in some cases, what seems to be a sudden vision loss may only seem sudden; perhaps the dog's vision has been deteriorating gradually over some time but, being an adaptable creature in a familiar environment, he has not been showing outward signs. Then you rearranged the furniture and suddenly discovered that your dog wasn't seeing anymore. What is going on?

Causes of Vision Loss

The cloudiness seen in the eyes of mature dogs is usually a result of sclerosis, or hardening of the lens of the eye. The lens of the eye is made up of fibers in a very precise physical arrangement. These fibers are formed throughout the animal's life on the outer portion of the lens. Over time, the innermost fibers get more and more compressed. This results in a hard center to the lens and a difference in how light is transmitted through it. The fibers then reflect a bit more light, and that gives the cloudy appearance (the same process, called presbyopia, occurs in people and leads to the need for bifocals). However, the light-transmitting capabilities of the lens are still intact, and the dog has lost little of his vision. Think of it like a cheap shower curtain—at a distance it is opaque and you can't see through it. But if you get right up next to it, you have no trouble seeing through to the other side. The sclerotic lens is the same way: although you are seeing the reflection off the fibers, which makes the eye appear opaque, the retina in the back of the dog's eye is close to the lens and is getting the picture.

The functional difference between this and a cataract is that with a cataract, the light is not getting to the retina. Your dog's eyes can be checked by your veterinarian, but you can get a rough determination that there is still light getting to the retina by looking for the tapetal reflection. There is a thin membrane at the back of animals' eyes called the tapetum lucidum that reflects light. We humans lack this, which is why animals' eyes seem to glow in the dark when a light like a flashlight or headlight strikes them, and ours do not. If there is a greenish yellow reflection from your dog's eye, then you know that light is getting through the lens to the back of the eye, where the retina containing the nerve cell receptors for vision reside, and is bouncing back through the lens again.

Because humans are very visual, some of us would have difficulties with this amount of sclerosis in our lenses. But dogs don't read and don't need to drive a car at night, so this usually has little impact on them. In fact, the best any dog ever sees is around 20/75 or so, compared with humans who, when they have perfect vision, can see 20/20. Although sclerosis and some retinal degeneration can happen due to age, the visual loss that occurs in dogs is generally not so much age-related but rather related to a specific disease condition. While the incidence of ocular problems may increase a bit with age, breed-related issues far outweigh age as a factor in the development of blindness in dogs.

Signs of Vision Loss

Things to watch for that indicate the occurrence of eye disease are redness, sudden changes in appearance, yellowish greenish discharge, squinting or sudden visual loss. If you notice any of these signs, it should prompt a visit to your veterinarian. If you have a breed that is known to have a higher incidence of eye diseases, you need to be extra vigilant and observant of changes.

Glaucoma is seen in dogs. It is mostly breed-related, that is, genetic in disposition, and increases in prevalence in middle age. Although a periodic measurement for intraocular pressure is a highly beneficial tool for early identification of glaucoma in people, recent research has shown that this is not effective for early identification in dogs. The mechanism of disease is different in dogs and, in a susceptible dog, glaucoma can come on rapidly and severely, whereas the most common form in humans is chronic and slow-developing. The aforementioned signs are the most useful in monitoring for this disease. Again, if you have a dog of a high-risk breed, increased attention, prompt identification and intervention are important.

Helping Your Dog

If a dog is diagnosed as having a cataract, cataract surgery is a possibility, provided that the dog is otherwise healthy, is a good anesthesia candidate and does not have any other ocular problems such as retinal disease, inflammation or corneal disease.

Unlike people, most dogs can adjust to loss of sight with relative ease. Because people are very visual and we use our sight all the time, the loss of sight can be very harrowing for us. In addition, people move by balancing on two teetering legs, which is not the easiest way to get around if you can't see. Losing their sight is just a bump in the road, not the end of the world, for dogs. Blind dogs never cease to amaze us with their ability to adjust, get around and keep their joyful love of life. These dogs will rely on memorized routes around the house, so moving the furniture or leaving objects in the dogs' regular pathways can be a problem. And, as mentioned previously, sometimes it is only due to changes in their familiar environment (such as rearranging the furniture) that owners become aware of their dogs' diminished vision.

It is important that your dog doesn't become socially isolated, especially if he is adapting to both vision and hearing loss. Remember that the dog can still feel vibrations from the floor and other kinds of touch, so physical contact can be comforting.

SMELL AND TASTE

Dogs have a highly developed sense of smell, 100,000 times more sensitive than that of people. Scenting capability plays a major role in how dogs interact with the environment, navigate and recognize individuals and places. There is not much research on if or how much a dog's sense of smell changes with age, but it appears that, even if some loss occurs, most older dogs are still within the normal range for dogs. It has been shown that certain diseases can cause a profound loss of smell. Some endocrine diseases, some canine viruses and periodontal disease can all interfere with a dog's ability to smell, although recovery from these diseases is thought to reverse the loss of scenting capability. Some things, like head trauma or tumors, may cause a permanent loss.

A geriatric dog may have only 25% of the taste buds that he had at one year of age. This, plus the reduction in saliva from the gradual drying of tissues that is common with age, has the potential to make food tasteless for a dog. If your old dog is losing weight due to reduced food consumption, increasing the tastiness of the food might stimulate his appetite.

PROPRIOCEPTION

Proprioception is the sense that tells you where your body is in space. It tells if you are sitting or standing, whether the surface under your feet is level or tilted, whether you are still or moving and, if moving, in what direction. It does this through a system of sensory neurons in muscles, joints and the balance portion of the inner ear, called the labyrinth, which is connected to the cochlea. Studies with elderly people have shown that this sense deteriorates with age, and clinical observations of elderly dogs suggest that this can occur in them as well. Problems with the sense of proprioception will affect gait and balance. With people, these proprioception deficits increase with age, and it is not always possible to find a medical cause.

Proprioception, however, is one of those senses that appears to respond favorably to usage. Studies, again with people, have shown that a program of muscle-strength and balance exercises can help improve balance in older people experiencing a reduction of this sense. Veterinary physical rehabilitators have developed techniques for aiding movement and balance in animals; even walking your dog on a variety of surfaces, like a level sidewalk and the uneven ground at a park, may assist in preventing some of the proprioceptive loss.

TOUCH AND PAIN

It is generally believed that the ability to sense touch and pain do not decrease with age. For example, a dog that is both blind and deaf can still detect his owner's approach by feeling the vibrations of the owner's steps upon the floor. However, an important factor to consider is that, while a dog's sensation of pain may not decrease, his ability to engage in adaptive responses to that pain may decrease with age. Because of that, pain may be observed as a slowing down or a set of disabilities (a cessation of things the dog used to do, like climb the stairs or hop up on the sofa to sleep) instead of the outward signs we are more likely to associate with pain, like whining or acting disturbed.

TIPS FOR HELPING A BLIND DOG

Getting Around

- A blind dog utilizes scent trails and memorized paths to navigate his home, so if you rearrange the furniture, relocate his bed or move his food and water bowls, he will need some help learning the new paths. It is best to keep the environment as consistent as possible. Some owners have used scented oils in hallways and on doorways to help their dogs navigate.
- When out on walks, use a flat collar or harness and allow your dog to use the leash for guidance. Trainers often say that your body language travels down the leash, and a well-attuned dog can become very aware of his owner's every move.
- Train a touch or auditory signal for "step up," "step down" and "wait" so you can alert your dog to changes in the terrain when out on walks.
- Going up and down stairs can be problematic for some dogs at first, but with encouragement and patience, most blind dogs will learn to do this.

Safety Considerations

Be alert to dangers that your dog will not be able to see, for example:
- Put a baby gate at the top of stairs to prevent falling.
- Make sure that the pool, garden ponds and other hazards in your yard are covered or fenced off from your dog.
- Keep his pathways through the house cleared.

Other Considerations

- A dog that is crate trained may feel safe and at home in his crate, especially if he is experiencing confusion or frustration.
- If your dog is showing some anxiety, be encouraging but don't coddle him, as this can reinforce his fears.
- Keep your dog's teeth clean. With diminished sight, your dog will be relying more on his sense of smell, and periodontal disease can hamper a dog's sense of smell.
- A good book is *Living With Blind Dogs* by Caroline Levine.

So with increasing age or conditions with chronic pain, the dog may be less and less able to show the pain he is experiencing and may be less able to engage in strategies that could bring relief.

In addition, with chronic pain, a "rewiring" of sensory neurons can occur. When this altered connectivity between different types of sensory fibers occurs, it is possible that the nerve fibers that used to carry the message of touch to the brain will now connect with an area that interprets this as pain. When this happens, mere touch can become painful. This is part of a process called "central hypersensitization," which amplifies chronic pain. So instead of the sensation of touch and pain diminishing with age, when a condition of chronic pain is present, this sense can become hypersensitive and turn, as it were, to the "dark side."

Because touch is a well-preserved sense, it is important that we use this to keep in close contact with our dogs through our own sense of touch, bringing comfort and companionship with our hands, using them to check in on the welfare of our companions.

CONCLUSION

A disability is not the same thing as an inability to participate in life. Any one of us can likely think of people we know who have adjusted to the diminishment or loss of a sense and gone on to live a full, rich and joyful life. The same is true of a dog who is experiencing a diminishment of his senses as an age-related change. A blind or deaf dog will not pity himself: he will go on about his life, learning to deal with his new circumstances. Therefore, you should not pity him either. Instead you should understand and give him the tools to assist him in continuing his journey. I think that it is with deep respect and great reward that we provide the necessary modifications and understanding to allow a dog's indomitable spirit to shine through the fog that diminishing senses brings.

5 Pain

Effects on Body and Mind

"Would getting older cause a change in personality in a dog?" my friend Donna asked me over coffee. "I've noticed that Bear has been acting different lately." Bear is her eight-year-old Labrador cross.

"What's different?" I asked.

"Well, it's like he has lost his sense of humor," she explained. "When we are out on walks, he doesn't want to play with other dogs like he used to. At home he seems, well, grumpy. Just not his old cheerful self. Would his personality be changing just because he is getting older?"

"The first sign of a medical problem is often a change in behavior," I said, "so I would suggest having him checked by his vet. Also, what you are describing could be because he is in pain. For example, he could be developing arthritis."

"That's something to consider," Donna said. "He has had a very active life."

Whether or not Bear's behavioral change is from pain, this conversation made me consider how hard it is for us to ask the question "Is he in pain?" when we notice that something has changed in our dogs. Why isn't it higher on our list of considerations? Even though Donna is a caring and conscientious dog owner, why hadn't she considered that her dog's "loss of sense of humor" might be related to pain?

If we initially miss that our dogs are in pain, it is not for lack of love, intelligence or desire to understand. It just isn't on our radar often enough. We don't think about it and don't know what to look

for. Denying that animals have thoughts and the ability to feel pain has been a part of Western science, medicine and culture for a long time.

SPLITTING THE MIND AND BODY

In the 17th century, scientist, philosopher and mathematician Rene Descartes proposed a philosophical concept called dualism. In this concept, the body is material and responds to the laws of physics, while the mind (or soul) is non-material and does not follow the laws of physics. This philosophy of dualism helped create the artificial mind-body split that still plagues Western medicine today.

Descartes additionally believed that only humans had minds and so concluded that animals lacked the ability to think or feel. He described animals as "mindless automatons," simply responding to stimuli with no capacity to feel pain. A dog that cries out when struck feels no more pain than a bell that rings out when it is struck by its clapper, he once wrote. Of course, that is nonsense, but this mistaken concept was carried forward along with valid scientific advancements that he and those who came after him made.

In the early 20th century, psychologist J. B. Watson said that to study behavior one could only look at observable effects. Humans can self-report their thoughts and feelings but because complex brain processes were not observable in animals with the technology of the time, it was concluded that thoughts and feelings in animals didn't occur. Any description of subjective states—that is, what was occurring internally—was avoided in scientific literature. Experimental animals weren't described as being hungry, they were described as being 24-hour food-deprived. Animals given electric shocks weren't described as being in pain and fear, they were described as vocalizing and showing avoidance behaviors.

Although there was no experimentation to support them, these concepts became codified in Western scientific thought. And so, based on the writings of an albeit famous 17th-century philosopher, the concepts that the mind and body are separate and that animals have no feelings have persisted. And based on almost 100-year-old writings of a psychologist, the concept that animals have no complex mental abilities and thus we are not to consider subjective states (thoughts, feelings) in them has persisted. Considerable scientific studies have more recently shown these concepts to be false. But, unfortunately, long-held beliefs, even bad ones shown to be untrue, die hard.

One of the things that we have come to learn is that the mind-body split is a myth. Health and disease affect mental processes, and mental processes, such as thoughts and emotions, affect health and disease. Chronic unresolved pain, for example, can harm your pet's physical health. Likewise, health problems can dramatically affect an animal's behavior.

CHANGING OUR FOCUS

Because of this history of denying that animals have feelings, we have not been taught to easily tune our eye to the signs of pain in animals.

So let's change the focus to a different perspective on pain and your dog with a few imaginary questions:

- Is your dog losing weight and his appetite because he has lost his zest for life, or is he in pain, making it difficult for him to eat?
- Is your dog grumpy and stubborn because he is a jerk (yes, I have heard this assessment), or is he in pain?
- Did he snap at you when you tripped over him because he has become dominant or aggressive and can't be trusted, or does he have arthritic hips and reacted in the extremes of pain?
- Is he senile when he wets in the house, or is pain making it hard for him to get to the appropriate potty place?
- Is he aloof and uncaring when he doesn't come sleep in the bedroom with you anymore, or has the pain in his hips made it too hard to negotiate the slippery stairs?
- Is he moving slowly from lack of interest or obedience, or is he guarding himself against further injury and pain?
- Is he disobedient when he sleeps on the furniture when your back is turned, or is his only alternative a cold hard floor, making him hurt? (We'll talk about geriatric bedding later.)
- Has he lost his zest for life and desire to play, or has it been driven out by pain?
- Has your dog slowed down, or has pain slowed him down?
- And, most importantly, if the problem is really pain, wouldn't we like to do something to help?

Of course, pet owners are the most aware of how their pets are doing, but sometimes fine-tuning our focus can open our eyes to a different way of looking at what is before us.

CATEGORIES OF PAIN

There are two major categories of pain: acute and chronic. Acute pain is severe pain that comes on suddenly and is what occurs after an injury or surgery, while chronic pain persists for a long time and occurs with things like cancer and arthritis. Acute pain is an adaptive, protective response to protect the body from further injury. For example, it was very painful if I put any weight on my recently broken foot—thus keeping me from using it and further damaging it. Pain causes avoidance behaviors, including slowing down and avoiding movements that cause pain, improving the potential for healing to occur. But chronic pain, which is long-term and continuous, can become maladaptive. It does little good and may actually cause harm.

EXPRESSIONS OF PAIN

It is important to realize that every animal is an individual and will express pain in its own unique way. And also, just as pain changes over time, so too may the animal's reaction to it. Frequently there will be a complex of behaviors. However, while there are characteristic behaviors and body postures that are recognizable in an animal experiencing pain, just because a dog doesn't display a specific pain-related behavior does not mean that he is not in pain. There are a number of circumstances that may cause an animal to temporarily mask its pain. Especially important to consider is that as a dog ages, his ability to engage in protective behaviors may be diminished or slowed. This slower response, however, in no way means that the dog is feeling less pain.

There are also personality factors to consider. As most dog lovers know, some dogs are stoic while others are more reactive and show their pain more readily. Depending on the circumstances, when a dog is out for an enjoyable day at the park with you, he may do what any of us do: become unaware of the pain while he is having fun and thus be less likely to show it outwardly. A shy and anxious dog may mask pain when others are around. The first sign of pain in our companion might be very subtle, like not chasing a ball for as long as he usually does or, as my friend noticed in her dog, a loss of his sense of humor.

Some behaviors that can be seen in an animal in pain are also seen with other diseases and due to other causes. For example, trembling can be seen in an animal that is in pain, but an animal also may tremble if he is cold, frightened, feverish, or suffering from a metabolic disease and so on. Whining can mean pain, anxiety or even anticipation of dinner. This is why you look for multiple signs. Recognizing pain requires that we heighten our attention and become careful observers. Possible expressions of a dog in pain can include changes in movement, body posture, behavior and expression.

Changes in movement. Limping or guarding an injured area, walking stiffly, slowness to rise or a reluctance to move may signal pain in an animal. These signs may be subtle and not easy to recognize. You may see a dog who doesn't come up the stairs to the bedroom anymore, doesn't greet you when you come home, seems slow urinating or defecating, changes posture while eliminating (for example, a male dog that no longer lifts his leg to urinate) or avoids the slippery linoleum kitchen floor (a sudden slip and recovery can cause pain). Your dog may be reluctant to jump into the car or onto the bed or couch, or he may require your help to do so. These changes can be more easily noticed if they come on quickly, such as after an injury. However, if these changes come on slowly, they may be just as indicative of pain, but harder for us to notice. Because of this, we need to be extra alert to these types of changes.

Change in body posture. An animal in pain might shift its body to bear more weight on its good limbs; for example, a dog with painful hips might shift more weight onto the front legs and move them more under the body for balance. This can also cause a change in muscle mass conformation. For instance, a dog with hip osteoarthritis will have atrophied muscles in his rear quarters and a somewhat barrel-chested appearance as he shifts his weight forward off the painful hip area. A dog may not raise his head as much or may carry his tail lower. Instead of having a straight back, he might bend his body to one side or the other. Back or neck pain may make it hard for a dog to lower his head to eat from a bowl on the floor, so he may eat for a while and then stop because he can't hold the painful position needed to eat the food.

Changes in behavior. These could include changes such as rest-lessness, increased irritability, loss of appetite or eating more slowly, being grumpy or anxious and even showing aggressiveness that is out of character, which might manifest as a dog who growls and snaps if children are playing too close to him. Your dog may decrease his interactions with you and with other dogs, no longer greeting you or trying to find an out-of-the-way place to sleep. He may start house-soiling. A dog who is in pain may start licking at a painful joint or he may lick or chew some other part of his body as a distraction from his pain, potentially causing injury at that location. Or your dog might stop playing as much. Instead of running the tennis ball into the ground, your dog may only fetch it a few times and then stop. Your dog may seem to have lost his pleasure in activities he previously enjoyed.

Pain-induced aggression, a behaviorial change of particular concern, is often a result of the instinctual "fear, fight or flight" response. When an animal encounters a threat to its security, these instinctual behaviors will take over and occur without conscious thought or intent. This can occur when a dog is placed in—or threatened with—sudden severe pain. This is a situation you want to make every effort to avoid, for all concerned.

Changes in facial expression. A dog may acquire a worried look or a fixed or glazed expression. He may look at or stare at the body part that is causing him pain. These facial expressions will be most obvious when the dog doesn't know he is being observed. A study that video-taped dogs postsurgery showed that the dogs exhibited much more pain behavior when they were alone than when their caregivers were present. This is an important point to remember—our dogs may be suffering in silence when we are not watching.

Vocalizing. This includes whining, crying, whimpering, groaning or growling. However, vocalizing is a nonspecific sign because it is seen for a number of reasons. Also, because people can talk, we tend to express our pain in human language ("Oooh, my aching feet!"). We are then trained by our experience to expect the expression of sounds as a reliable indicator of pain. But animals are not able to talk, and some may not vocalize until pain is moderate or severe. This kind of sign is therefore more reliable with people than it is with animals, because an animal is more likely to be silently experiencing pain than a person is.

AGGRESSION AND PAIN

"I don't know what happened, doctor. He has always been so gentle, so steady with the children. He always seems to love them. How could this happen?"

This woman's children were playing in the room and stumbled over the sleeping dog, who, completely out of character, woke with a roar and snapped at one of the children. Now a child could be injured or at least badly frightened, and the family is devastated and torn between their love for their child, their need to be responsible, their fear it will happen again and their love and loyalty to their old dog.

Worse still, it could have been a neighbor's child who was involved, and now the neighbors are clamoring for the family to get rid of "that vicious dog." After all, "everyone knows" that once a dog has bitten, he can never be trusted again.

Fear and pain can stimulate an instinctual fight or flight reflex that includes, among other things, lashing out at the source of the pain. (After all, if the source of the pain were something attacking you, this would be a matter of survival.) Imagine how it must be for a dog to be woken up in sudden, unimaginable pain with his only thought being to get away from this threat. Imagine if you were asleep and a 300-pound person stepped on your foot. You would likely wake and, without thought or deliberation, you would strike out and kick at the source of the pain. A dog lashing out in the extremes of pain is not the same thing as an aggressive, untrustworthy dog.

If your dog has shown aggression, take precautions to prevent injury to others and have him examined for illness or painful conditions. If necessary, consult a veterinary behaviorist to determine the causes, evaluate the risk and make a plan and recommendations. If the aggression was sudden and out of character for this dog, and this is a dog that is in pain and was put in a situation of immediate severe pain, then managing the pain and managing the dog (including giving him a place to sleep where children will not disturb him) are reasonable options. All dog bites (or near bites) should be taken very seriously. But an overreaction to a reflexive protective action on the part of the dog can result in a tragic irreversible decision to end an innocent dog's life.

PHYSIOLOGICAL EFFECTS OF PAIN

Managing your pet's pain is more than just an issue of welfare and compassion. Pain can have a deleterious effect on the health and longevity of your pet. Pain, both acute and chronic, is capable of causing a stress response in the body. In the short term, the stress response is designed to mobilize resources to help an animal in a fight or flight situation. But as stress becomes prolonged, it starts harming rather than helping the body.

Suppression of the Immune System

Pain can cause suppression of the immune system, impairing the dog's ability to fight infection or cancer effectively. The chemical mediators of the stress response act to break down protein, which causes damage to muscle tissue. The stress response can lead to poor wound healing and increased wound infection. It can impair learning patterns and memory. Chronic pain can cause weight loss, poor haircoat conditions and an acceleration of aging. Because of the effects of pain on the immune system, pain management is also a vital part of cancer therapy and management. Pain, in reality, can steal time from your pet's life and life from that time.

Rewiring the Central Nervous System

One of the inevitable consequences of chronic pain is a rewiring of the central nervous system's response to touch and pain receptors. As the painful condition continues, the chemical mediators that are produced cause the growth of some nerve fibers in the spinal cord. Usually the nerve fibers that conduct the sense of touch are separate and terminate in a different location than the fibers that conduct the message of pain. But when this new growth occurs, the nerve fibers that used to carry the sense of touch to the brain now interconnect with the fibers that carry the message of pain. When this occurs, pain is amplified and even mere touch can become painful. This process is called central hypersensitization (*central*, meaning it is in the central nervous system and *hypersensitization*, as mentioned previously, meaning that the sense of pain increases).

Pain from an affected area can also interconnect with neurons from other geographic areas of the body, so eventually the pain seems to emanate from wider areas than the spot actually causing it. Another kind of rewiring causes the pain receptors to have a lower threshold so that what was previously minimally painful is now moderately or severely painful. In addition, because it "winds up" the ability to feel pain, this effect increases the sensation and duration of pain after an injury. And lastly, this sensitization and the stress response to pain increase the likelihood of creating a permanent memory of the pain and its surrounding circumstances so that similar circumstances can trigger pain.

These changes and others are more likely to occur the longer the painful condition is present. How much, when and to what degree they occur are individual to each dog. All dogs with chronic pain from osteoarthritis will develop some manifestations of central hypersensitivity, though not all dogs will begin to associate pain with touch. Experience with people, who can verbalize their sensations and perceptions, shows how this can occur with some individuals. This and other processes can lead to pain that is amplified in duration and intensity and becomes increasingly difficult to treat.

This information emphasizes why we should treat pain sooner rather than later. If you take the long view, you will see that whatever you do to reduce pain when your dog is first starting to show the signs of pain (like being stiff in the morning) will not only help now but also help years from now.

PAIN MANAGEMENT

Pain is like the multi-headed Hydra of Greek mythology. The best way to combat it is to get the jump on it and go after it with a diversity of weapons. Pain management is not just about using pills, although drug intervention is one part of the approach. It is instead about taking the broad view and intercepting pain on its many fronts. It is a multimodal process, a change in philosophy and lifestyle. The different modes of pain management work in concert with each other, so using more than one approach can produce a synergistic, and thus more beneficial, effect.

Start by being proactive in detecting pain, remembering that dogs do not always show obvious outward signs. Once every day, run your hands completely over your dog from the tip of his nose to the tip of his toes. Pay special attention to detecting any areas of tension, heat, swelling or other concerns.

When utilizing any form of pain management, keep track of some concrete objective indications of progress. These indications should be individualized to your particular dog and circumstances. For example, you might want to monitor your dog's ability to walk up a specific set of stairs or make note of how many times he will retrieve a tennis ball. You may want to record this information in a notebook or on a calendar so that you can refer to it later, enabling you to adapt and re-evaluate as needed.

Keeping Your Dog Comfortable

Owners have many options to help keep their old dogs comfortable and help with pain management. Consider some of the following topics:

Physical rehabilitation: A common avenue in human recovery, physical rehabilitation is an often overlooked, but powerful, branch of medicine with proven benefits in pain relief and improved mobility for dogs, too. Included under this would also be acupuncture and massage.

Changing the set-up: Your dog's comfort may be improved by items as ordinary as the right pillow or bed or a higher bowl. Take a "dog's eye" look around your home and think about what it is like for your dog to live there. What can you do to make it more comfortable for your dog?

Proper exercise: Are you exhausted by those people who recommend exercise for everything? Just the sight of a Jazzercise class or treadmill makes me weary, but dogs, even old ones, welcome a certain amount of exercise. Exercise can loosen tight muscles, strengthen muscle tone, flex tight joints, oxygenate the tissues and release "feel good" hormones. However, exercise is beneficial only if it is consistent with your dog's abilities.

Nutrition and diet: Both can play a role in pain management, too, especially if you have an overweight beast at home. Sometimes the reduction in weight in an overweight dog is all that is needed to take a dog from needing considerable intervention (surgery for an orthopedic condition or extensive pain management) to being a dog who requires much less intervention and enjoys life more. Further, some nutritional supplements are showing promise in helping to manage inflammation and modify pain.

Drugs

Nonsteroidal anti-inflammatory drugs (NSAIDs) are often the first line of defense among drugs commonly used to control pain and inflammation. But drug therapy for pain management does not stop there. Another important category of drugs to manage pain is the opioids. Morphine and codeine, for example, are human preparations of drugs in this family; there are others available for dogs. Some forms of antidepressants are sometimes prescribed— not because of their effect on depression but because they appear to alter how the nerves in the brain perceive and react to pain. In addition, there are a number of exciting developments in recent years for novel pain therapies. In the future, the choices for pain-management drugs approved for dogs will likely improve.

CONCLUSION

No one knows your dog better than you do. Once you know what to look for and tune your senses to these things, you can become more aware of when your dog is feeling pain. With awareness and compassion comes the ability to help. No one therapy is best for treating pain; instead, by using a variety of pain therapies, they act synergistically with each other.

6 Arthritis

The Vicious Circle

As an old Chinese proverb puts it, "A man dies from the feet up." You can almost say that movement is life, and for a dog this is probably even truer than it is for people. Without the ability to move, a dog can't get to his food and water, get to a comfortable sleeping place, get to a potty place or even get to the window to see what is happening. While we use speech, dogs use movement for communication. Without movement, it is hard for a dog to be a dog and to engage in any of the behaviors that give joy or have meaning. For a dog, movement is life and gives life meaning.

When difficulty in moving is coupled with constant, unrelenting pain that intensifies with every step, life can become very difficult indeed. Arthritis, which causes pain and hampers movement, can suck the life and vitality out of your beloved companion. If the signs of arthritis are not recognized or if nothing is done to treat the disease until it is too late, the dog will suffer. It is when their dog is in constant pain and hardly able to move that many compassionate dog owners will choose to help a beloved dog through euthanasia rather than allow him to continue suffering this existence. Slowing the process of joint destruction and pain that can lead to this frozen endpoint is a very important part of care for the mature dog.

VICIOUS CIRCLES WITHIN CIRCLES

Arthritis is a disease but also a process. Instead of being a single vicious circle, looking at arthritis is like looking into the innards of a complex Swiss watch, with everything interlocking and interacting.

The arthritic process most often starts with some form of injury or insult to cartilage, the cushioning tissue that covers the ends of the bones at the joints. Cartilage has extremely limited healing or regenerative capability. It develops during embryogenesis and matures as the puppy grows to adult size. After that, "what you see is what you've got." The cartilage cells (called chondrocytes), which have limited blood supply, are kept healthy—fed and oxygenated—by the joint fluid within the joint capsule. Thus there is an integral relationship between the quality of the joint cartilage and the joint fluid. When an injury occurs to the cartilage, the chondrocytes release chemical signals that stimulate inflammation (redness, swelling and pain) and degradation (loss of cartilage quantity and quality).

Inflammation is a double-edged sword. Early in a disease process, it may have some beneficial effects by limiting continued overuse of the joint and inducing reparative processes. But chronic inflammation does more harm than good. Chronic inflammation causes production of chemical mediators that increase the rate of degeneration of the already damaged cartilage, and a vicious circle of damage, begetting inflammation, which begets more damage, starts. The ultimate results are pain, swelling, dysfunction and loss of quality of life in affected dogs.

The pain causes another vicious circle to form: the pain leads to less movement, which leads to further degeneration, which leads to more pain. That is because movement has numerous benefits for the joint, keeping it flexible, keeping the muscles that stabilize the joint strong and helping to circulate the joint fluid, which is needed to keep the chondrocytes healthy. In addition, it has been shown that appropriate exercise can actually reduce pain. Being frozen into immobility by the pain of arthritis only increases the rate of degeneration and ultimately causes more pain.

Pain is also debilitating, and chronic pain has the ability to up-regulate its own receptors, causing an intensification of pain and worsening a bad situation. The pain and reduced mobility from the arthritic process produce another vicious circle: reduced activity encourages weight gain. Obesity greatly accelerates the rate of the arthritic process through increased demands on the weight-bearing joints, reduction of mobility, reduction of flexibility of the joints and chemical signals produced by fat cells that encourage inflammation.

Another vicious circle involves proprioception, the sense of where the body is in space. It is a complex web of nerves in the muscles, skin and joints that interact with the areas in the brain that detect and coordinate movement. The sense of proprioception is what allows a being to move in a smooth and coordinated manner. Studies have shown that the arthritic process interferes with this system. If the sense of proprioception is not functioning optimally, some of the smoothness of movement can be lost. This has the potential of increasing the stress and concussion on the cartilage at the joints, increasing the potential for micro-injuries, thus increasing the potential for degeneration and pain. In a "use it or lose it" circumstance, movement can help reduce the proprioception deficits.

Increasing age is also a factor in the degeneration of cartilage. The cartilage matrix, which is a complex mixture of large protein molecules, is maintained by the chondrocytes. Aging diminishes the ability of the chondrocytes to synthesize and maintain the cartilage matrix. The cells become less able to produce matrix and the matrix that they do produce is substandard in both quantity and quality. The tissue loses its normal strength and resiliency, becoming unable to withstand the normal wear and tear of daily life, and begins to break down. You can then understand that when you put injury, degradation, obesity, inflammation and inadequate movement on top of this, the progression can be severe and rapid. Increasing age in a dog ramps up our need to be proactive in treating arthritis.

RISK FACTORS FOR ARTHRITIS

Age

Any vertebrate animal, domesticated or wild, will experience arthritic changes in its joints to some degree if it lives long enough. This is not just a result of being a domesticated animal, as demonstrated by several research reports by wildlife biologists researching wolves and coyotes. Most wild-dog relatives do not live long enough for arthritis to develop. One report, however, cited an aged wolf with considerable arthritic changes, which resulted in significant gait restriction, who still managed to kill two deer during the study time. Arthritis is the result of wear and tear on the joints and the endpoint of the damage accrued from living life. With dogs, given their various sizes, lifestyles and life expectancies, there can be a lot of variation in the age of onset, severity, joints affected and speed of progression.

Although age itself is not a disease (no matter what your mother used to tell you), the tendency to develop arthritis, which is a disease, increases with age. Simply put, the more time a dog (or any animal, including your mother) has on this hard-surfaced planet, the greater the opportunity to stress and damage the cartilage in his joints. Nonetheless, at any time in a dog's life, anything that damages or stresses the cartilage in the joints can cause small changes that can go on to become arthritis. Thus some dogs will develop arthritis when young because of injury or predisposing conformation. More commonly, however, it is a progressive disease that becomes more prevalent and severe with increasing age. Perhaps mom was right when she talked about her "old bones," as there is indeed an age-related change seen in older cartilage and joints, which are not as forgiving of physical insults as are younger joints, making it easier for arthritic changes to start and progress.

Weight and Size

There is probably no greater contributor to the development of arthritis than excess weight on the dog. Not only does obesity put additional stress on the skeleton that is carrying that extra weight, but also the fat cells themselves secrete substances that encourage inflammation and the development of arthritis.

Large-breed dogs have a higher incidence of arthritis than smaller dogs. This is due to the amount of stress that is put on the skeleton by the size of the dog and may also include factors relating to the speed of growth he experienced when young, as well as genetic predispositions in some breeds. However, this is not to say that osteoarthritis is not a concern for small-breed dogs as well.

Body Shape

The dog's skeletal frame was designed by nature to function optimally (although other wild canids still get arthritis with age). We humans took the shape that nature gave the dog and started tinkering with it. Given the variations in dog body types, the exaggerations sought after in some breeds and random breeding practices, we can end up with individual dogs whose joints are not at the optimal angles and who don't always develop into congruent, stable adults, which increases their risk for arthritis. For example, the confirmation of some German Shepherd Dogs' rear quarters may contribute to the development of arthritis. But this is not a problem seen only in purebred dogs, as some "oddly shaped" mixed-breed dogs may have a unique conformation that results in suboptimal joint angles, just due to the random assortment of genes. Dogs with orthopedic problems such as hip or elbow dysplasia, or those who have torn cruciate ligaments in the knee, will develop arthritis in the affected joints.

In addition, accidents and injuries can change the conformation of a joint. An injured joint can lead to damaging alterations in loads placed on other joints on that limb or on a compensating limb. An accident, such as being hit by a car, may cause the initial damage to the cartilage, setting the stage for a cascade of changes.

WHAT AN ARTHRITIC DOG LOOKS LIKE

Too often owners dismiss a dog's reduction of movement with the simple presumption, "Oh, he is just getting old and slowing down." Erase that concept from your consciousness. Instead of observing and just accepting that your dog is slowing down, ask yourself this question: "Why is my dog slowing down?" Dismissing the dog's slowing down with "he's just old" will cause you to miss early warning signs and may allow your dog to live in unnecessary pain.

Conditions that develop slowly are harder to recognize than something that causes a sudden change. Arthritis is a disease that has a chronic (long-standing) component but also can have acute (recent) flare-ups. So it is important to recognize that, just because your dog has recovered from an acute flare-up and looks good in comparison to his condition a short time before, it does not mean that he is no longer dealing with an underlying chronic condition that needs treating. The chronic disease makes the dog more susceptible to having acute flare-ups, so make sure that you are looking for evidence of both.

SPORTS AND ACTIVITIES

Just like a human athlete, a performance or working dog or a super-active dog who has spent a great deal of time bounding on hard surfaces, jumping in and out of trucks or twisting and turning through obstacle courses is more likely to pay the price of arthritis down the road. Any activity that smashes the joints together repeatedly has the potential to do small amounts of injury that can accumulate with time and lead to degenerative changes.

There's no doubt that dogs love vigorous, exciting activity, which can be pleasurable for both the dogs and their owners. By all means, young and in-shape adult dogs should enjoy this type of activity; in fact, keeping in shape and maintaining adequate muscle tone can help protect a dog's joints from injury when the dog does engage in physical activity. Canine athletes, like their human counterparts, benefit from warming up and stretching prior to taking part in vigorous activity. Keeping the dog in fit condition with frequent workouts is always better than sporadic hard exercise of the type that "weekend warriors" engage in.

Be aware, however, that as your dog approaches his mature years, you will need to lessen his participation in activities that can be stressful on the joints and increase your arthritis surveillance to be proactive about recognizing the onset and pursuing treatment.

Additionally, be cognizant of the fact that your aging dog can still get caught up in "the joy of the moment" and may try to do the same vigorous activities he did when young. Curb his enthusiasm, no matter how soul stirring it is to watch. A dog's unabashed enthusiasm can lead to cartilage damage and joint injury, so it is up to you to monitor your eternal puppy and step in when his enthusiasm gets the better of him.

Remember, too, that a dog may easily mask signs of arthritis when he's around you or doing something he loves. He may be so excited that you're tossing a Frisbee for him that he'll forget how sore his back legs were all day or he may be so happy to see you come home that he'll jump on his hind legs or tear around the house, forgetting all about his aching back and neck. Be sure to look out for the things you might see in a dog that is developing arthritis.

Early Changes in Behavior

Since your dog will be doing his best to compensate and modify his movement to minimize his pain, behavioral changes early on may be fairly subtle and thus difficult for you to recognize. Initially the arthritic dog may be shortening his stride or slowing his gait. He may develop alternative routes that put less discomfort on his joints, like going around something he used to jump over or finding an easier way to get around an obstacle. He may slow his speed, running for shorter periods of time, trotting when he used to run, walking when he used to trot. Generally he will reduce the distance he travels and the amount of time he plays. For instance, he used to chase a ball 20 times before wanting to take a break, and now he wants a break after 5 or 10 times.

An important early sign of arthritis that you should look for in your dog is the tendency to be stiff when rising and then warming out of the stiffness. You might also notice him hesitating slightly before jumping into the car or onto the sofa, things that he used to do effortlessly. He may change his regular resting areas and start to avoid contact with boisterous family members (such as youngsters of both the human and canine variety) who might knock into him, grab him or engage in rough play. What used to be fun and exciting can now cause pain. Instinctively your dog has been limiting his activities, interactions and routine to reduce the pain caused by movement. Take a close look at his muscle mass, as you may see that it's reduced along with his activity level.

Later Changes

As the damage and pain worsen, the signs you can see will be far more apparent. Now your dog may have difficulty going up or down stairs. He may start lagging behind when walking with you on lead. He may show increased stiffness after resting and lameness after strenuous exercise. He may be slow or have difficulty rising, sitting or squatting to eliminate. The pain could cause him to have sleeping problems and be restless at night. He may become grumpy or short-tempered and might whimper, yelp, growl or even snap when you touch him in certain areas. By this time, he is likely to be in constant

SKEPTICALLY OPTIMISTIC

"Slow-acting, disease-modifying osteoarthritis agent" is a term that refers to a number of compounds found in nature that are commonly called chondroprotectants. Some are given in the form of injectable compounds (like Adequan), others are marketed as nutraceuticals and given orally and still others are applied topically. Nature's pharmacopoeia is complex and diverse, and some of these compounds are showing great promise in slowing the progression of osteoarthritis and perhaps having beneficial effects with other conditions as well. There is a great deal of variation in how these compounds work and how much testing has been done with them. Some of them work, but not at the dosage, interval or amount that we are giving. Some are the modern equivalent of "snake oil." And some are really beneficial.

Although called chondroprotectants, there is much diversity in where these compounds actually have their effects. A given compound may affect more than one part of the vicious circle of cartilage destruction, inflammation and pain. Some compounds are said to improve the quality and quantity of joint fluid. Others appear to be taken up by the chondrocytes and stabilize the cartilage matrix. Some appear to help control inflammation. Some may do little or nothing at all (except empty your wallet).

Currently the research data looks promising with glucosamine and chondroitin combinations and the omega-3 fatty acids. Research is ongoing with a number of other compounds, and hopefully new findings will add new weapons to our arsenal.

The best thing that you can do as a pet owner is to be skeptically optimistic. Look for reliable research data. Talk to your veterinarian. If you start using these compounds, watch closely and measure improvement objectively. Most of these compounds take around a month to have an effect. Those that are showing promise appear to act synergistically with other treatment modalities, so don't rely on the compounds only. There is no harm in being hopeful provided that we, as my mother used to say, "put on our thinking caps."

and worsening pain. The vicious circles are all coming together to make him miserable and disabled.

DAMAGE CONTROL: A MULTIMODAL APPROACH TO ARTHRITIS MANAGEMENT

Because the cartilage cannot repair itself, it is not possible to heal arthritis once it has started. Our aim instead is to slow the degeneration, reduce the inflammation and limit the pain. Maintaining the ability to move and freedom from pain are our primary goals in an effort to improve the well-being of our beloved dogs. There is no single treatment that unequivocally works, in part because this is such a multifactorial disease, intermeshing at so many levels. Surprisingly for such a common disease, arthritis is also a poorly understood disease on many fronts. It is the subject of considerable research, with each finding a tiny stone to be placed in a huge mosaic—only with time will a coherent picture develop. As the owner of an aging pet, you should keep up on the latest treatments. Some sources where you can find these research reports include the Arthritis Foundation, veterinary medical teaching hospitals and the American Veterinary Medical Association (AVMA).

Guiding Principles

There are two guiding principles for arthritis management. First, because there are so many factors influencing the process of arthritis, our best approach is one that focuses on more than one factor in the disease progression. Second, we emphasize the importance of getting started with intervention sooner rather than later. By the time the dog is showing signs of pain and restricted movement, irreparable damage has already occurred to the cartilage. The clock is now ticking; the degenerative process has begun. The longer you go before you start treatments, the more damage, inflammation and pain will be present. Even if you can't extinguish the flame, it is easier to control a campfire than a forest fire.

Steps to Take

The general rationale behind arthritis management is to control inflammation (to reduce pain and degeneration), reduce obesity, support the chondrocytes and joint fluid, reduce pain and keep moving. Let's look briefly here at the strategies and treatments that promise the best results.

Manage weight. The most effective known treatment for arthritis is weight control, which can slow damage and reduce the amount of pain medication needed. You should be able to feel but not see the ribs on your dog, and when looking at your dog from above or the side, you should see a waist.

Exercise the dog. Maintaining muscle tone, maintaining flexibility, improving blood flow and keeping ligaments, bones and tendons strong can all benefit an arthritic dog and help slow the progression of the disease. Strong muscles, ligaments and tendons function to stabilize joints and prevent further damage. Maintaining flexibility helps the dog utilize his joints to the maximum and continue to use the parts of affected joints where the cartilage is not as damaged. Improving the blood flow helps reduce inflammation. In addition to regular exercise, more specialized techniques like physical rehabilitation, massage and acupuncture can assist with improving movement.

Control inflammation. Since inflammation is an integral part of the degenerative process, controlling inflammation can slow degeneration and reduce pain. Some strategies for controlling inflammation are nonsteroidal anti-inflammatory drugs (NSAIDs), glucosamine, omega-3 fatty acids, antioxidants, acupuncture and physiotherapy.

Control pain. To improve the quality of life and well-being of your dog, controlling pain is essential and encourages more movement, which in itself has positive benefits. Some strategies for pain management include NSAIDS, analgesics, acupuncture, physical rehabilitation, massage and environmental modifications such as ramps and cushioned sleeping pads.

Support the cartilage and joint fluid. How can owners improve the function of cartilage and joint fluid in older dogs? Substances such as glucosamine, chondroitin, MSM, New Zealand green-lipped mussels, hyaluronic acid, omega-3 fatty acids and antioxidants may actually benefit cartilage and joint fluid. The jury is still out on how these compounds work and which are the most effective. Dog owners have to be cautious, as they are not regulated by the Food and Drug Administration (FDA) and there is considerable variety in their quality.

CONCLUSION

An aging dog with arthritis is not "just slowing down," he is being slowed down by a nasty disease that will get nastier with time. Only your attention and intervention can help.

7

Obesity

The Thief of Time

Oh, beautiful, for spacious size! America, the land where the streets are lined with super-sized junk food meals and fad diet books. In what other country could the word "biggie" be adopted as a verb!? Could anyone miss that American waistlines have ballooned over the past decade? It's no mystery that overeating, underexercising and poor food choices are not good for our health, not to mention the health of our family members (human and canine). And, yes, the waistlines of our pets have expanded, too.

An estimated 25% of the dog population is overweight; however, if you look at average weights of dogs over their lifetimes, this weight gain peaks in the middle years. In fact, more than 40% of dogs between 5 and 10 years of age are overweight or obese. And while excess weight is just as deleterious to the health of our dogs as it is to the rest of us, we see the effects more quickly and dramatically on our canine family members because of their shorter lifespans. Obesity damages the health of our dogs and lessens the time that we and our precious pets have with each other. Time is one thing we cannot buy, borrow or steal. Once wasted, it can never be reclaimed. And time together is what we lose if we allow our dogs to become or stay obese.

THE DANGERS OF OBESITY

Concern about obesity is not just a matter of esthetics or wanting your dog to look his best. Obesity can have some serious implications for the health of your dog. The reason why obesity is of particular concern is that many diseases are associated with it. Numerous studies have shown

that obesity can affect both the health and longevity of dogs. The medical problems that are more common in obese dogs read like a "Who's Who" in detrimental diseases. These include an increased likelihood of orthopedic disease (arthritis, hip dysplasia, spinal disc disease), abnormal insulin response (called insulin resistance), abnormalities in circulating lipid profiles, cardiovascular disease, urinary disorders, reproductive disorders, cancer (particularly mammary tumors and transitional cell carcinoma of the bladder), skin diseases and a higher likelihood of complications during anesthesia.

How can a few extra pounds do all that? Recent scientific research is starting to shine a light into that bewildering fog, and a new picture of fat metabolism is emerging. We used to think of fat as simply a place where the body stored away its extra calories—a well-stocked pantry or larder. If you had more food than you needed immediately, having a fat-cell pantry meant that you could tuck away the extras for later use. The fat cells were seen as being like the canned goods in the pantry— saved for later but not actively involved in anything else.

Recent research has squashed this view. Research has shown that fat cells are nothing like the inert cans of food waiting on the shelf for eventual use. Instead, fat cells actively produce chemical signals that affect other parts of the body and can have a profound effect on both behavior and health.

One kind of chemical mediator produced by fat cells is called leptins. Leptins serve an important function in the normal animal by regulating hunger and food intake as well as energy metabolism. But in some obese animals, the brain does not respond normally to leptins, and overeating continues.

Leptins are just one of many kinds of compounds, called adipokines, secreted from the fat tissue. The adipokines include several chemical messengers that promote inflammation in many tissues in the body. Inflammation is a physiological double-edged sword: in the short term, inflammation is an adaptive response to cellular injury; however, inflammatory products are also very destructive, and chronic inflammation produces chemical mediators that can be carried in the bloodstream and are harmful wherever they reach. In other words, obesity is an inflammatory condition. And this long-term, low-level inflammatory state can have widespread detrimental effects throughout the body.

PERCEPTIONS

Our perceptions are a major risk factor when it comes to obesity in our dogs. Most people simply do not perceive their pets as being overweight. Our culture is geared toward seeing round and ample as a sign of affluence and adequate care. Roly-poly puppies are seen as cute. When we look at a dog at his optimum weight, he may actually seem lean to us. Plus it is difficult for us to systematically evaluate our pets to determine if they are at their optimum body weight—we have not trained our eyes to see the parts of our dogs where they carry extra weight. In addition, because weight is a loaded issue in our culture, many veterinarians feel uncomfortable giving it the emphasis that they should. This is especially difficult for the veterinarian to discuss if the owners themselves are overweight, which is too often the case.

As your dog approaches his mature years, the law of averages indicates that a number of diseases are going to become more common. High on the list are orthopedic diseases and cancer. A dog who is obese in his middle years or younger will have a higher likelihood of having difficulties with these diseases as he matures into old age. So by combating obesity when your dog is middle-aged, you are giving him a higher likelihood of having less pain and debilitating disease as he enters his geriatric years.

A recent study showed the importance of maintaining an optimum weight for dogs. A lifetime study was conducted in which two sets of related dogs were assigned to two feeding groups. The first group was called the "control-fed" group. From weaning until three years of age, they were allowed to eat all they wanted. After that point, they were fed a regular maintenance amount (in fact, in photos of these dogs, their overweight condition is not so obvious). The siblings in the "limit-fed" group were fed 25% less than what the control-fed dogs had received. In everything else, these dogs were treated similarly. They were monitored for their entire lives, receiving proper care for health problems if they arose.

The many results of this study were absolutely stunning. For example, by eight years of age, osteoarthritis affecting multiple joints was significantly more common in the heavier dogs. The onset of chronic diseases requiring treatment was delayed in the limit-fed dogs. The median age of death was almost two years later in the limit-fed dogs. The kinds of diseases that led to death were generally similar; it was the time of onset of the diseases between the two groups that differed. For example, although cancer was seen in dogs in both groups, age of death due to tumors was an average of nearly two years later in the limit-fed group. While this study looked at a lifetime of feeding restriction, studies from rats, mice and monkeys have shown that there are benefits even when the calorie restriction starts at various points later in life.

The benefits of weight loss in an obese dog are both long-term and immediate. The dogs who have lost weight to return to their ideal body condition appear to feel as if they have a new lease on life; they are often more active and playful. You will notice that those who were developing orthopedic disease will have their gaits and ability to move improve. They will require less pain medication to combat disabilities caused by orthopedic disease. Some dogs that were being considered for surgery for a painful orthopedic condition have been able to forgo the surgery at that time, simply because of the weight loss. We give our dogs a better chance for the future and greater enjoyment of the present when they are at their ideal body condition.

FACTORS CONTRIBUTING TO OBESITY

Feast or Famine Mechanism

First of all, we have to realize that it is not a common situation to have a surplus of easily available food, as we currently have now in this part of the world. This has rarely occurred at any time in the evolution of dogs (or us, for that matter). As a result, canine metabolism, physiology and behavior are geared toward a feast or famine circumstance. In the wild, dogs eat what they can when they can, and they gain weight to tide them over in the lean times. And the lean times always came, whether brought about by winter, drought, flood, overpopulation, disruption of food supply because of war, natural variations in prey species or other events.

Being designed to eat what they can when they can has kept dogs surviving as a species for thousands of years. Historically, until the Industrial Age and now the fast-food nation, it has been a fail-safe mechanism. Today, this is a detriment to our dog population because it means that few dogs have a good feedback mechanism to tell them to stop eating when they have had enough for maintenance. Although they will stop eating when their stomachs are full, they will usually always eat a bit more than they need. And we give our dogs more than enough.

The majority of dogs will always be striving to eat more than they need, and their metabolism will be geared to saving the extra calories in a storage compartment (fat cells) to use later. In other words, many dogs don't have a sensitive enough "off switch" when it comes to appetite. They are genetically geared to eat more than they need for

THE JOY OF FEEDING

The feeding relationship we have with our pets is an emotional one. We are a species that loves to nurture, and there is no greater way to feel this nurturing joy than to give nourishment to another creature that obviously appreciates it. Think of the happiness seen in the face of a small child feeding ducks at a pond and you will recognize that we are hard-wired to nurture those around us. And our dogs can approach each feeding with the gleeful anticipation of a child on Christmas morning. Where else are we so appreciated? Your supervisor may want you to redo the report you just handed in, your students may not like the homework you are assigning or your children may not like the food you prepared for supper, but your dog quivers in delight whenever you fill his bowl. Want to feel like you are the center of another creature's universe? Just start your dog-feeding ritual. And while it seems that the times when we are able to completely please others are few and far between, we get that opportunity twice a day with our dogs, who dance with delight at every mealtime. Where else can you get such ecstatic adoration for such an easily completed task? To say "Whoa!" to that delight, to be the source of restriction, can be really hard to do, but necessary in order to be truly nurturing and caring for the needs of your dog.

maintenance. Plus, if the food is very palatable, even the cautious eaters may overeat. For this reason, "free-choice feeding," that is, letting your dog eat how much he wants when he wants, is a large risk factor for obesity because few dogs will self-regulate and consume the right amount of calories for a healthy weight. However, even if you regulate the amount of food that your dog is given, realize that he will likely want more than is necessary for a healthy weight.

Sedentary Lifestyle

Sedentary lifestyle is a problem not only for people but also for dogs; everyone in this industrial/information age moves less and does less, to the detriment of all. There was a time when dogs worked alongside their owners, herding sheep, hunting, working in the farm fields, killing vermin, guarding the homes, protecting the livestock. Dogs had jobs, most of which required them to be on their feet and active.

Recently, I visited a goat ranch in central Washington State that had two working Great Pyrenees livestock-guardian dogs. As the goats left on a foraging foray that took them over a half-mile from their barn, the tall dogs ambled along with them. The herd was constantly in motion throughout the day, searching for grass to graze and then, when full, returning to the barn for shade and water, and the guardian dogs stayed with them. This is traditionally how dogs have lived: doing something.

Now we have stay-at-home-and-sleep dogs. They remain inside the house or apartment while we are at work (or at our feet for those fortunate owners who work at home). Few of us have jobs that keep us constantly on the move, and even those of us who do rarely take our dogs with us when we work. It is probably no surprise to anyone that there is a correlation between the activity levels of dogs and owners: people who do not exercise much tend to have dogs that get little activity.

Treats

At the same time that owners are being less active with their dogs, they appear to be compensating by giving them more treats. One can't help but wonder if we are trying to make up for not spending time and doing things with our dogs by tossing them more treats.

Are we becoming like parents of those poor little rich kids who spoil their emotionally neglected children with gadgets and long vacations instead of spending actual time with them?

This is not to say that you shouldn't offer treats to your dog, but treats should be given for *doing something*—not just for *being*. And don't give a handful when a single small treat will do. You have to remember that those treats are not made of nothing. They contain real elements, a.k.a. calories, and many of them have lots of calories (which is why they taste so darn good that the dogs dance—or waddle, as the case may be—every time they hear the canister clinking!).

Do the math: any calories given as treats need to be subtracted from calories given in the food bowl, or you will be giving a net increase in calories. What if you were on a well-balanced weight-loss diet, but every evening you splurged by eating a bowl of ice cream or slice of cheesecake that was not included in the plan? Suffice it to say, you wouldn't be very successful. Even things you don't often think about, like rawhide bones, can be calorie-dense if your dog consumes them. So limit treats, including table scraps, to no more than ten percent of the calories your dog should be consuming. Don't be one of those owners who gives his chubby dog a biscuit every time he barks at the treat jar or looks at you with pleading eyes.

Table Scraps

Sharing morsels from your healthy dinner, rich in vegetables and lean protein, with your dog can be a part of his healthy diet. If, however, your dinner consists of pizza, donuts and fried chicken, this wouldn't be a good choice under any circumstances. In addition, there are human foods that should never be fed to dogs, as they are actually toxic to dogs. Additionally, too many table scraps could lead to nutritional deficiencies in dogs, and even good (healthy, balanced) table scraps still contain calories.

As with doggie treats, any increase in calories via table scraps needs to be balanced by a decrease in the food bowl or you will be feeding a net increase in calories, with a corresponding weight gain. So again, the recommendation from veterinary nutritionists is that no more than ten percent of the calories given to your dog be in the form of treats and table scraps. Remember also that fat and oils are

HUMAN FOODS THAT SHOULD NOT BE GIVEN TO DOGS

According to the ASPCA Animal Poison Control Center, human foods and drinks you should not give to your dog are alcoholic beverages, chocolate (this is a species sensitivity that is dose-dependent), coffee (species sensitivity, particularly a problem if they consume grounds or chocolate-covered coffee beans), fatty foods (can cause GI upset and possibly pancreatitis), macadamia nuts (significant species sensitivity, mechanism unknown), moldy foods, raisins/grapes (species sensitivity, mechanism unknown), onions/garlic (intraspecies sensitivity, usually when a large volume is consumed), yeast dough (because of the anatomic position of dog's stomach, a large volume of rising bread dough can cause an obstruction) and anything containing the sugar substitute xylitol (species sensitivity), such as sugar-free candy and baked goods.

denser in calories. So when you trim that bit of fat from your meat so that it doesn't end up on your waistline, think of your dog's waistline too and resist the urge to feed it to him. Likewise, you shouldn't share your fatty meats, meat trimmings, bacon, sausage or pan drippings with dogs. In addition to adding pounds, ingestion of a large amount of fat can cause pancreatitis in dogs, a severe life-threatening condition. Foods containing fats and oils are highly palatable and dogs are highly motivated to consume them—some-times with fatal results.

Time Spent Eating

How long does it take for your dog to eat the food in his bowl? While some dogs are nibblers, most will wolf down their food in a matter of minutes, cleaning their bowls faster than a Kentucky Derby winner can cross the finish line. Just as dogs used to work alongside people, they also used to work to get food. According to Ray Coppinger, a biologist who studies dog evolution, many dogs in the past and still today in other parts of the world get a lot of nutrients from scavenging, a time-consuming process. The dog's ancestors, wolves, spent a lot more time getting to the edible portions of the carcass of their prey than a dog spends eating a bowl of kibble.

The speed of consumption is important when you consider that the nervous system and hormone signals that tell an animal that it has eaten enough, the signals of satiety, take a while to register. Rapidly eaten food is simply not as satisfying because the satiety centers haven't been adequately triggered by the time a dog is finished eating. So a way to help your dog is to make his food more difficult to get, through the use of food puzzles and food-searching games. This has the double benefit of slowing down the feeding process and providing cognitive enrichment, which helps keep the brain alert.

Change in Food Quality

Most dogs are fed commercial pet foods for at least part of their meals. Over the past 20 years or so, there has been an increasing number of "premium" or "super premium" pet foods introduced to the market. Many of these foods are both more palatable and higher in fat and calories than less expensive foods. This may have contributed to an increase in the number of overfed dogs. Pet owners (your author included) tend to fill their dogs' bowls to a specific level without regard to what food we are putting in the bowls, rarely referring to the feeding charts on the back of the bags. This can get us and our dogs into trouble. For example, if we switch to a new food with a higher nutrient density and continue feeding the same volume, it means a net increase in calories fed to the dog, with a resulting weight gain.

Better flavor also can lead to more enthusiastic consumption and higher feeding motivation in our dogs. If fed free-choice (meaning that you leave a full bowl of kibble out all day), most dogs will overconsume. This will also increase their will to work harder to get more food than they should eat, be it by more begging or finding ways around our food-storage systems. For instance, if I forget to latch the pantry door when we leave the house, my dog Rosie will open both the door and the dog-food container and stuff herself. She might not do this for boring, tasteless food. (But she might!)

Does this mean you should feed a low-quality food? No! What it means is that you should recognize that you should not feed the same volume of a calorie-dense food as you would of a lower-calorie food. Don't let habit and the size of the food bowl determine how much you feed your dog. Measure how much food you are actually giving and check the labels. Be aware, however, that even if you do feed only the amount shown on the label, you may still be overfeeding your dog. Each dog is an individual, and dogs can vary dramatically in their energy needs. The labels on cans and packages of food are based on the average needs of average dogs. Is my Rosie average? (Not if you ask her.) Theoretically, then, that means that nearly half of all dogs need less than the amount shown (and about half need more). If your dog is one that needs less, he will gain weight unless smaller portions are given. If your dog has a tendency toward weight gain, like my Rosie does, a smaller portion or a lower-calorie food should be given.

Canned Versus Dry Food

There has been a shift toward feeding dry dog foods instead of canned foods to our dogs. One of the constituents of canned foods is water, which contains no calories, while with dry dog foods, the filler is often a grain-based product, which does contribute calories. When water is consumed along with the food, it might help the dog feel more full and satisfied without contributing additional calories. So there is the potential that with some dogs, feeding canned foods may help them feel more satisfied. If dry food is fed, it can be moistened with warm water. This not only encourages water intake—something that may be beneficial for aging dogs—but also can enhance the food's palatability.

Spaying and Neutering

Spaying/neutering is a good and responsible pet-owner practice. It can be highly successful in controlling excess pet populations (helping to prevent the unfortunate end result of euthanasia of homeless animals), plus it helps to control some unwanted behaviors, like heat in females and marking and roaming in males. But removal of the ovaries or testicles and the accompanying sex hormones is not without physiological consequences, one of them being that the animal gains weight more easily. With spayed or neutered dogs, owners need to be additionally aware of their pet's tendency to gain weight and cut calories accordingly.

FOOD FOR THOUGHT

Sometimes the biggest risk to those we love is right under our noses. There are a lot of things that we simply cannot control. Sometimes, no matter how well you prepare and safeguard, a problem will come out of left field that you never expected. But obesity is a known risk with known consequences. Dogs live in the moment, and their spontaneous joy is one of the reasons we so love to share our lives with them. But because they live in the moment, they do not have the understanding of how their actions, including how much they eat, will affect their future health. Obesity is more of a threat to a dog's well-being than many people realize. But now that we do recognize it, our responsibility is to be aware, to evaluate and do something about it. Maintaining an ideal weight for your dog is one of the most loving and powerful choices you can make for him.

8 Hypothyroidism

The Great Masquerader

One summer, a friend of mine worked in a western resort town. "It was funny," she later told me. "It seemed that every one of the little shops, most of which catered to tourists, had a laconic Labrador Retriever as a shop dog. It was almost like they were the official mascots of the town, and everywhere you looked there was a sleeping Labrador—on the porches, on the floors next to the cash registers, everywhere. And none of them seemed to do anything but lie around. As the summer continued, I developed a fantastic theory about those Labradors. I figured they all belonged to the Lazy Lab Service that the tourist town operated to maintain rustic appearances. I imagined that if I got up early enough in the morning, I would see a van marked LLS drive up in front of each of the shops, unload a semi-comatose Lab and arrange it picturesquely inside the shop."

Although my friend's story still makes me chuckle, it always also reminds me of "the great masquerader," which is my name for hypothyroidism. My first encounter with this disease was years ago with my Labrador Retriever Shaina, whose pre-treatment demeanor would have made her an ideal shop snoozer. Even though there are a number of endocrine disorders that older dogs can get, this one is of particular importance because many of its signs mirror what we envision to be the effects of old age. Thus it is easy to miss or dismiss the signs of hypothyroidism—one more reason to say, "Oh, he is old and just slowing down." In reality many dogs who appear to be "just slowing down" are suffering from an illness that can and should be treated. Hypothyroidism is a disease in which the body doesn't produce enough thyroid hormone. That sounds clear and simple, but it isn't.

Eternal Puppy

THE MASTER CONTROLLERS

Thyroid hormone can be viewed as the master controller of the body's metabolic system. It influences the concentration and activity of many enzymes, which in turn influence the metabolism of vitamins, minerals and proteins and regulate all aspects of carbohydrate and fat metabolism. It influences the secretion of all other hormones and the responses of their target organs to them. It has marked effects on the biochemical function of the heart and lungs and the production of red blood cells. It influences turnover of the skeletal system and is necessary for optimal function of the nervous and immune systems. Essentially, there is no tissue or organ system in the body that is not affected by thyroid hormone nor will escape adverse effects if this hormone is not secreted in the proper amounts.

One would think that with a hormone that is so important and does so much, it would be easy to notice when it is not present in the correct amounts. But it is the very widespread nature of the effects of thyroid hormone that make it difficult to detect problems initially. There is such a wide range of signs of this disease that are possible; in addition, the onset of the disease is often gradual. The severity of the signs increases as less thyroid hormone is released. But a slow onset is hard to notice. So in the early stages of the disease, there can be a slow progression and there can be many possible signs, both of which make hypothyroidism difficult to identify.

SIGNS OF HYPOTHYROIDISM

The most commonly reported signs seen in a hypothyroid dog include lethargy and weakness, mental dullness, irritability, weight gain and skin and coat changes. As we've mentioned, these very signs are too often dismissed by owners as normal, even expected, signs of aging. They may also be signs of other disease processes. Hence, hypothyroidism can masquerade as another problem or simply as old age, when in fact the dog is suffering from a widespread illness that is sapping his energy and vitality. To add to the confusion, there is a great deal of variety in what the hypothyroid dog will look like.

Frequently we find hypothyroid dogs who are lethargic and mentally dull, who tend to gain weight, who have little tolerance for exercise, who exhibit muscle weakness and become fatigued easily and who have poor tolerance for the cold. Essentially they turn into the equivalent of slow-motion heat-seeking missiles, always looking for warm places to sleep, a lot like the laconic Labs sleeping in the sun at a resort town. All of these characteristics are related to the generalized reduction in metabolism. The dog is running out of steam because his internal biochemical furnace can't process its fuel efficiently.

Sometimes owners notice changes in the coat and skin of the hypothyroid dog. A classic change seen in some hypothyroid dogs is a symmetrical loss of hair over the body (but not the head and legs); sometimes the tail is affected (the so-called rat tail). Other external changes that are associated with hypothyroidism are a dry scaly coat, excess pigmentation (the skin gets darker), recurrent ear and skin infections, excessive shedding and an inability to grow hair after clipping. Thus, hypothyroidism may be masquerading as chronic skin problems. There may even be a secondary bacterial infection present due to the impaired immune function brought on by hypothyroidism.

Sometimes hypothyroid dogs will develop a condition called myxedema, in which there is a thickening of the skin on the forehead and face, leading to puffiness and increased thickness of facial skin folds and drooping eyelids. This will give the dog what is called a "tragic expression" on his face, a downcast mask with a sad and sorrowful look.

Alterations in nerve-cell function in the hypothyroid dog can lead to hind-limb shaking, weakness, walking in circles, knuckling at the joints or dragging feet and even seizures. There may be changes in the eyes with abnormal fat deposits in the corneas or within the eyes, increased eye infections, insufficient tear production and glaucoma. Cardiac changes can include irregular heart rhythm, slower heart rate and reduced cardiac output. And again, all of these signs may be mistaken for signs of other illnesses.

Hypothyroid dogs are sometimes described as grumpy, irritable or sad. While these signs are well described, there are some reports suggesting that additional behavior changes may also be seen in hypothyroid dogs. We've already mentioned mental dullness, and affected older dogs may also show loss of learning. Hypothyroidism can present as cognitive dysfunction, anxiety or behavior that people might describe as "neurotic."

While hypothyroidism is slowly progressive and the signs seen in the early stages are still a threat to a dog's welfare, a severely affected dog can experience the severe signs of profound weakness, slow heart rate, hypothermia and a coma that progresses to death if not appropriately treated. Obviously the hope is that the hypothyroid dog will be recognized and treated long before the disease gets to this point. However, as long as hypothyroidism is mistaken for other things, as long as we are blinded by the masquerade, we can't get the dog the help he needs.

Not only is hypothyroidism difficult to recognize, it is difficult to diagnose. A factor that interferes with the ability to easily diagnose hypothyroidism is that many things affect thyroid hormone and its circulating blood levels. Factors such as drugs, circulating levels of other hormones, dietary components and other diseases can cause the levels of thyroid hormone to fluctuate or to interfere with our ability to measure what is functionally present. Levels that you measure in the blood serum may not reflect what is in the tissues, which is where the hormone is needed to have its effect. Since the blood levels can fluctuate, a single measurement may not accurately show what is present. There is no single diagnostic test that gives a definitive diagnosis, so the accurate diagnosis of hypothyroidism is neither simple nor straightforward. Rather, diagnosing hypothyroidism is a complex combination of raising your index of suspicion, observing clinical signs and performing a variety of laboratory tests that may even at times seem to contradict each other. Sometimes, if the clinical picture and test results are ambiguous or don't agree, the diagnosis has to be made by doing a short six- to eight-week trial therapy of supplemental thyroid hormone and looking at the response.

TREATMENT OF HYPOTHYROIDISM

Because of the difficulty in diagnosing hypothyroidism, there is also controversy about the prevalence of this disease: some believe that it is overdiagnosed while others feel that it is underdiagnosed. Both viewpoints are likely correct, with some dogs who are not hypothyroid being diagnosed as such while many actual hypothyroid dogs are not diagnosed due to the aforementioned factors that can complicate recognition and diagnosis. However, keen observations by the owner, good communication with the veterinarian and patience and persistence are factors that influence a correct diagnosis.

Considering the confusion and difficulty in diagnosing hypothyroidism, it is nice to hear that it is fairly easy to treat if present. Treatment consists of supplementing with synthetic T4 (thyroxine) under the supervision of a veterinarian. In this case, if thyroid supplementation is discontinued for any reason, the dog needs to be weaned from the supplement gradually so that his thyroid can increase production to the extent of which it is capable. If thyroiditis has destroyed the thyroid gland or limited its function, the dog will need to have thyroid hormone given to him for the rest of his life.

When a hypothyroid dog starts getting supplemented with the proper levels of thyroid hormone, it may seem like a small miracle has occurred. It can look like spring returning after a long, cold winter. Your dog will regain energy and vitality and have a sparkle in his eyes that you will realize you haven't seen for some time. You can even imagine a dog's gratitude and relief at having his energy back again, no longer shackled by the heavy chains of weariness.

There are a number of endocrine disorders that can be seen in an old dog, including diabetes and disorders of the adrenal gland. The reason for the focus on this particular one is because of its prevalence and the tendency for it to be overlooked and mistaken for the signs of aging. You can't stop the clock, and an old dog will always be an old dog who, like ourselves, is not getting any younger. But it is a real shame when a dog is struck with a disease that is not diagnosed or treated because the disease is masquerading as old age. Hypothyroidism, if treated, will give the dog a lot more life to live and many more times to enjoy.

ABOUT THE THYROID

A hormone is a substance that is produced in small amounts by an endocrine gland and that travels, usually via the bloodstream, to other locations in the body where it has its effect. This effect consists of changing the output or function of other cells or organs in the body. Hormones are the chemical controllers that keep the body in balance and operating smoothly. Because a little bit of these chemical signals can have a large effect, hormones are under a lot of feedback control, with checks and balances. When there is an endocrine disorder, either this feedback mechanism isn't working properly or the gland itself is producing too much or not enough of a particular needed substance.

If there is too much of a substance produced, the resulting condition will have the prefix *hyper-* and if there is not enough of the hormone produced, it will have the prefix *hypo-*. So *hyperthyroidism* is the production of too much thyroid hormone and *hypothyroidism* is the production of too little thyroid hormone. Hyperthyroidism is seen more commonly in older cats and is rare in dogs; hypothyroidism is the most common endocrine disorder seen in dogs, and its incidence increases with age.

For the thyroid, the first layer of control is at the hypothalamus, which is in the lower part of the brain. Cells there detect the circulating levels of thyroid hormone and if the levels are too low, the cells release a control hormone called thyrotropin releasing hormone (TRH), which stimulates cells in the pituitary gland (located at the base of the brain). The pituitary gland releases thyroid-stimulating hormone (TSH), which travels through the bloodstream to the thyroid gland and stimulates the production and release of thyroid hormone. The thyroid gland lies in the neck and requires dietary iodine to make thyroid hormone.

After release from the thyroid gland, most thyroid hormone is bound to specific binding proteins in the bloodstream. It is only the unbound (free) thyroid hormone that can enter cells and have an effect. The bound form makes up a circulating reserve. There are two thyroid hormones produced by the thyroid gland. Most of the hormone produced contains four atoms of iodine per molecule, T4 (thyroxine). A smaller amount of hormone with three atoms of iodine per molecule, T3 (triiodothyronine), is also produced. Both travel both bound and free.

There are several places where thyroid hormone production can be impaired: the hypothalamus, the pituitary gland or the thyroid gland itself. The most common kind of hypothyroidism is a result of some problem with the thyroid gland. A condition called thyroiditis (inflammation of the thyroid) is the most common cause of hypothyroidism, being responsible for at least 80% of cases. This is actually an autoimmune condition. Over a period of several years, the thyroid tissue is invaded by cells of the immune system, which results in destruction of thyroid tissue. The causes of this autoimmune disease are not known. Since hypothyroidism is seen in some breeds more than others, there could be a genetic component, and environmental factors are likely also playing a role.

Although less common, the problem could be at the level of the pituitary gland or hypothalamus, and there could also be tumors of the thyroid gland or in or around the pituitary gland.

Tests exist to measure the amount of free T4 and T3, as well as the total (combination of free and bound) amount of T4 and T3 hormone in the serum. Levels of TSH and TRH can also be measured as well as levels of autoantibodies against T3, T4 and the master molecule thyroglobulin, from which they are produced in the thyroid gland. While the presence of elevated levels of these autoantibodies confirms autoimmune thyroiditis, their absence does not rule it out. Perhaps this gives you a better appreciation of why getting a "simple" diagnosis of hypothyroidism is not a simple task at all.

9 **Cancer**

A Case for Hope

Hearing the word *cancer* conjures up frightening images of pain and loss. We all know someone who has died of cancer—a loved one, friend, family member. It is a word that fills us with dread and sends an icy chill up our spines. It makes us feel helpless, impotent, unable to protect those we love the most. And unfortunately this is something that many of us will experience because cancer is a disease commonly found in older dogs.

Yet although the fear of cancer is very real and understandable, having hope is also realistic. Medicine, technology and drug therapies have all undergone dramatic improvement. We know more about the immune system and nutrition and how to influence healing. If the thought of cancer is frightening, we can place in our minds the image of cancer survivor Lance Armstrong, winning his sixth Tour de France. We've come a long way. In recent years there has been an explosion of new cancer therapies that have become available, and the discoveries made in the treatment of cancer in companion animals is even speeding up the availability of new therapies for people.

COMBATING THE FEAR OF CANCER AND ITS TREATMENT

When a cancer diagnosis is heard, fear grasps people in a two-handed grip. On one hand is the fear of the disease itself; on the other hand is the fear of the cancer-fighting therapy. In few other diseases do we have such a destructive combination in which the treatment for the disease is feared almost as much as the disease itself. Combined,

these fears feed each other, crippling us, hampering our ability to reason, evaluate and make effective choices. They create a barrier that might delay early appropriate intervention. Or, conversely, they can cause you to make snap, ill-considered decisions. The way to combat this destructive duo is with the sword of knowledge, the shield of hope and the strength of love.

It is important to recognize that, while cancer is a single word, this word covers a number of different disease conditions. There are many different kinds of cancer, some of which are easy to combat and some that are more difficult. There are some cancers that have a fairly high complete cure rate, some that we can hold at bay for a length of time and some that we may not be able to control easily. But even with the kinds of cancer that are more difficult to control, our best guess at the course of the disease could be wrong and the particular animal might be able to combat the disease better than expected. And we can still provide support, relief from symptoms and hospice to keep our pets comfortable and give us quality time together.

Many people, upon hearing the word cancer, immediately envision the specter of the grim reaper and imagine the most severe and damaging forms of cancer. They may feel powerless, immobilized by the fear and hopelessness that wash over them. But in reality we are not in a position of being powerless against an invincible foe—there is a lot we can do. Many dogs with cancer can be cured or at least rendered free of their disease for a significant period of time. In fact, some veterinary oncologists have said that cancer is the most curable of the chronic diseases your pet may face.

Treatment Fears

The other ugly face of fear is the misconception that cancer treatments will be expensive, ineffective, inhumane or intolerable for your dog. Often such beliefs as these are wrong or out of proportion. Just as the therapeutic options for cancer have improved, so too has the knowledge of how to administer and monitor them. Likewise, there are many options for controlling pain and discomfort during the treatment itself. Dog owners will be relieved to learn that, according to veterinary cancer specialists, the crippling effects of chemotherapy so common in people are rarely seen in dogs. Dogs are better able to tolerate the effects. And with appropriate care, dogs undergoing cancer treatment experience not only little to no toxicity but also an improvement in their quality of life from controlling the cancer.

Another factor that needs to be considered when comparing cancer therapy between humans and dogs is that generally our goals are somewhat different. Humans are very long-lived in comparison to dogs. When we fight cancer in a person, generally he is not close to the end of his normal lifespan, so the therapeutic choices are made to fight hard and go for a complete cure or measure success by at least five years of remission. However, in a dog who is already middle-aged or older, a remission of two years is often quite reasonable. When caring for a dog with cancer, the issue of quality of life is paramount, while with humans, there are those people who are willing to make the choice to go "through hell and back." So comparing people's experiences with cancer therapy to what your dog will experience is not a valid comparison.

The advancement in therapeutics and diagnostics for cancer has also spawned an increase in the availability of advanced-care veterinary centers. It used to be that advanced cancer care was only available in veterinary schools. However, now there are a number of private practice specialty centers that are staffed and equipped to a degree comparable to or better than the university veterinary hospitals. This gives owners a greater availability of hospitals with specifically trained doctors and staff, more experience and a wider range of therapeutic options.

The Decision to Treat

Still there is the mistaken view of "Oh, I wouldn't do that to my dog." You might hear from others that treating cancer in your dog is somehow a foolish and cruel thing to do to your loving companion. It is not. And if people express this opinion and pass judgment on you, you should recognize that they also are likely operating from a position of outdated information and ignorance.

Treatment decisions need to be based on many factors, including age of dog, type of cancer and stage of advancement of the disease. There are three basic levels of cancer treatment: treatments designed to cure the disease; treatments designed to slow the cancer's progression and give you and your pet more time together; and when cure or control of the cancer is not possible, palliative therapies designed not to fight the cancer but to help the patient feel more comfortable. Remember that dismissing treatment as "not an option" or something that "will cause too much suffering for my dog" without knowing all the information is not a kind or reasonable approach.

We humans bring to this partnership with our canines the gift of abstract reasoning, language and an intelligence that dogs, despite their many, many talents, do not have. We have the ability to assimilate and understand knowledge and we have the ability to choose. When we think of chemotherapy, too often we think of the worst-case scenario, perhaps based on what we've heard about other people's experiences or possibly from our own experience. Fearing the worst, we dread any harm coming to our beloved dogs and we want to protect them. But our trusting and loving dogs are counting on us to live up to our end of the partnership, to use our greater intelligence and make rational, informed decisions. For their sakes, we have to see beyond our fear.

Dogs live in the moment: they fear neither cancer nor chemotherapy. That in itself gives them an advantage that we don't have. Their world is already eternal.

WHAT IS CANCER?

Most cells in the body grow and reproduce. Like leaves on a tree, the cells of the skin, blood, digestive tract and many other organ systems are constantly turning over. Old cells die while new cells take their place: there needs to be a balance between loss and growth. This growth is tightly controlled by numerous factors in the body, and growth of any one cell is mediated by these factors from outside the cell interacting with its own DNA. But in some cases, there is damage to the DNA and the cells stop responding to normal growth-control factors. At its core, cancer is the result of damage to the DNA of a cell that causes it to grow and reproduce in an uncontrolled way.

Of course, cells are bombarded daily with things that damage the DNA. However, there are cellular mechanisms that repair damaged DNA, and there are also specialized cells in the immune system that recognize and remove damaged cells. So it only becomes a problem when the cellular repair mechanisms and "surveillance system" are not able to keep up with the wear and tear of living in a world surrounded by potential sources of DNA damage.

Cancer is seen more frequently in older animals for several reasons. First, it is simply an issue of numerical averages—if cancer occurs at a certain low frequency per year, the more years the animal is alive, the higher its lifetime likelihood of getting cancer. Second, in older animals there can be the cumulative results of years of exposure to low-level carcinogens in the environment and of DNA transcriptional errors from repeated divisions. Third, the cellular DNA repair mechanisms and immune surveillance system in an older animal do not work as well as they did when the animal was younger.

Types of Tumors and Diagnosis

A cluster of cancerous cells all growing in one location is called a tumor. A benign tumor is one that is slow growing and not likely to spread. However, a benign tumor can still present a problem due to its location or if it presses on another part of the body. For example, a benign tumor near the esophagus can impede swallowing, or one near a nerve can impede nerve transmission.

Malignant tumors are generally more serious than benign ones. The cells grow more wildly and can spread to other locations. The process of spreading to other locations is called metastasis. It is thought to occur when cancerous cells break off from the primary tumor and then travel in the blood or lymphatic system to another location, where they then set up shop and start growing.

When a veterinarian makes the diagnoses of cancer, he looks at a number of factors. The physical appearance of the cancer cells from a biopsy gives a lot of information: what type of cells they are, how much they have changed from the original cell type, how rapidly they are dividing. Many kinds of cancer follow somewhat predictable pathways of growth and spreading, so knowing the type of cancer gives some predictive ability. The doctor will also look at the lymph nodes and other common metastatic sites for indications of whether the cancer has spread and, if so, how far. Based upon all of that information, the cancer will be assigned a stage, which indicates the progression of the disease.

Tumor cells can also secrete substances that affect how the individual feels. Called tumor cachectins and interleukins, these substances can make the individual uninterested in eating, experience fatigue and feel sick. In addition, invasion of the normal tissue by cancerous cells can be painful. This is why it is never OK to pursue a "let nature take its course" or "wait and see" approach. Treatment for cancer, even if it is palliative and doesn't change the ultimate conclusion, can prevent your dog from living in pain.

RISK FACTORS IN THE DEVELOPMENT OF CANCER

It is important to realize that usually no one event or element will cause cancer. Epidemiology is the science of how diseases appear in populations and is used to look at correlations—do things happen more commonly together? Risk factors are just that; they are factors known to increase the risk of developing cancer by harming the DNA of cells or cellular mechanisms that repair DNA. It is rare that one can point to a single factor or time or exposure to something and say with any certainty that this specific event caused the cancer to form. Instead, there is a subtle interplay between genetics, the immune status of your dog and your dog's exposure to known environmental carcinogens. However, because we do know that certain substances are harmful and have been shown to increase the incidence of cancer, it is wise to do our best to eliminate them from our dogs' environment.

By paying attention to the risk factors and striving to reduce your dog's exposure to known and suspected carcinogens, you can reap benefits in improving the odds for your pet as well as for you and your family. Realize, however, that you can only at best improve the odds; many variables are simply out of our control. You can help your pet lead a healthy lifestyle and avoid known risks and still eventually face cancer in your pet. All we can do is strive to reduce the risk factors and lower the probability of cancers forming.

Cancer research is ever-continuing, and new risk factors and possible cancer preventives are coming to light all the time. Because cancer is a common disease, there are a lot of snake-oil salesmen and crazy theories out there as well. This is a time when it is important to be skeptical and get your information from well-known and trusted sources.

Genetics

There is genetic link in the development of cancer. Some popular breeds, such as the Golden Retriever and the Boxer, have a higher incidence of developing cancers of any type. Some other breeds have a higher probability of developing certain kinds of cancer; for example, Scottish Terriers have a higher incidence of developing bladder cancer. However mixed-breed dogs, while having a lower incidence rate, can also develop cancer. These breed prevalences are of interest to cancer researchers because they may offer an insight into genetic factors in relationship to the development of certain diseases.

While this is of interest on the research level, what the dog owner really wants to know is what the risks of cancer development are in his own dog. The most important action you can undertake is to research your dog's breed (or dominant breed/breeds if he is a mixed breed) and learn what cancers are more common in your dog's breed or background so that you can increase your surveillance in those areas.

Weight Control

Maintain your dog at his optimal weight. Studies have shown that dogs who are obese have an increased risk of cancer. Not only has increased weight been linked with an increased incidence of some kinds of cancer, but it appears also to have an influence on the age at which cancer develops. In the aforementioned study in which sibling pairs of Labrador Retrievers were fed either a regular diet or a diet reduced by 25%, data from the lifetime of these dogs showed that, while a similar cancer rate and type was seen in both experimental groups, the limit-fed groups had the cancer develop an average of two years later than the control-fed group.

Other Dietary Considerations

A balanced diet designed for dogs can prevent nutritional deficiencies that can hamper your dog's ability to fight disease and is better for his long-term health. In addition, the long-chain eicosapentaenoic (EPA) and docosahexaenoic (DHA) acids, both of which are found in fish and flaxseed oil, have been consistently shown to inhibit the proliferation of breast- and prostate-cancer cell lines experimentally and to reduce the risk and progression of these tumors in many species.

A recent epidemiological study was reported in the *Journal of the American Veterinary Medical Association* that looked at the effects of vegetable consumption on the development of a common type of cancer in the Scottish Terrier. The study compared vegetable consumption, as remembered by the owners, between dogs who had and dogs who had not developed cancer. Of course there are many variables to consider, but the study suggested that the dogs who had consumed more green leafy and orange-red vegetables had a lower incidence of cancer. Although it is unknown at this time how much of an effect this is, if you wish to add vegetables to your dog's diet, think colorful and nonstarchy.

Environmental Carcinogens

A number of environmental factors are known to increase the incidence of cancer. To determine what factors are relevant to dogs, we can extrapolate from those things known to be harmful to humans and look at specific scientific studies with dogs. For example, dogs that have been exposed to coal and kerosene heaters and those exposed to secondhand smoke have a higher incidence of cancer of the respiratory tract, especially the lungs and nasal cavity. Dogs whose owners worked in the asbestos industry have a higher incidence of mesotheliomas. There is an increased risk of several kinds of cancer in dogs whose owners used chemicals including paint, asbestos, solvents, insecticides and herbicides such as 2,4-D. For example, a link has been found in Scottish Terriers between the development of bladder cancer and exposure to herbicides and insecticides. We need to think twice about spraying these chemicals on our lawns and then letting our dogs out to play on them a short time later.

A correlation between increased cancer rates and exposure to radiation, strong electromagnetic fields and direct constant sunlight also has been found.

THE IMPORTANCE OF REGULAR VETERINARY CARE

There is no more powerful tool in veterinary care than the trained hands of a veterinarian on your dog. Regular semi-annual senior wellness visits to the veterinarian can improve your dog's chances by increasing the likelihood of catching cancer early in the game. The sooner a cancer is detected and treatment started, the less the likelihood of the cancerous cells' becoming more undifferentiated and out of control, the less damage to surrounding tissues, the less the chances for spread and the greater our ability to control it. Time is of the essence when treating cancer, and being proactive about your dog's veterinary care is a way of getting the jump on it.

In addition, get in the habit of doing a "tip of the nose to the tip of the toes" careful sweep with your hands over your dog at least once every day. Pay attention to the wisdom of your hands; they will notice if something is not right. If something doesn't feel right, pay attention and monitor that spot carefully. Be aware of the signs of cancer in dogs and go to your veterinarian any time your concerns are piqued.

The American Veterinary Medical Association lists on its website (www.avma.org) ten common signs of cancer in small animals:

- Abnormal swellings that persist or continue to grow
- Sores that do not heal
- Weight loss
- Loss of appetite
- Bleeding or discharge from any body opening
- Offensive odor
- Difficulty eating or swallowing
- Hesitation to exercise or loss of stamina
- Persistent lameness or stiffness
- Difficulty breathing, urinating or defecating

IF YOUR DOG IS FOUND TO HAVE CANCER

Seek a Specialist

Talk to your veterinarian about getting a referral or consultation with a veterinary oncology specialist. Your primary-care veterinarian should be able to give you a referral to a cancer specialist or, if this is not feasible, at least consult with a specialist. Oncology specialists see cancer far more frequently than your vet; in fact, it's all they see. You can rely on their greater level of experience and trust that they are up to date on the most current therapies. Your primary-care veterinarian may see your dog's tumor type several times a year, while the cancer specialist may see several every week. The specialist will have access to a greater variety of therapies and be better able to predict the course of the disease. When practical, the specialist will consult with your primary-care veterinarian for assistance in managing your dog's case. A coordinated approach between your primary-care veterinarian and a veterinary specialist is often the best approach.

Write Things Down

It is hard to remember everything, and when you have a lot of worries, more details will slip out of your mind. When you go to your veterinary visits, it may be hard to remember exactly what and how often things are happening at home. During the veterinary visit, you will also be given a great deal of information in an emotionally charged setting. Even if it all made perfect sense at the time, you may find that you don't remember it all when you get home. Keep a journal. Write down what you are observing. Take it with you to your veterinary visits and write down what you discuss with your vet.

Enlist the Whole Family

Some people worry about letting their children observe the process of disease, treatment and eventual death of their canine family member, afraid that it will affect them negatively. But I think the reverse is true— our children stand to gain a lot from being gently led through this process. There are many things that we need to protect our children from in this world, but feeling the love and watching the compassionate care for an ailing family member is not one of them. Instead, if you, as an attentive and caring parent, go through this together with your child, gently explaining as you go, this can be an important lesson for that child about the value of compassion, empathy and kindness.

While we adults are busy keeping all the balls we juggle in the air, children can be far more observant of the details. If we tell them what to look for and listen to their observations, they can be powerful allies in a cancer care team. Your children may also surprise you with their approach and attitude to the "c" word. Recently a friend of mine went through a breast cancer scare of finding a lump and getting a biopsy. While we waited for the results, I told my daughter what was happening. Her reaction was a lot different from mine. "Oh, she said, "Mrs. Wilson, my science teacher, had breast cancer five years ago, and she is still OK." She went on to name several other teachers at her school who were cancer survivors. That made me realize that our children, raised in a world of greater medical advancements than what we experienced in our youth, would have a different and refreshing outlook. Perhaps this is why we are encouraged to "see things through the eyes of a child."

Keep a Positive Attitude

As closely tuned as they are to our moods and feelings, our dogs know when we are worried or frightened. They won't know why and may interpret your behavior to mean that you are angry or displeased with them. That is an additional burden that dogs should not have to bear, one that can even interfere with their ability to heal. In other words, your attitude and coping strategies can affect the quality of your dog's very life. Does that mean that you should be Pollyanna-ish about everything? Of course not. But at the same time do not give in to despair or constant worry. If need be, empower yourself by learning positive coping strategies, if not for yourself, at least for your family and canine companion. There is no doubt that the positive attitude, approach and spirit with which we care for our pets and each other can make an amazing difference in the quality of life for dogs as well as for people with cancer.

Keep Him Pain-free

It is imperative to have an active, preemptive and ongoing pain management and prevention program for a dog with cancer. Our greatest worry for our dogs is that they have the best possible quality of life, and utilizing a multimodal plan to manage pain is the best way to assure this. This could include oral medications, transdermal patches, acupuncture and even injected pain medications. The important thing is for your family and the veterinary team to work together to recognize, prevent and manage pain.

Check on Supplements

Be sure that, when your dog is undergoing cancer treatment, you discuss with your veterinarian any and all supplements you might be giving your dog, be they nutritional, natural or given as treats. (They may even be in the dog food you are feeding.) Although it may seem paradoxical, some of these healthful substances can actually interfere with efforts to remove the cancer cells from your dog. For example, vitamin E is a powerful antioxidant and a necessary part of a healthy diet. But vitamin E supplementation given during some kinds of chemotherapy can actually reduce the effectiveness of the anti-cancer treatments. It is thought that what is occurring is that in order to combat the cancer, chemotherapy drugs need to kill the diseased cells; these drugs are generally designed to damage the fastest growing cells, a characteristic of cancer cells. The antioxidants in the vitamins, may, in fact, block some of the biochemical ways in which the chemotherapy drugs attack the cancer cells.

Loving, responsible owners always struggle with the desire to do something. And it is easy to want to jump in and try to support your dog with every trick and healthful intervention that you can think of. But unfortunately, in doing this you might be hampering the effectiveness of the chemotherapy in doing its job. So to prevent this interference from occurring, make sure that you provide complete information to your veterinarian.

CONCLUSION

It is because of the bond we feel with our older dogs, the sense of companionship and familiarity, the unconditional love and affection we share, the desire to protect and nurture that we feel so strongly and have such a sense of loss and fear when we find that a beloved dog is suffering from cancer. And embarking on the journey of treatment may seem as uncertain as launching a ship into uncharted waters, hope as remote as the stars. But it is that same love and togetherness that enables us to approach cancer therapy with a sense of inspiration and challenge. The journey you are embarking on can be one of celebration of life, trust and a deepening of the bonds of love you have with your dog and others around you. Some owners of dogs with cancer have found that walking this pathway with their dogs has allowed them to heal in ways they never expected, some finding emotional resolution for unhealed pain or sorrow they have suffered in the past. This needn't be looked upon as a journey down a pathway of sorrow and despair but rather as an affirmation for our understanding of how precious life is and how deep and nourishing is our love. Looking cancer unflinchingly in the face is a way we can truly understand how each day we have together is a gift. Our pets are so innocent in their trust that it is sometimes harder to consider cancer in them than in ourselves. But in our role of guardians and caregivers of our pets, we must make compassionate choices for them.

10 Heart Disease

The Heart of the Matter

According to the Centers for Disease Control (CDC), cardiovascular disease (CVD), primarily heart disease and stroke, causes more deaths in Americans of both sexes and all racial and ethnic groups than any other disease. Since this is so prevalent in people, and we are very aware of it, veterinarians are often asked if older dogs have heart problems, too. The answer to that question is no and yes.

Dogs do not generally get the CVD that humans get, with hardening of the arteries, elevated blood pressure and heart attacks from blocked cardiac arteries. They rarely get the heart-clutching, falling-on-the-floor cardiac arrest problems we all have come to recognize through greater public awareness. But dogs do have heart problems, and these do increase in prevalence as they age. They are just different kinds of heart problems from those usually seen in people.

At its simplest, the circulatory system (heart, lungs and blood) is a matter of fluid dynamics. Blood-carrying oxygen from the lungs is pumped out to the tissues of the body, which need the oxygen and other blood components to function. Blood from the body returns to the heart and is pumped back, along with metabolic waste products, to the lungs to pick up more oxygen and dump off its carbon dioxide—and around and around it goes again.

The system has to stay in balance between the lungs and the rest of the body for it to operate correctly. Oxygen and all of the important fluid constituents of the blood have to stay in balance. Important components for keeping that balance are the heart valves, which are like one-way pressure valves; they keep the blood going in

Eternal Puppy

the correct direction and not backflowing, where it shouldn't be headed. Another important component is the strength of the heart muscle itself and the balance between the part of the heart that pumps just to the lungs and the part that pumps to the entire body.

The lungs are a lower-pressure system than the body. Blood from the lungs should move through the heart and out to the body, not directly back to the lungs. If the heart valves don't function properly or the pump itself doesn't function in a balanced way, things get out of kilter. And the result of that imbalance is that oxygen doesn't get where it is needed and fluids build up where they should not.

HEART PROBLEMS IN DOGS

Research has shown that approximately 10 percent of dogs seen by a veterinarian have some form of heart disease and that the severity of this can increase with age. Dogs can develop heart problems from mitral valve regurgitation (where the heart valve doesn't seal off properly and a backflow occurs), dilated cardiomyopathy (a condition that causes the heart to dilate and not pump efficiently), lung diseases and even, though rarely, from arteriosclerosis, a condition similar to that seen in humans. Other problems that can be seen involve the pericardium, the fibrous sac that surrounds the heart. However, regardless of the underlying cause, the goal of therapy will be to do the best to keep the system as much in balance as possible and treat to achieve specific goals based on the problems these conditions cause.

Mitral Valve Regurgitation

Mitral valve regurgitation (backflow of blood through the valve) is the most common cardiac abnormality seen in dogs. The mitral valve (so called because it was thought to look like the miter, a headdress worn by Catholic bishops) is located between the left atrium and left ventricle. When this one-way pressure valve fails to close properly, small amounts of blood can backflow with each contraction of the heart. This condition is reported to increase with age in dogs, being seen in about 10 percent of dogs at 6 years of age and possibly in as many as 60 percent of dogs at 12 years of age. It is more often seen in small-breed dogs, and some breeds, like the Cavalier King Charles Spaniel, are more susceptible, indicating that a genetic predisposition is possible.

The development of mitral valve insufficiency is likely a result of both genetic and environmental factors. The valves can develop a set of small nodules that crinkle the valves. The presence of the nodules allows bacteria to more easily colonize and reproduce, further distorting the valve and showering bacteria into the bloodstream. There is some suspicion among researchers that chronic dental disease may seed the bloodstream with bacteria, contributing to progression of the disease. This is another good reason why good oral health is of benefit to the overall health of your pet.

When the blood backflows through a faulty valve, it makes a whooshing sound called a heart murmur that can be heard with a stethoscope. Your veterinarian can pick this up during a routine physical exam. There is more than one heart valve, and the veterinarian can tell which one is making the noise by the placement of the stethoscope. Some heart murmurs are of lesser concern. Also important is to determine whether they are worsening with time.

Dilated Cardiomyopathy

The second most common type of heart disease is dilated cardiomyopathy (enlarged heart). This is very much a breed-related problem and is seen more frequently in larger dogs and certain other breeds, including Dobermans, Boxers, the giant breeds and Cocker Spaniels. What is observed in an affected dog is an irregular heart rhythm, which is detected during a routine physical examination or after a fainting spell.

SIGNS OF HEART PROBLEMS

While we have a vivid picture in our consciousness of what a heart attack in humans looks like, we may be surprised to find that heart problems in dogs are more likely to be seen as either a dry hacking or a soft but persistent cough (especially at night), exercise intolerance, difficulty breathing and even fainting. The dry cough is usually due to an enlargement of the left atrium, as it enlarges in response to the abnormal pressures and the extra work required of it, thus putting a squeeze on the large airways in the chest. The soft, moister cough is due to the weeping of fluid into the air sacs as the body attempts to relieve the pressure in the blood vessels of the lungs.

WHAT CAN YOU DO?

- Be aware
- Take your dog for regular veterinary exams (preferably twice-yearly senior wellness visits)
- Maintain good oral health in your dog
- Recognize the signs of heart problems in dogs
- Keep in good communication with your veterinarian during treatment (know how your dog is being treated, be observant, write things down, stay in contact)
- Monitor your dog's comfort level

Many times both components are present, which can then cause a myriad of other difficulties. The exercise intolerance is a result of the tissues in the body getting insufficient oxygen to function optimally. A gradation of signs is often seen: initially these signs are not seen at all (asymptomatic), then seen after severe activity, then the signs are seen with slight activity and then, in a severe heart condition, they are seen even when the dog is at rest.

HEART TREATMENT

Regardless of the cause, the goal of therapy is to make your dog more comfortable and to give drugs that attempt to slow the disease from progressing. A number of drugs are available that can combat various parts of the disease complex and try to bring the system back into as much balance as possible. To prevent the problem that is already present from creating worsening conditions, this is one of those situations in which sooner is better than later. An asymptomatic dog, meaning a dog whose veterinarian has found a new heart murmur during a routine medical exam, without any complaints or observations by the owner to suggest it might be there, may only require monitoring. Some heart murmurs do not go on to develop into congestive heart failure, and the dog will live with his murmur for many years and die from unrelated causes. However, a dog showing symptoms will likely need some kind of medical management. This is a situation in which you must keep a close eye on your dog and stay in good communication with your veterinarian. Like any chronic disease, the goal is management to give your dog the best quality of life possible and to give you and your pet the most time together.

Currently, surgery such as valve replacement is not a frequently recommended option. Surgical treatments are still in the experimental stages and are currently associated with very high risk. Let's hope that this will improve with time and research.

CONCLUSION

Cardiac disease in older dogs underscores one of the most important Eternal Puppy lessons: owners of older dogs must take their dogs to the veterinarian more frequently than other dog owners, preferably twice a year, and be sure that the vet has a good senior-care program. We've mentioned that heart problems can be asymptomatic early in the disease progression, but problems in one part of the circulatory system may already be remodeling or changing other parts of the circulatory system. This means that a veterinarian may detect a developing cardiac problem a great deal sooner than the actual signs appear and thus be able to recommend appropriate medical intervention and medical management for your dog. Thus, the sooner you start monitoring a potential or developing cardiac problem, the better likelihood you have of preventing or slowing these changes.

As with all disease processes, there is also the quality of life issue to consider. No one should think about euthanasia at the first hint of an age-related problem in his dog. Even if the disease does progress, medical management can usually keep a dog comfortable for some time to come. Even with the best medical management possible, however, your dog may become less comfortable at some point in time. And this turns out to be the bottom line: keeping your dog comfortable. Close and honest communication between you and your veterinarian, along with your trusted support network (family, friends, fellow dog owners), will tell you when the disease can no longer be managed well enough and when there is nothing more you can do to keep your dog comfortable. Until that time has come, remember that life is a gift and that we should treasure and enjoy each day we have with our dogs.

Dentistry

Tooth or Consequences

Let's face it: no one really likes to go to the dentist. It puts you in funny, vulnerable positions while things happen that can hurt. We know it is good for us, but that doesn't mean we like to do it. However, we certainly prefer it to a toothache.

Dentistry is good for our dogs as well. Not only does it keep their breath fresh, so that we enjoy being around our dogs, but it also plays a valuable role in maintaining our dogs' overall health.

"Doggy breath" is not normal. Most of the time it is a sign that there is a problem in the dog's mouth. This problem could be in the form of periodontal disease, a broken or infected tooth or, more rarely, a tumor in the mouth.

General practice veterinarians have training in dentistry and can handle basic dentistry problems in their patients. There are also specialists in veterinary dentistry who are board-certified through the American Veterinary Dental College. In addition to their veterinary training, they have rigorous training after obtaining their veterinary degree. Also a number of veterinarians who are not board certified have practices limited to dentistry or make dentistry a high priority in their practice. The advantage to going to these more specialized practices is that they have more specialized training and specific tools for the practice of veterinary dentistry. They sometimes also have more advanced anesthetic protocols and equipment than a general practice. They can handle more involved procedures and have a greater number of options available to them. The preferred choice is dependent on the specific

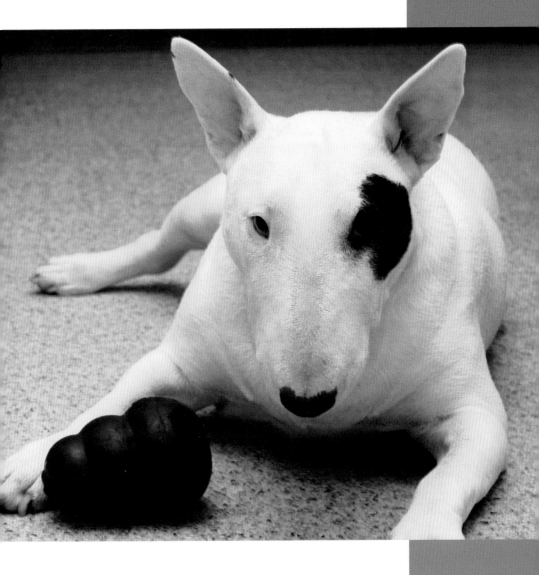

needs of your dog. Talk to your veterinarian about whether referral to a dental specialist is a good plan for your dog.

PERIODONTAL DISEASE

Periodontal disease affects the structures that hold the teeth into
the mouth. By 4 years of age, 85% of dogs will have some form of
periodontal disease. Periodontal disease starts with the formation
of plaque on the teeth. Plaque is composed of sloughed skin cells,
food particles and bacteria. Plaque can start forming as early as 12
hours after the teeth have been cleaned. If the plaque is not
removed, mineral salts from the dog's food will combine with the
plaque to form a hard calculus (also called tartar) on the teeth. This
calculus forms both above and below the gum line and is irritating
to the gum tissue. It also changes the pH, which allows more bacteria to live below the gum line. The inflammation and by-products
from the bacteria eat away at the support structures of the teeth.
When enough of the support structures are damaged, the tooth
loosens and eventually is lost.

Older dogs may be at an increased risk for dental disease
because they have reduced salivary production compared with
what they had when they were younger. The saliva functions to
wash and clean the mouth and even has some antimicrobial functions. With a drier mouth, the dog may have more food sticking to
his teeth and less natural cleaning action, thus increasing the risk of
dental disease.

Periodontal disease does more than just cause bad breath and
tooth loss. The constant inflammation and infection at the gum set
up a situation where bacteria from the mouth are able to enter the
bloodstream. These bacteria can travel far and wide in the bloodstream until they lodge in a distant organ, where they may cause
damage. Periodontal disease has been implicated in the development
or acceleration of diseases in the kidneys, heart, liver and brain.

Periodontal disease can also be painful, and this chronic pain can
affect your dog's well-being and behavior. He might be grouchy (just
think how cheerful you are with a toothache), avoid things that
could come in contact with his face (like petting or fetching toys)
and even eat less because it is painful to chew his food.

BRUSHING YOUR DOG'S TEETH

There are excellent homecare products made for dogs' teeth. Your dog won't like the "minty fresh" toothpastes made for people, but these should not be used with dogs anyway. Human toothpastes are not designed to be swallowed (and rinse and spit is not something you will likely teach your dog!). Instead, there are toothpastes formulated for dogs, available in flavors such as liver and beef that your pet will enjoy. Start by getting the dog to lick a bit of the paste from your finger. Progress (over a period of days if your dog is resistant) to extending your finger back along the outside of the molar teeth, between the lip and the teeth. Don't worry about the inner surface of the molars; dogs don't typically build up plaque there. Then sweep around the base of the canines. Don't worry too much about the little incisors in front. Keep everything upbeat and happy, and don't force it. Watch your dog for signs of discomfort and give him the time to adjust to this new ritual, which he will probably come to enjoy as time spent getting attention and affection from you.

Most dogs will think that what you are doing is pretty weird at first, but will come around when they realize that they get their owners' undivided attention and tasty treats. When the dog starts accepting your touching the inside of his mouth, you can move on to using dental devices like a doggy toothbrush or a fingertip brush. For tiny dogs, you might need to use a cotton swab (but don't let him grab it and chew it up) or your littlest finger.

The time that it takes your dog to accept the home dental-care routine will depend on his personality and past experience. It may be too painful for your dog if you start brushing his teeth after he already has periodontal disease; in this case, you will need to get him used to just licking the toothpaste from your finger and having you handle his mouth until after he has had a veterinary cleaning. Brushing the teeth can reduce the degree of periodontal disease but will not eliminate it, so veterinary dental cleanings will be necessary along with your homecare routine. Some dogs develop tartar more quickly than others.

BONE OF CONTENTION

In recent years, there has been a natural-foods movement for feeding pets a "back to nature" diet. Proponents of these diets sometimes recommend giving dogs big meaty bones to chew on as part of that diet. They argue that dogs evolved for millions of years as predators and that returning to a more natural diet is healthy for a dog.

Veterinary dentists, by contrast, are concerned about the risk that hard bones as chew objects pose to a dog's teeth. Chewing objects that are harder than a dog's teeth leads to tooth fractures. Broken teeth can't heal the way broken bones do. A broken tooth is a tooth that will die and eventually need to be removed. Broken teeth allow bacteria to enter the root canal directly and travel into the bloodstream. Preventing broken teeth should be a high priority in preserving the health of your dog's mouth and perhaps his overall health, they argue. For this reason, they recommend that the dog not be allowed to chew on natural bones and other hard objects such as cow hooves and nylon chew objects.

Of course, dogs are not wolves. Even though they derived from this species, major anatomical, behavioral and physiological differences have occurred over the tens of thousands of years that they have lived with us. Scientists who study the domestication of dogs have suggested that dogs diverged from the wolves when they started scavenging from humans rather than exclusively hunting. Further, since their domestication, dogs have eaten what we have eaten, from a hunter-gatherer diet to a pastoral diet to an agricultural diet to an industrial diet, each step moving them further away from the diet of their wolf ancestors.

I became curious about the teeth of wolves that eat the "natural" diet. Scientific research on this topic is generally lacking, but I was able to inquire about a captive wolf population to see what had been observed. At Wolfpark outside Battleground, Indiana, the wolves are kept in a group housing arrangement. Off to the side are pens that house the senior wolves that no longer live with the pack. None of the wolves this age would be alive in the wild. They wouldn't be able to keep up with the demands of travel and hunting and may, in some cases, have been killed or driven off by their pack. However, here the elderly wolves are kept individually or in pairs, are fed and cared for and are allowed to live out their lives.

At Wolfpark, the wolves are given a natural diet of whole animal carcasses (frequently in the form of road-killed deer). I asked Pat Goodmann, head of wolf research at Wolfpark, about the condition of the teeth of these older wolves that have eaten this natural diet for their entire lives. "I see less tartar than is generally seen in dogs of a similar age," she told me, "but a lot of broken teeth." The broken teeth come from fighting with each other and, you guessed it, chewing on bones. Of course this observation is not the same as scientific evidence, but it suggests that with the natural diet it is also natural to occasionally break teeth. Wolves in the wild rarely live past middle age for a variety of reasons. Loss of teeth and chronic low-grade infections from broken teeth may be contributing factors limiting the life span of the wolves in the wild. Further research is needed.

If you feed a natural diet with large bones to your dog, there may be some other benefits, but be prepared to have him monitored more frequently for broken teeth and be prepared to follow through with the necessary dental procedures when these occur.

Unfortunately, it is not possible to determine the condition of the teeth in an awake animal. Sometimes, once an accurate and complete exam under anesthesia is done, the veterinarian will find teeth that are loose, infected and have no hope of staying in the mouth. It is better that these teeth are removed instead of being left in the mouth as a constant pain and infection source. Further, the dog's stomach does a pretty good job of masticating food, so a dog doesn't need his teeth for chewing as much as he needs his mouth to be pain-free and healthy.

FRACTURED TEETH AND EXTRACTION

If the dog has a fractured tooth, it needs to be taken care of for several reasons. First of all, the tooth can be painful. With time, the pain may decrease, but not the health risk from the broken tooth. Just because the dog resumes eating normally does not mean that a broken tooth is no longer a concern. With a broken tooth, the pulp cavity containing blood vessels and nerves is exposed, creating an open thoroughfare for bacteria from the mouth to enter the bloodstream. Either the broken tooth needs to be extracted or a root canal procedure needs to be performed to prevent this chronic infection risk.

Sometimes the thought of tooth extractions can disturb some pet owners, but it is important to consider this from the dog's perspective, not our own. Dogs are not vain and don't care how they look and so wouldn't be bothered much over missing a tooth or two. They'd surely much rather be missing a tooth than be in constant pain.

SAFETY OF ANESTHESIA

"But my dog is too old for the anesthesia" is a common concern veterinarians hear from owners. Age itself does not pose an increased anesthesia risk. The condition of the patient is the more important factor, and this can be assessed through blood tests and a comprehensive physical exam prior to the procedure. Proper anesthetics, procedures and monitoring need to be used. However, as one veterinary colleague of mine put it, the risk from anesthesia is a theoretical risk; the risk from not getting dentistry is a known risk—like standing in front of an oncoming car.

While cleaning teeth without using anesthesia is a procedure being touted by some veterinarians and even non-vets, veterinary dental specialists warn against this. Considering that the plaque that causes periodontal disease is below the gum line, it cannot be removed without anesthetizing the animal. In addition, as the plaque is scraped from the teeth, it aerosolizes bacteria that are part of this plaque and tartar complex. When a dog is anesthetized, he has a breathing tube, and the air that he is breathing comes in through the end of the tube. If the scaling is done without intubation, there is an increased risk that the dog will inhale those bacteria right into his lungs.

PREVENTION OF DENTAL PROBLEMS

Of course the best way to minimize the cost and anesthesia risk from dental procedures in your older dog is to minimize the need for dental procedures to start with. By getting in the habit of brushing your dog's teeth at home, you can greatly reduce the frequency with which he needs veterinary dental cleanings. Good dental care at home also decreases the deleterious effects of periodontal disease.

You can reduce the probability of broken or fractured teeth by not allowing your dog to chew on anything that is harder than his teeth. This probably seems obvious (like the old joke about not eating anything bigger than your head), but unfortunately many of the treats and common doggie chew toys are in fact too hard for dogs' teeth. Dogs have powerful jaws and can actually damage their teeth by chewing on hard objects. On the "do not chew" list are bones, cow hooves and nylon bone products. On the generally safe list are Kong toys, the Busy Buddy line of toys from Premier Pet products and some kinds of rawhide chew toys. Go to www.vohc.org, the site run by the Veterinary Oral Health Council, to see a description of some chew products. Obviously no chew toy is 100% safe for your dog, so be sure to supervise your dog with any chew product.

12 Skin and Coat

Staying in Touch

Most of us can recognize an older dog by the color of his hair—the old fellows turn gray in the muzzle just like gray-bearded grandpas. But gray whiskers aren't the only change that age brings to your dog's coat and skin. Many age-related changes occur so slowly and subtly that you may not even notice them at first. While some hair-coat changes are a normal part of aging, it is important to not dismiss or ignore it if you see changes in your dog's coat, particularly if it happens rapidly. Many endocrine disorders will also cause alterations in the haircoat. Gradual age-related changes need to be distinguished from signs of disease.

AGE-RELATED CHANGES

There is drying of all of the tissues in an older animal. This occurs everywhere in the body: the salivary glands produce less saliva; the lacrimal glands secrete and discharge fewer tears; and even the amount of water in the cartilage is reduced, causing it to lose some of its elastic properties. The skin also is affected. This natural loss of moisture means that the skin will dry out more and can become flaky. In addition, there is a loss of sebaceous glands on the skin, and those that are present work less efficiently. The sebaceous glands produce the oils and waxes that lubricate the haircoat and give it its glossy shine, springy texture and protection from the weather. The drying of tissues and the loss of protective oils combine to make the haircoat and skin of an older dog drier, less shiny and less resilient.

Eternal Puppy

There is a gradual loss of hair follicles, the structures in the skin that make hair. The haircoat of dogs is made up of two kinds of hair: the guard hairs and the softer insulating undercoat. When the older dog experiences a natural age-related hair loss, the loss, or reduced hair production, will primarily happen in the insulating undercoat layer (the coat that you can't readily see). That's not trivial information; it is important to remember because the loss of undercoat compromises your dog's ability to keep himself warm.

Skin can also become hyperpigmented and thickened. There is an increase in the keratin on the pads and nose, so the dog's nose can get a crusty feeling. In the winter the nose and pads can crack and bleed. You will also see an increase in the calluses on the elbows from the dog's lying down more.

EFFECTS OF IMMUNE SYSTEM CHANGES

Another consequence that is very important to understand is how the changes in the older dog's immune system make skin diseases more common but also harder to notice.

When an individual has a bacterial infection, it is not the bacteria themselves that cause the signs you commonly associate with infection: redness, swelling, pain and itching. All of these are a part of the inflammatory response, controlled by cells in the immune system, and are a part of the body's mechanism for fighting disease. Think for a moment of your reaction to a mosquito bite. The swelling and itching are a reaction produced by your body in response to the small amount of foreign substance that the insect introduced under your skin. Your reaction to that substance was one kind of inflammatory response.

In an older dog, the immune system does not function as well as it used to and therefore the inflammatory response is muted. The itching or redness that you would expect to see in reaction to a skin problem is not as obvious. In addition, the sebaceous glands that secrete oils and waxes that are a part of the skin's protective system are also working at a reduced capacity. This reduction of immune response and reduction in the protective barrier make the dog more susceptible to infections of the skin even though the common signs that you would look for (the itching and redness) can't be detected readily.

IN TOUCH WITH YOUR DOG

Putting our hands on our dogs and maintaining a physical connection with them is one of the greatest joys of living with our pets. When we feel this warm, living creature beneath our hands, it is good for us and it is good for them. Studies have shown that people's blood pressure drops and they become more relaxed when they stroke an animal. But there are also positive effects for the animal, as they also benefit from that loving connection. It is easy, as a dog ages, to become "out of touch" with him as our lives are busy and the dog may be less active. But staying "in touch" with your dog, both in an abstract and in a very real and practical sense, is one of the most important things that you can do to look after the health of and maintain the bond with your dog.

The skin is also the place where you may encounter lumps and bumps as you are running your hands over your dog. Some of these may be completely innocuous, but some are not. Because of the reduction in immune response, older dogs are also more susceptible to tumors. The best rule of thumb is to be sure that you run your hands over your dog's entire body at least once every day. In some ways, our fingers are our best "eyes" and the best, most sensitive, tools we can use to monitor our dogs' health. Besides, our dogs will love the undivided attention.

LONGER AND MORE BRITTLE NAILS
An old dog's toenails may get longer and more brittle. Part of the reason for this is that the dog is exercising less and not wearing down his nails. There also can be a laxity of the ligaments and tendons of the legs. When the ligaments in the back of the leg become lax, the back of the foot drops a bit and the front of the foot rises a bit, and this raises the toenails up to a point where they will wear down less.

VET AND OWNER EXAMS
Be sure to take your dog to the vet for twice-yearly senior-wellness checkups as well as anytime something seems "not quite

CONFESSIONS OF A BINGE GROOMER

Brushing your dog can be a wonderful bonding experience for you and your dog. As the brush strokes the dog's body, removing dead hair and debris, it is like getting a combination body massage and back scratching. The problem is that many dogs don't like to be groomed by their owners. I have two of them that don't like it, and I realized that this was my fault entirely.

Remember back to your childhood: it was lovely getting your hair brushed by a grownup, but not if the comb caught in a tangle. Especially not if it was your Aunt Matilda and she was rough with the comb and insisted on getting that tangle out right then and there. It was even less enjoyable if your Aunt Matilda would scold you and yank harder if you squirmed because of the pain. Pretty soon, if you saw pesky Aunt Matilda with a comb in her gigantic hand, you would slip out the door and find a tree to hide in.

I realized I was the problem when I was petting Rosie one day and noticed a mat in the hair on her hindquarters. I picked at the mat with my fingers for a moment and then went to the pet drawer to get a brush. When I came back with the brush, Rosie, who was usually completely underfoot, was nowhere to be found. Rosie had vanished. And when I found her, she was under my desk with a hangdog expression on her face.

That was when I realized that I was that pesky, yanky Aunt Matilda with the fire in her eyes and the comb in her hand and I had been focusing completely on the coat, not the dog. I would go too long between grooming sessions and then try to fix it in one sitting, making my dogs miserable, all the while convincing myself that this was for their own good. I had become obsessed with removing every tangle and loose hair, had made my grooming sessions last way too long and had made my dogs squirm and hurt. No wonder Rosie hid under my desk!

This had to stop. I had to shift my focus away from the perfect coat and back to my dog and her comfort. I had to make grooming enjoyable again.

So I started my 12-step program as a recovering binge brusher. I started by feeding a treat with the brush in my hand, then one stroke with the brush followed by another treat. Then I started leaving a brush out on the front porch and would brush the dogs before and after taking a walk, when they were in a pleasant frame of mind. I got some brushes with bumps and nubs that are designed for massaging and invigorating the skin, not just working on the hair coat. And I would restrict myself to filling up the brush only one time with hair and then stopping (this was easy with Rosie's long hair and Raven's thick double coat—only a few strokes and the brush would be full, and that was my mandate to stop). I would watch my dogs for signs of discomfort and stop immediately if I saw them.

At the time of this writing, we are all doing much better. Oh, sometimes I fall off the wagon and try to go for a second brushful of hair. But changing my goals was the key—no longer is my goal to get the perfect coat, but to have a grooming session with a happy dog. If my dog is not happy or becomes unhappy, I am not meeting my goal no matter how nice her coat looks.

right." Especially with an older dog, the earlier you intervene with a medical problem, the better your chances of helping. Owners frequently have a little voice that says "something is wrong." This little intuitive voice can get drowned out by the voice that tells you "there's nothing to worry about," "don't rock the boat," etc. Learn to listen to the little intuitive voice. Changes in the skin or hair are sometimes the earliest changes that a dog owner will notice that can point to an underlying disease process. Your hands may notice these changes before your eyes do, so make it a point to run your hands over your dog's entire body every day. If your fingers detect something unusual, pay attention.

TREATMENT FOR YOUR DOG

Coat and Skin Care

Soaps, shampoos and detergents all have the same thing in common: they are chemically designed to remove oils. Even a moisturizing shampoo will still remove oils. In an older dog, the oils are not being produced at the same rate as when the dog was younger. These oils are needed to coat the individual hairs, create a protective layer on the skin, give the coat luster and body and protect the animal from elements and infection.

To make the most of a limited resource, it is better to bathe your dog less often but brush your dog more often. Bathing your dog less will leave more of the oils and waxes where they can do their job. Brushing more often will do a better job of distributing the natural oils that are present and may help stimulate the glands to produce more. You may also look for a variety of brushes to use. Not only do you want to brush out loose hair, but you also want to massage and stimulate the skin. Different brushes may accomplish this task more handily than just one type, and you may find a brush that your dog really adores.

In addition to reduced bathing and increased brushing, you may be able to assist your dog with the use of humectants and emollients. These can both add moisture to the skin and coat. Ask your veterinarian for recommendations.

Remember also that, if your older dog now has less of the insulating layer of his haircoat, he will get cold more easily. If your dog has always slept in a location like a garage or outdoors, be aware that as he gets older it may become more difficult for him to stay as warm as he once did and that you will need to provide better means for your dog to stay warm. Even dogs who sleep indoors may become uncomfortably cold when they sleep, and this can interfere with their sleep.

If your dog's nose or calluses are getting harsh and crusty, you can soften them by rubbing a non-toxic lotion into these areas several times a day. Ask your veterinarian for a recommendation of what to use.

Nail Care

We may get used to hearing an old dog's nails' going clickety-clackety over the floor, but it is actually not good for him to have his nails this long. Dogs should walk on their pads, not their toe-nails. Walking on their nails spreads out the toes and stretches the ligaments in the legs, neither of which is good for the feet and legs, and puts abnormal stress on the joints and muscles.

In addition to the potential pain that overgrown toenails can cause, standing up on tippy-toes, like a ballerina, is not a secure way to move. The toenails are more prone to slip and slide than the pads. Arthritic older dogs may become worried about slipping, as this can be painful, and thus become reluctant to move as much, especially on hard, slippery floors. Older dogs also have a reduced sense of proprioception (the sense that lets a body know where it is in space). A reduction in proprioception makes the world feel less secure under the dog's feet and his balance harder to find, which could cause a dog to exercise less. Overlong toenails only add to this problem.

Another real problem with overlong nails involves the quick, the part of the nail that contains the nerves and blood vessels. In a normal nail, the quick will not grow to or near the end of the nail, but it will in a neglected or overlong nail. This starts a vicious cycle, because trying to cut a nail back too close to the quick will hurt, making the dog reluctant to have his nails trimmed. The best solution is not to try to fix the problem all at once. Frequent small trimmings, just clipping a little bit off the end of the toenail at a time, will cause the quick to recede. As you trim the nails, be careful that you aren't putting your dog in an uncomfortable position or wrenching a joint abnormally as you focus on the toenail that needs to be cut rather than on the whole dog. A dog with painful arthritis may struggle to get away and be reluctant to cooperate when you approach with a nail trimmer if you inadvertently cause him pain.

13 Behavior

Changes in Aging Dogs

"It is the brain, the little gray cells on which one must rely."
—fictional detective Hercule Poirot, created by Agatha Christie

Behavior is of paramount importance to those of us caring for aging dogs. Behavior is where the mind-body-spirit connection is the most apparent, and as your dog ages, it becomes increasingly important to look at your dog as an integrated whole. Virtually any medical condition can affect behavior. In fact, a change in behavior, be it something as subtle as increased thirst or decreased activity, is generally the first sign for a pet owner that something is not right with the health of his dog. Paying careful attention to changes in behavior gives us the ability to get the jump on developing disease conditions and be able to intervene at more optimal times.

Although the body can affect the mind (the consequences of which we see as behavior), the mind can also affect the body. For example, chronic anxiety and stress can adversely affect the immune system while positive mental stimulation can improve mental and physical health.

Behavior also includes the personality of your dog and how you interact together, how your dog responds to you and what you do together, so this is the place where the bond we have with our dogs resides. If aging or disease conditions affect the personality of your dog and what you can do together, it can erode the human-animal bond and the degree of happiness that you derive from each other's company.

Behavior is where we put it all together: who our dogs are, how they feel and how they act.

Eternal Puppy

PAYING ATTENTION TO CHANGES

There are several difficulties when trying to pay adequate attention to behavior changes in aging dogs. First of all, behavior changes can come on slowly, which means they may not be noticed. Dramatic and rapid changes are very apparent, but subtle and gradual changes often are not. Perhaps more insidious, however, is the perception that the behavior changes seen are just a normal part of aging, when in reality many things thought to be age-related changes are instead age-influenced diseases that are treatable, partly treatable or at least manageable.

This point was brought home during a field study with a drug that is prescribed for cognitive dysfunction (senility) in dogs. In the trial, more than 600 aged dogs and their owners were enlisted in a field study of a drug that improves neurotransmitter function and has antioxidant activity. Owners were asked to assess their dogs' behavior at the beginning of the study, then again after 30 days of treatment and again after 60 days of treatment. Based on previous studies, it was expected that improvements would be observed in some dogs that were reported to be showing signs of cognitive dysfunction. What was not expected, however, was that a number of dog owners who had reported their dogs as "normal" at the start of the trial also reported improved behavior at the 30-day evaluation. Even more notable was that the behavior classification that showed the most improvement was "decreased social interaction," which is a category directly related to our bond with our dogs. What this indicated was that, because of the slow and insidious nature of age-influenced neurological problems and because we have a mistaken expectation of reduced interactions in older dogs, these owners hadn't realized that their dogs had problems until a medication that specifically targeted these problems was given and the dogs returned to more normal behavior.

The point that I want to make in mentioning this study is not that drugs can solve behavior problems; that would be an oversimplification, and drugs should never be the first or only modification made for behavior problems. Rather, I wish to highlight the fact that a percentage of the participating owners did not notice the behavior changes that had occurred in their dogs until after the dogs improved.

So we need to be very careful when looking at the behavior of an aging dog and realize that there are a number of things that we can do to help our dogs live richer lives. We also need to recognize these changes early, because this is when intervention is the most useful.

AGE-RELATED CHANGES IN THE BRAINS OF DOGS

No organ in the body goes unchanged by age, and the nervous system is no exception. There is an overall reduction in brain mass in older dogs, including a reduction in both neurons and support cells. There are changes in the blood and oxygen supply to the brain, from changes in both the brain and the circulatory system, the latter from decreased heart output and decreased physical activity. There is a reduction in the production of some of the neurotransmitters (chemical communicators in the brain). There is also a reduction in the function of the mitochondria of the cells in the brain. Mitochondria are the parts of cells that function with energy metabolism—they are like the furnace of the cells, where the fuel is burned.

While some things diminish, other things increase with age. When the brains of older dogs are specifically examined, it was found that they contain a larger amount of a substance called beta-amyloid plaques than that found in younger dogs. While beta-amyloid plaque formation is not completely understood, it is believed to be toxic to nerve cells and associated with cognitive dysfunction disease in dogs and Alzheimer's disease in people. In both humans and dogs, more extensive beta-amyloid plaque formation is associated with more severe cognitive impairment.

Toxic free radicals (also called reactive oxygen species) are by-products of cellular metabolism. To utilize fuel energy, a cell uses oxygen. The oxygen is needed to efficiently burn the fuel, but a small amount of the oxygen is converted to these reactive oxygen species. It is a lot like burning wood in a campfire. The beneficial light and heat are produced, but so too is the detrimental soot and smoke. These toxic free radicals (the "soot and smoke") can interact with DNA and proteins and lead to cell damage, dysfunction, mutation (possibly leading to cancer) and even cell death. Of course, the body is also well equipped with mechanisms to defend itself against toxic free radicals. In addition to making enzymes that break down free radicals, the body utilizes dietary free-radical scavengers such as vitamins E and C (called antioxidants).

However, as the mitochondria age, they become less efficient, producing more free radicals and less energy (more smoke and less light). The brain is particularly sensitive to free-radical damage because of its high oxygen demand and because it has a limited antioxidant defense and repair ability. All of this can then lead to an accumulation of oxidative damage in the canine brain as it ages. Oxidative damage is thought to be part of the mechanism behind age-related changes in learning and behavior and also the degenerative changes that lead to the disease of canine cognitive dysfunction. That is what is going on inside the dog…what do we see on the outside?

DOG APPEASING PHEROMONE (DAP)

While we often think of behavioral modification or drug therapy as the main treatment options for anxiety, there is a new and different treatment modality with interesting possibilities. A pheromone is a substance that is produced by an animal and can change the behavior of another animal who detects its odor. The natural world is full of these chemical signals, like the foraging trails laid down by ants or the sex-attractant pheromones released by female mammals when they are in estrus and ready to mate. Pheromones communicate with very primitive and powerful parts of the brain to influence emotion and behavior.

A group of French researchers has been investigating the use of pheromones for therapeutic purposes: to calm and reassure. Dog appeasing pheromone (DAP) is one of these. This pheromone comes from the mammary glands of lactating bitches and it identifies the source of nourishment and comfort essential to the survival of newborn puppies. Studies have shown that DAP, when used in a spray, diffuser or slow-release collar, reduces anxiety in many dogs when they are in stressful circumstances. It appears capable of dialing down anxiety: bringing it to a manageable level for some dogs or reducing the amount of anxiety medication needed in some others. DAP must be used correctly for success, and, as with all behavior drugs, environmental management and behavior modification will be needed along with it, but pheromone therapy gives us another tool to help us keep our dogs comfortable.

CHANGES ON THE OUTSIDE

Psychological studies that were designed to ferret out different learning strategies in a controlled experimental environment have shown that there are differences in the way that older dogs learn versus how younger dogs learn. These studies were done with laboratory-reared Beagles and have found a number of interesting things. Younger dogs generally outperformed older dogs on many learning and memory tests. Yet in some kinds of learning, older and younger dogs did equally well.

What this means at home is that your older dog is still able to learn new tasks but perhaps will take a few more repetitions to do so than a younger dog will. However, there are some learning circumstances that will not be different between young and old dogs. At the same time, an older dog will likely be more resistant to change, more likely to try to continue to do what he has previously learned(what we call "being set in their ways" in humans). This is not a result of deliberate stubbornness; it just means that the older dog is functioning with different operating equipment. New habits can be learned, but doing so may take longer. If, however, your dog starts forgetting well-learned behaviors, things he has reliably done for a long time, like finding his food bowl or the house-training routine, this is an indication of a medical problem (including, but not limited to, canine cognitive dysfunction) and means that he should be checked by his veterinarian.

Remember also that there are sensory deficits and medical conditions that can interfere with learning or performing a specific learned behavior. A dog with age-related hearing loss may not come when he is called because he can't really hear you. He may not retrieve quickly if arthritis pain is interfering. So there may be a difference between what your dog knows, what he can learn and what he is capable of doing.

Another behavior change seen in older dogs is an increase in anxiety and anxiety-based disorders (like separation anxiety, phobias or a dog that won't settle down). As with learning, sometimes it is not easy to tell if this is a result of a neurological issue, a disease or an environmental stressor. An older dog may be more disturbed by changes in routine, like a new pet or a change in your work schedule. Additional stressors can be increased pain and disability from arthritis and loss of senses such as hearing or vision. Sometimes it is not one thing, but a

SOME PROBLEMS COMMONLY SEEN IN CANINE COGNITIVE DYSFUNCTION

Disorientation: Does your dog get lost easily in a familiar environment? Appear confused? Go to the wrong side of the door (not accounted for by visual deficit)? Does he have trouble maneuvering around or over obstacles, even though he is physically able to do so? Has he gotten stuck in a corner and can't figure out the way back out?

Sleep-wake disturbances: A dog developing cognitive dysfunction may experience alterations in his sleep-wake cycle, becoming disconnected from a normal 24-hour day/night schedule. He may sleep more throughout the day and then show increased restlessness and wakefulness at night.

Social interaction changes: Cognitive dysfunction may cause decreased social interaction, such as reduced interest in petting or failing to greet you when you enter the house. Your dog may have problems with social relationships with other pets. Alternatively, instead of socially withdrawing, he may become clingy and have an increased need for attention and affection.

Activity changes: A dog showing signs of cognitive dysfunction may become apathetic and have reduced responsiveness to stimuli. Alternatively, he may show increased restlessness and purposeless movement, like pacing, licking, vocalizing, wandering and staring into space.

House-soiling: House-soiling can have a number of causes, one of which is cognitive dysfunction. The house-soiling difficulties commonly seen with cognitive dysfunction include eliminating in odd places or in the view of the owners, going outside and then eliminating when he returns inside or soiling in his crate or sleeping area. It is as if he no longer remembers what he is supposed to do.

Look at the whole picture: A dog that is developing CCD will not necessarily show all of these signs nor will one dog look just like another. In addition, other conditions can also cause these signs.

number of little things that, added up together, tip the balance. Correcting some of these things may bring stress and anxiety back to a manageable level for the dog.

RESPONDING TO BEHAVIOR CHANGES

Your response to these anxieties can make a difference in how they progress. Anything that can generate more fear, like punishment or forcing the dog to confront what he fears (called flooding) can make the overall anxiety worse. However, too much comforting of a fearful dog can potentially reinforce the fearful behavior. Like Goldilocks, you have to look for the calm, confident balance that is "just right." Keeping the environment consistent can reduce anxiety in an older dog. Living in constant fear is a miserable way to live and if your dog's anxiety is worsening, a consultation with a qualified behaviorist can be of great assistance.

Your training and handling methods should focus primarily on positive reinforcement. It is not fair or kind to punish a dog for something that he cannot help, and concepts of dominance do not apply. And it is counterproductive to handle your dog in a way that might generate anxiety, due to how the incidence of anxiety disorders increases in older dogs. Punishing your older dog for something he can't understand to begin with can only increase anxiety and all of the disturbing behaviors that go along with it.

CANINE COGNITIVE DYSFUNCTION

When a cluster of specific behavior problems is seen that are due to the effects of brain aging, this is a disease condition called cognitive dysfunction syndrome. It is roughly equivalent to senility in humans.

It is hard to say where along the continuum brain aging becomes a disease process, or even whether this represents a continuum of changes or separate entities. It is tempting to try to draw the line and decide that on one side are normal changes and on the other side is disease, but this is an impractical exercise in most cases. The important point is to catch these changes early because there are environmental enrichment, dietary and even drug and nutraceutical options that appear to slow the disease process and can help maintain your dog's quality of life. Although brain cells do not regenerate,

YOU CAN TEACH AN OLD DOG NEW TRICKS... IT JUST TAKES A BIT LONGER.

I love to sing folk music and used to be able to memorize words to a song in a heartbeat—twice through the song and I had it down. So it was a rude awakening for me when I started singing songs with my children and found that they could memorize words quickly while I lagged way behind—often to a chorus of "Mom, that's wrong" whenever I sing the wrong word. Apparently my middle-aged brain doesn't memorize song lyrics like it used to. But while my rapid memorization skills don't seem to be up to their par, I can still come up with new harmonies, figure out guitar chords without seeing the music and pick out the melody on a piano…all with better faculty than my word-memorizing teen-aged kids. There is, after all, more than one kind of learning, and experience matters.

The songs that I learned as a teen, back in my rapid-memorization stage, are seared in my memory, and some I could probably still sing even if I hadn't heard them for a decade (including the ones I would prefer to forget).

So while I can't memorize words as I used to, I have made more connections to other things. Maybe if I had continued to learn new songs at the rate that I did as a teen, when I had more time and fewer responsibilities, I would have retained this mental skill. Maybe if I tried to memorize a new song every day, I would regain it. And I have an impressive library of songs already learned that I can still draw from memory.

A similar process appears to occur in older dogs as well. When tested in specific facets of memory and learning, younger dogs learn faster at a number of specific categories. In other facets, old and young dogs are similar. And when dogs are continually challenged with learning tasks, they retain more learning ability and can utilize more flexible problem-solving skills. Does an old dog remember something from its teenaged years as if he learned it yesterday? Anecdotes would suggest this is likely, but systematic experimentation hasn't been done. Still, I think it is likely that old dogs not only are still learning new things, albeit slower, but they also have a good ability to remember what they've learned previously. What they know, can utilize and can learn from scratch just looks different from what you see in a younger dog. And the same is true of us as well.

it is possible for some to take over the function of cells that are lost and to protect what is left, so the objective is to catch this disease when there are still enough healthy cells left to maintain function. While treatment is important, the best approach is prevention, because by the time signs are seen, there could already be significant deterioration.

Cognitive dysfunction disease is a diagnosis that is made by exclusion. That means that for a veterinarian to make this diagnosis, the dog must exhibit a set of specific behaviors. The veterinarian then rules out other diseases and circumstances that might be contributing to the behaviors seen. However, cognitive dysfunction can also take place hand in hand with other diseases, so finding one doesn't completely exclude the other. In trying to pinpoint cognitive dysfunction, the veterinarian looks for some characteristic changes in the dog's behavior that suggest that this disease is occurring. Important to consider as well is the severity of the behavioral signs—is this not present, is it mild, or is it severe? Because we can not look into the brains of dogs and see how much beta-amyloid plaque formation is occurring, without injuring the brain (or killing the patient) to do so, the studies that found a strong correlation between the severity of specific behavior signs and the degree of beta-amyloid plaques in the brains of dogs post mortem are the strongest evidence we have to go on. In this case, analysis of the behavior and ruling out other things that could cause it is the "laboratory test" for this disease in the same way that looking for a blood component would be the test to use in some other disease.

THE BOTTOM LINE

The bottom line is that it is important that you do not dismiss behavior changes as: "Oh, this is just what an old dog does." While changes in the brain are inevitable as the dog ages, disease states are not. There is a lot you can do to delay the onset and slow the progress of these changes, improve your dog's well-being and maintain the precious bond that you share with your pet.

Section III

Strategies for Maintaining a Vital Senior

14 Exercise

A Magic Bullet?

People are often looking for a magic bullet, a golden egg, a perfect cure-all, a wonder drug that leads to good health and heals every pain. Of course, there is no such thing, but the closest we can come is a powerful tool that is at every pet owner's hands and feet: exercise.

Dogs were never designed to be sedentary. For most of their evolutionary history, they have been on the move, doing something, often working alongside their human partners. While the progression—from active helpers who lived mostly outdoors and earned their keep by working with people to beloved pets who live inside our homes—has become a normal, even cozy, arrangement for human and dog, there are some drawbacks for our naturally active, hard-working canines. What has happened in recent decades is that the human half of the pair, in this technological age, has become increasingly less active and, since the human end of the leash has virtually complete control over the canine end, the dog has been forced to lead a near-sedentary existence as well. A feral dog may cover a five-mile range every night, while many of our largely indoor pets are lucky to be outside for five minutes several times a day. Most dogs today do not live on large expanses of property. Many suburban dogs are limited to small yards and city dogs are restricted to on-leash exercise and the occasional visit to the dog park. In other words, it is rare these days for a dog to get the level of exercise that he is genetically designed to get.

This problem gets even worse as a dog ages. Puppies are self-exercising: driven to play and move. I always wince when I see a

normal, active, adolescent dog disparaged by his frustrated owner as "hyper," when actually the dog is exhibiting a normal activity level for a young dog. Today's dog owner simply expects a dog to live his life in too restrictive an environment, where he can't expend the energy he's programmed to. But dogs can adapt to this unfortunate circumstance of inadequate exercise. By the time they reach maturity, they are pretty used to it; the puppy drive has diminished and they are no longer striving as hard to get the exercise their bodies and minds need to be their healthiest. As they enter their senior years, other complications, like the pain from arthritis, further slow them down.

Since we create the environment in which our dogs live, it is up to us to see that they get the exercise they need. Exercise has a myriad of benefits, both mental and physical, for an aging dog, and it is one of the most powerful tools you have to help your dog age gracefully.

BENEFITS OF EXERCISE

Exercise stimulates the brain. Getting your dog out into a change of scenery and allowing him to sniff new smells, feel the breeze, walk on uneven surfaces and so forth stimulate many different pathways in the brain. It rejuvenates and invigorates. Exercise can improve the oxygenation of tissues, including those in the brain. As my mother used to say when she booted me out the door to play outside: it gets the cobwebs out.

Exercise also improves the proprioceptive sense, that unconscious sense that tells the body where it is in space. As a dog ages, this sense diminishes. One thing that can slow this loss is for your dog to experience a variety of uneven surfaces that challenge the proprioception parts of the nervous system and help keep the neurological pathways functioning.

Exercise is an integral part of an obesity-management program. Maintaining a dog at his recommended weight, or helping him to lose weight when needed, is the most effective treatment we have for arthritis. It has been well demonstrated that weight loss, even in a moderately obese dog (who doesn't even look overweight to many of us), can reduce the impact of a number of painful conditions and improve mobility and overall health.

Generalized muscle loss is seen with advancing age. This geriatric muscle-wasting syndrome is a multifactorial problem in which researchers observe a number of hormonal and metabolic changes, but the picture of how they all interrelate is still not clear. Exercise is one factor found to help slow this process and give your dog more strength to get around. However, while gradual muscle loss is a part of normal aging, if you see rapid muscle loss, you should schedule an appointment with your veterinarian, as this could indicate the presence of a medical problem.

In the arthritic dog, there are many benefits seen from exercise that appear to slow the disease process or at least the amount of pain and infirmity it can cause. Exercise stretches the joints and improves flexibility. It strengthens the muscles around a joint, which then function like a shock absorber and stabilizer, protecting the joint from overload and helping to circulate the joint fluid, which is necessary to maintain healthy cartilage in the joints. And exercise reduces pain, which in turn encourages more movement.

GUIDELINES FOR EXERCISING AN AGING DOG

Here are the basic guidelines for safe and effective exercising.

Be mindful. Watch your dog and make sure that you are setting a pace that is appropriate for him and that you are paying attention to when he needs a rest. People tend to be very goal-oriented when they exercise. We have goals or benchmarks in mind that measure our progress. When we go out to exercise, we have a plan of where we intend to go and what we intend to do and we set out to implement that plan. For example, we might decide to walk around the block a certain number of times or walk to the park and back. We may stop or slow down and rest once we reach a benchmark and then we continue on to complete the distance we have mentally set up as our goal.

When exercising an old dog, we need to change our concept of what our goals are. The goal now is not where and how far are you going today, but how your dog looks and how he is doing. We need to walk at the rate and distance that our dog needs to walk comfortably. We notice and monitor whether or not he appears uncomfortable. We take the time and go the distance that our dog can handle. Our goal now becomes doing what is best for our dog and determining

A HOMECARE EXERCISE PROGRAM FOR DOGS WITH ARTHRITIS

Begin the day with a 15- to 20-minute warm-up session, applying warm water bottles or heated wet towels to the dog's stiff joints. You can heat up the towels using the microwave oven, making them only as hot as is comfortable for you on your own skin. After the warm-up, slowly flex and extend the dog's joints. Do not force them beyond the range that is comfortable for your dog. Watch closely for signs of discomfort. Slowly do 15 to 20 repetitions on each affected joing.

During the course of the day, take your dog on a few short walks, allowing him sufficient rest in between. Let your dog set the pace and distance. Several short walks are better than one or two long walks. If your dog shows reluctance, fatigue or stiffness, cut the level of activity in half and work up gradually from there.

As your dog's endurance improves, begin to include activities to improve mobility, increase muscle strength and reduce pain. Some suggestions are to walk up and down ramps or stairs or walk a serpentine pattern up and down a curb. Don't push your dog beyond what he is comfortable doing.

Your dog should cool down after any exercise. Massage and use an ice pack (or a bag of frozen vegetables) on the arthritic joints to minimize any swelling that may occur following exercise. If the program is continued, your dog should show improvements in movement and reduction in pain. However, if you don't continue, you will lose the benefits gained. Consultation with a veterinarian trained in canine physical rehabilitation is also highly recommended, as he will have additional techniques that he can employ and that can assist you in tailoring your plan to your dog's condition and needs.

Adapted from information in *Canine Rehabilitation and Physical Therapy* by Daryl L. Millis MS, DVM; David Levine Ph.D., PT; and Robert A. Taylor DVM, MS.

this by paying attention to him. We have to change our focus from the destination to the journey.

Take it easy. If you are starting an exercise routine with your dog, ease into it—don't go for a marathon. Look for low-impact activities. Don't take on strenuous new activities; instead do variations of what the dog already knows and has been doing all his life. Particularly if your dog is arthritic, exercise should be increased gradually so that his pain and stiffness are not intensified after the activity. If you see this occurring, cut back and increase even more gradually. If you can't find an exercise level or activity that doesn't cause your dog more pain, you should get a referral for a veterinarian with training in canine physical rehabilitation. Such a professional can employ techniques to help your dog regain strength and mobility in a more controlled way.

Get variety. Like muscles, proprioception is also a use-it or lose-it resource. Loss of balance and fluidity of movement can make it difficult for an older dog to get around and can really compromise his quality of life. Stimulating the nerve pathways slows this loss. Have your dog walk on a variety of surfaces to the degree that he is able. Guide him up and down inclines, do a serpentine pattern along a curb while stepping up and down, walk on trails and fields. Look for walking routes with different surfaces and terrain (within reason—no need to go bushwhacking). Look for interesting things to step over and around. Set up low parallel poles (no higher than the dog's wrist) for the dog to walk over (like cavaletti used in horse training). By increasing the variety, you are stimulating both the unconscious proprioceptive part of your dog's brain and the conscious problem-solving part.

Put on the brakes. Because dogs live in the moment, it is hard for a dog that is playing and having fun to realize that he is going to hurt a lot the next day. (This is not unlike the way you feel following your first day back to the gym after a long holiday or hiatus!) At the same time, play is important and provides great mental, physical and emotional enrichment, so you need to look for balance. You may need to step in and moderate his activities. If you go to dog parks, be careful about energetic young dogs who might bowl your oldster over in their enthusiasm. Intervene if playing gets rough.

Get wet. Swimming is great exercise, provided you take a few safety precautions. Be aware that in cold waters, older dogs will get chilled more easily. Remember that dogs can drown, and older dogs have less reserves of energy. Even if he was a powerful swimmer when young, don't let him overexert himself and get exhausted. Choose safe calm waters and use a life vest made for dogs.

Bring it indoors. Exercise indoors when the weather is bad. Many people go to the gym or do mall walking for indoor exercise, both activities that do not include dogs. Some communities do have indoor exercise facilities for dogs, but if you don't have access to one of these, there are still many activities you can do at home. Play hide and seek. If your dog is able, do stair laps (with a treat or cuddles at the top and the bottom). Use food puzzles. Once your dog knows the concept of "find it," you can hide toys or divide his dinner into a number of portions and hide them for him to find. And how about doggie calisthenics? A great muscle builder is to do lie down, sit and stand exercises. Keep all of your activities light and upbeat, with a lot of praise and laughter, and it will be fun instead of work.

Don't be a weekend warrior. It is far better for an older dog, particularly if he has arthritis or is just starting an exercise program after a long reign as the "royal couch potato," to have steady, frequent, low-impact exercise than sporadic, strenuous exercise. The weekend-only exercise schedule is potentially damaging to unaccustomed joints and muscles. Although it may seem fun at the time, the sudden burst of activity could result in substantial pain a day or so later and can cause an arthritis flare-up. Joints are more likely to get injured because the muscles aren't in condition. Steady exercise through the week may be able to get your dog in shape for some weekend fun, but be sure to watch your dog during times of more vigorous activity and put on the brakes to avoid overexertion. If your dog is stiff and appears to be in pain on Monday, then you know that you overdid it and that you'll have to moderate his activities more the next time.

Don't forget his thermals! As a dog ages, he will likely experience a thinning of his coat and changes in his metabolic rate and subcutaneous fat layer. These natural changes will make him less able to tolerate the cold than he could in his youth, which can make going outside in cold weather uncomfortable for him. When bad weather hits, your old pal may cut his trips outdoors to potty as short as possible, getting less exercise than usual. And he may become chilled while out on a walk. If he is showing signs of discomfort in the cold, slip a doggie sweater or coat on him. Intolerance to cold is also a sign of hypothyroidism, so be sure to report this observation to your veterinarian.

Stay in the cool of the day. If cold can be a problem for an older dog, heat can be doubly so. Dogs do not dissipate heat as well as humans (which is why canine endurance races such as the Iditarod are held in the frozen North—similar strenuous activities in a temperate climate would likely kill the dogs). Whereas humans use sweating to cool the body, dogs only sweat from the pads of their feet. Their primary form of cooling is to pant—pulling air over the evaporative surface of their tongues (by contrast, humans use their entire bodies as an evaporative surface). The canine cooling system is less efficient and requires energy to perform (which generates more heat). Plus dogs are covered with a fur coat that insulates them, holding the heat in. Effective cooling requires an effective respiratory system, and as dogs age, their respiratory capacity is reduced, thus reducing their bodies' cooling capability. So while all dogs are more susceptible to overheating than people, this is even more of a danger for older dogs.

To protect from overheating (and a potentially fatal case of heat stroke), don't exercise your dog during the hot parts of the day. High humidity also increases the potential for overheating. Pay close attention to your dog in warm weather. Make sure that he stops to cool off and that he has plenty of water (carry a water bottle and portable doggie bowl). A dog that is having fun is capable of literally running himself to death in hot weather, because he often won't stop until he is in serious trouble. Having fun with their pet, children will keep throwing the ball until Beethoven rolls over from exhaustion, so be sure that you supervise and intervene to keep your dog from overexerting himself in hot weather. Take your walks in the cooler parts of the day.

Exercise benefits the body, heart and spirit of your dog and the relationship you have with each other. Don't look upon it as a burdensome task, but rather a source of joy and quality time for both of you. Enjoy!

THE DOG DAYS OF SUMMER

One of the things we humans have in common with dogs is that we both evolved for endurance activities. However, there is an important difference: humans are adapted to dissipate heat, while canids are not. Biologist Dr. Ray Coppinger sums it up: "Dogs are good at retaining heat but they are lousy at dissipating heat."

Humans and dogs both evaporate water to cool their bodies. But humans can use the entire surface of their body, while dogs only sweat a tiny bit from the pads of their feet and primarily use the evaporative surface of their tongues. Dogs increase their breathing rate to pull air over that evaporative surface—we recognize it as panting. Panting requires energy and generates heat. Dogs' richly vascularized muscles give them great athleticism but also generate large amounts of heat. The metabolic process for cooling that we both share is that when we are getting hot, the body floods blood vessels near the skin to aid in cooling—but while our skin is mostly bare, dogs are covered with fur. Cooling down properly requires a well-functioning respiratory system, and therefore older dogs are at a higher risk for heat stroke since their lungs aren't as elastic as those of young dogs and they can't breathe as deeply or as easily.

Likewise, overweight dogs are at higher risk as well. Dr. Coppinger says "The best way to dissipate heat is to radiate heat from the skin, but if you add a layer of fat to that, such as in an overweight dog, the dog is in real trouble."

A human usually will quit when he is getting overheated, but a dog, so caught up in what he is doing and enjoying quality time with his owner, may not. Or a dog will try to quit, but his human exercise partner either doesn't notice the signs of exhaustion and overheating or won't let the dog do so.

So when a dog trots behind a jogging owner, chases a ball in a park or goes out hunting, his body temperature can become so elevated that he is in serious trouble before he can recognize it and stop. Put simply, on a hot day, a dog can literally run himself to death.

Prevention, therefore, is the most important step that you, the pet owner, can take. Recognize when conditions are too hot, and don't exercise your dog. And realize that being left in cars that get hot or tied in the direct sunlight can also be dangerous. "Also be aware of the danger of humidity," advises emergency veterinarian Dr. Karol Mathews. "This is the killer, as heat dissipation is reduced as the humidity increases." It is especially bad for dogs and cats as their main (really only) source of heat dissipation is from a relatively small area of the body, their tongue.

If your dog has become overheated, here are some things to know:

An overheated dog might be prostrate and panting, unsteady on his feet or actually lapse into unconsciousness. Lack of panting may occur if the dog is going into shock. The dog might vomit or have diarrhea and the mental status can vary from alert and anxious to depression, stupor, unconsciousness and even seizures.

If you suspect hyperthermia or heat stroke in your dog, call an emergency veterinarian immediately. Take a rectal temperature, as it will give the veterinarian valuable information. Cool the animal by gentle hosing with cool water or immersing for a short time (no more than 15 minutes) in cool water. (Don't let his head get in the water.) Wet his fur and blow air over him with a fan. Use cool or tepid water, not ice cold water.

Be careful of overcooling your pet. Once the dog has overheated, the thermoregulatory centers in his brain are impaired and it is possible to overshoot and get them too cold. Both conditions, overheating and underheating, can cause shock and multiple organ failure.

A case of heat stress in a dog may resolve on its own, once conditions for cooling are provided. But a moderate to severe case, called heat stroke, will need the services of an emergency veterinarian, as this is a very serious condition potentially causing death, and very expensive to treat. Remember, you can save your dog's life by keeping him cool in summer heat.

15 Nutrition

No Easy Answers

The feeding relationship is a powerful aspect of the human-animal bond, providing emotional pleasure to ourselves as well as nurturing to our dogs. This is one of the ways that our eternal puppy stays an eternal puppy—our dogs are dependent on us for nourishment. Not just nutrition, but good nutrition. We know that good nutrition has an influence on health, so this is one area where we can have a positive impact on our aging dogs.

What, then, should we feed our senior dogs? What is the one perfect diet for older dogs that meets all their nutritional needs? The short answer is that there isn't one perfect diet that suits every senior dog. There is no easy answer to the question of what is best to feed our aging dogs.

This is not to say that there are no good diets for older dogs or that nutrition is not a critical factor for keeping old dogs healthy. The confusion comes in trying to determine the specific combination of nutrients needed, in what amounts, by a specific dog.

Even though senior diets have been sold for some time, initially these diets were based on best guesses and supposition, not a lot of actual research. And because different companies were marketing foods based on their own best guesses, there was a lot of variation between the pet-food companies regarding how their senior diet should differ from their regular adult diet. The Association of American Feed Control Officials (AAFCO) feeding standards recognizes only two different life stages for dogs: puppies and adults. All senior dog foods fall under the "adult" category of nutritional

standards, and those standards were developed for the average adult dog without consideration of whether the nutritional needs of the average senior dog might be different. So while senior pet foods are very common, unfortunately there is no legal definition of what constitutes a senior pet food—it just has to meet adult requirements. Only in recent years has senior food become an area of focused research.

The second confusing factor is that every dog is individual in his needs, and those needs change as the dog ages. For example, two dogs of the same size can have different energy requirements. Just think of every 40-year-old person you know: each one has his own activity, health and energy needs, and the same is true of each 7-year-old dog. Plus there is a great variation in body types in dogs. An extreme example is the difference between a Chihuahua and a Great Dane, but there are differences between all breeds, as well as natural variations among dogs within the same breed. Additionally, a dog's needs will change with time. Again to draw the analogy to humans, a 40-year-old person will likely not have the same nutritional requirements when he is 70 years old. The same is true for a 7-year-old dog, whose needs will likely be different at age 10, 12 and so on.

One must also recognize the power of food fads. People are always being told what to eat and what not to eat in order to be healthy, and it seems as if there's always a new "superfood-of-the-moment." These trends have spilled over into what we are advised to feed our pets. Then there are the food-fad gurus—charismatic people who have seen the light and want to lead you on the path they have blazed (not that some of them haven't had valuable revelations, but too often they have an axe to grind, something to sell, and they use testimonials instead of testing to back up their claims).

Myth is also a powerful element. Once something is thought to be possible, it is passed around until it is believed to be true—sometimes blown out of proportion or with very little real data to back it up. The Internet has accelerated the tendency by which misinformation gains credibility and becomes widely accepted. Myths are also used in advertising, giving the illusion of truth.

And then—to be completely skeptical about what information is available—one must examine the pet-food companies themselves.

These are billion-dollar industries who want your loyalty almost as much as your money. How do you know who and what information to trust?

In the middle of these minefields we and our hungry canines walk, looking for the best food to feed our aging pals. We know that what we provide for our dogs to eat is important for their health. The difficulty lies in knowing how to decide what is best. The reality is that there is no single best diet for older dogs, only the diet that is best for your dog at this particular point in time. And since aging is a process, there are times when your dog's nutritional requirements change; when this occurs, you will need to change your dog's diet to match these changing needs.

Until recent years, nutrition was not a consistently required or even frequently offered field of study in veterinary medicine. This has changed in recent years and not only are veterinarians getting nutrition training, but veterinary nutrition has also become a specialty field. Some veterinarians go on to get advanced training and become board-certified in veterinary nutrition. This has led to increased research, more learning and teaching and to the availability of specialists for clinical consultation.

THE BASICS OF DIETS

Before trying to determine which diet is best for your aging dog, it is important to understand basic facts about foods. What do we mean by nutrients? What is protein and what is its dietary importance? Do dogs need carbohydrates just as people do? Are there good fats and bad fats for dogs?

Nutrients Versus Ingredients

It is important to recognize that there is a difference between an ingredient and a nutrient, although these terms are sometimes used interchangeably. A nutrient is an ingested substance that the body needs and utilizes to promote growth, maintenance or development. An ingredient is a specific type of food, such as chicken, rice and vegetable oil, which generally contributes more than one kind of nutrient. Dogs have absolute requirements for certain nutrients; they don't have absolute requirements for specific ingredients.

To understand what is meant by this, let's consider meat, arguably the key ingredient in the canine diet. Most people will say that dogs are carnivores and need to have meat protein in their diet. This statement is not completely true—dogs need amino acids, the building blocks of protein. Meat is composed, in a large part, of muscle protein, which is made up of amino acids. But there are other sources of amino acids besides meat. Eggs, for example, have an excellent complement of amino acids, and all plants have some amino acids. What is critical is that dogs get an adequate amount of a specific set of amino acids. It is the nutrient that matters. The ingredient is of importance only insofar as it is able to provide the nutrients needed, in an available and tasty form, while not providing undesirable substances.

Protein and Amino Acids

As important as the amount of protein is the quality of the protein. What is meant by protein quality is that the protein contains usable amino acids in the proper amounts.

Proteins are made in the cells by amino acids connecting together in a specific order to make a specific protein. If an amino acid type is not present in sufficient numbers, then the protein can't be made—it is as though you are decorating for Fourth of July and your design called for alternating red, white and blue light bulbs. If you run out of blue light bulbs, you are stuck, because you can't continue without the missing color and still make the desired color pattern. The same happens if the body has limited amounts of an amino acid—the proteins requiring that amino acid in their structure can't be made.

An essential amino acid is the name for an amino acid that the body must get in the diet—these amino acids can't be manufactured by the body. Nonessential amino acids are manufactured in the body from the essential amino acids, so there has to be an adequate supply of the essential amino acids to make the rest. All 20 amino acids are needed and must be present in a functional form.

Individual protein sources are not equivalent in having a full complement of amino acids. For example, meat and eggs (called high-quality protein sources) have a fairly full complement of the necessary amino acids, while plant proteins are often lacking in a few amino acids. However, if you feed two different plant proteins, each one being high in the amino acid that the other is lacking, they will balance each other. If you compare that to the light bulb analogy above: one protein source might have a lot of white bulbs, some red and no blue, while the other has a lot of blue, some red and no white. Put them together and you can have enough to make a long string of red, white and blue.

In addition, how the protein source is processed is of importance. The bottom line is that you need a full complement of functional amino acids. The more processing done to a protein source, the greater the risk of denaturing or damaging the amino acids, making them unusable. So chicken meat usually is a higher-quality protein source than meat and bone meal, which undergoes considerable processing. It is worthwhile to look at the ingredients list on the food you are feeding your dog. Ingredients are listed in descending order according to the amount of that ingredient in the feed—those at the top of the list make up the highest percentage. Look to see what protein sources are listed in the first several ingredients. (Meat by-products are the by-products of US human food consumption, meaning what the public doesn't usually eat, like kidneys, liver, tongue and heart.)

Carbohydrates and Glucose

A carbohydrate is a substance that breaks down into glucose (a basic form of sugar). Simple carbohydrates are made up of sugars while complex carbohydrates are starches, which are long chains of simple sugars. Some people feel that carbohydrates are not needed in the diet of dogs because dogs are carnivores and evolved from the meat-eating wolf. However, while dogs belong to the scientific order *Carnivora* (which includes everything from the mongoose to the grizzly bear and refers mostly to tooth type), they are very much omnivores (eating food of both plant and animal origin). The wolf is actually more cosmopolitan in its eating habits than many people realize, and feral dogs around the world most often live as scavengers at the edges of human settlements, eating what people discard, including many plant-based carbohydrate foods. Some scientists have put forth the theory that the domestication of the dog was primarily the selection for animals that scavenged at the edges of human civilization and eventually lost their fear of humans, which allowed taming and genetic alterations to take place. Certainly for the past 10,000-plus years, dogs have lived alongside people and have primarily eaten what we have eaten. When grains and other plant-based foods made up the bulk of our diets, they made up the bulk of our canine companions' diets as well. (Although perhaps not optimal for either of us if lacking in other nutrients.)

When looked at on a cellular level, cells of the body need glucose to function. This is the primary energy source for most cells; for some cells, like those in the brain, glucose is the only energy source that they can utilize. In other words, cells need to have glucose to function. If the cells don't get the glucose they need from carbohydrates in the diet, they will tear up amino acids and fat for their carbon skeletons and utilize these to make the necessary glucose.

So having some carbohydrates in the diet can be protein-sparing. In an older dog that is already experiencing some degree of muscle wasting, the last thing we want is for the body to be breaking down muscle to provide it with glucose. There is nothing wrong with providing carbohydrate in the diet so long as there is sufficient protein and fat to meet the dog's other needs.

Good Fats/Bad Fats

You have probably heard that there are health concerns for humans regarding the consumption of unsaturated versus saturated fats. You have probably heard these described as good fats (unsaturated fat, or fat that is liquid at room temperature) and bad fats (saturated fat, or fat that is solid at room temperatures). Recent studies have shown that this dichotomy doesn't exist for dogs. There are not bad or good fats for dogs: they can handle saturated and unsaturated fats equally well. Nor is there any reason—expect for calories—for a dog to be on a low-fat diet either. Fat in proper amounts is required in a healthy diet and also gives the food flavor and imparts a sense of fullness. While low fat and low saturated fat are dietary guidelines given to some people, these concepts do not generally apply to dogs. They do have a need for certain essential fatty acids in the diet.

Fat is high in calories, of course, which needs to be considered if your dog is overweight, as many older dogs are. A lower-fat diet usually is lower in calories, so your dog can enjoy the same or even a larger serving for the same or fewer calories. There may be a reduction in satiety (feeling full) with a low-fat diet. However, even if feeding a reduced-fat food, giving fatty treats will hamper weight loss efforts. It is also important to know that a sudden increase in fat consumption (like giving your dog the grease from your leftover turkey) is neither safe nor healthy and can trigger a dangerous disease called pancreatitis, which can make dogs very ill and possibly even cause death.

DIETARY CONSIDERATIONS FOR YOUR AGING DOG

Many factors must be taken into account when determining which diet is right for your eternal puppy, including the special needs of the aging body, specialized medical conditions and food allergies. You may also want to consider whether an unconventional diet is the way you want to go. Because his body is changing as he ages, a dog's nutritional needs change as well. Changes to lean body mass, fat content of the body and decreased intestinal motility all make a difference when it comes to diet choices for your dog.

Change in Lean Body Mass

As dogs age, they tend to lose muscle mass. Geriatric muscle wasting is an age-related change that occurs in every species. Diet, as well as other physiological processes, not all of which are known, has some influence on the muscle-wasting process This muscle-wasting syndrome can be worse if there is insufficient protein in the diet.

Protein is always being turned over and rebuilt. In older dogs, the protein synthesis (rebuilding) becomes less efficient than the protein turnover, so there is a gradual loss of lean body mass.

Studies now suggest that for older dogs to maintain both protein turnover and lean body mass, they need more high-quality protein than young adult dogs do. This is the reverse of what was believed to be true until recently. It used to be believed that older dogs needed reduced protein as a way of sparing the kidneys, which are the organs that clear the waste products of protein metabolism from the body. Recent research, however, has suggested that reduced-protein diets may actually be too low in protein and may contribute to muscle wasting. The optimal protein levels are still controversial topics among nutritionists, but it is wise to avoid reduced-protein diets for your older dog (unless your dog has significant kidney disease and this type of diet is prescribed and monitored by your veterinarian).

Because of the nutritional variation in ingredients, it is better to purchase a feed that actually was tested in animal feeding trials to show that it provides balanced nutrition, not one that was formulated simply to meet a certain standard.

Change in the Body's Fat Content

Along with the reduction in lean body mass (muscle), there is an increased percentage in fat content in the bodies of older dogs. Muscle tissue is more metabolically active (burns more calories), so a reduction in lean tissue results in lower energy needs and thus lower calorie requirements. Several studies have shown that maintenance energy requirements decrease about 20 to 25% in senior versus young adult dogs. However, the need for other nutrients is unchanged, so the nutrient-to-energy ratio needs to change. This is highly individual, though; if your dog is losing too much weight, a calorie-restricted diet would not be appropriate.

Decreased Intestinal Motility

A normal change seen in aging is that there is decreased intestinal motility, decreased absorptive capability and decreased fluid in the intestines, which can make an older dog prone to constipation. In this case, increasing soluble and insoluble fiber can help. However, a high-fiber diet would not be appropriate for a dog that is having trouble maintaining weight, because this type of food is generally low in calories. Many dry foods have a moderate, but not excessive, fiber content.

Specialized Diets for Specialized Medical Conditions

An important element in choosing the optimal diet is the overall health of the dog. If your dog has one of the diseases that is commonly seen in aging dogs, such as heart disease, kidney disease,

A CAUTIONARY WORD ABOUT RAW-FOOD DIETS

Raw-food diets are very controversial. Listen to a proponent and opponent discussing the relative merits and deficits of a raw-food diet, and you'll feel like you've stepped into a political debate. Unfortunately there is not a lot of good research, so the opinions being expressed are just that: opinions. However, there are a few points to consider: while raw-food advocates say that some valuable nutrients are destroyed by cooking, the situation is not black and white, because there are some nutrients that are made more available by cooking the food. If your older dog is having difficulties absorbing nutrients due to age-related changes in intestinal motility and structure, a cooked food might actually make it easier for him to assimilate the nutrients he needs. There also is a safety factor that needs to be considered, and here there is research. Because the food is uncooked, organisms like parasite eggs and bacteria like *E. coli* and *Salmonella* that have not been denatured by the cooking process may be present in raw foods. So there is a potential of transmission of these disease agents. You will need to be scrupulously clean and careful in your food preparation areas and follow safe food handling methods. If there are immune-compromised people in your household, such as the very young, the very old or those with a disease or on medication that modifies the immune system, then feeding a raw-food diet to your dog at this time might not be the best choice. Studies have shown that feeding raw-food diets does increase the likelihood for contamination in the household with bacteria such as *Salmonella* and *E. coli*.

cancer, diabetes, arthritis or cognitive dysfunction, to name a few, then specific dietary intervention may improve the symptoms and could even slow the progression of the disease. In this case, you will need to discuss specific dietary recommendations with your veterinarian.

Food Allergies

Sometimes a dog will develop an allergy to a specific ingredient or set of related ingredients in the food. A food allergy is most commonly noticed as non-seasonal itchy skin or as gastrointestinal signs such as diarrhea or vomiting. Of course, there are many other problems that also produce these symptoms. If you or your veterinarian suspects a food allergy, then you will need to devise and follow a specific elimination feeding plan to determine the specific ingredients to which your dog might be allergic. There is a systematic process used to diagnose food allergies, so ask your veterinarian for assistance in developing a plan. What is generally done is to switch your dog to a diet made up of some less usual food ingredients that the dog is unlikely to have encountered before, and so is less likely to have an allergic reaction to. Once the dog has stabilized on this diet, it is "challenged" by feeding certain specific food ingredients and then observed for a return of allergic signs, indicating a food allergy to that ingredient is likely.

Unconventional Diets

A number of homemade, boutique and "natural" diets are becoming popular for feeding dogs. Of course, food is food and there is nothing sacrosanct about food for dogs made by pet-food companies. Dogs have been domesticated for approximately 10,000 years, and it's been only in fairly recent times that we've had the option of feeding our dogs commercial diets prepared especially for them. Prior to that, they ate more or less what we ate (or in some cases, what we chose not to eat) or what they could hunt for themselves.

The development of prepackaged pet foods is as much about convenience and expense as it is about providing the correct nutrients in the proper proportions. The major pet-food companies have greater resources to do research, manufacturing and distribution. Still it is possible to feed a homemade ration to your dog, made from whole ingredients, that rivals (and may improve upon) anything that the pet-food companies can provide. However, it also is possible to feed an unconventional diet to your dog that has nutritional deficiencies, if you have not done your homework and researched what your dog should be fed.

The important factor is going to be how good is the information about designing a homemade diet or purchasing a product made by a boutique company. Many small companies do not actually have their own processing plants, but subcontract the manufacturing.

TURN THE BAG OVER!

Madison Avenue and marketing specialists know what strings to pull to get people to buy what they need and maybe even what they don't need. When buying dog food, you are presented with a dizzying array of choices in attractive, eye-catching packages—all designed to get you to notice and buy them. But your dog doesn't eat the package (well, some might try, but shouldn't). Your dog eats the food in the package. And the old adage of not judging a book by its cover holds true here. Instead of succumbing to marketing tomfoolery, turn the bag over and look at what actually is in the food. The back of the bag—not the pretty, colorful front—is where you should be looking. Ingredients are listed in descending order according to their percentage in the food, so check the primary ingredients used.

Somewhere buried on the back of the dog-food package will be an AAFCO statement. The Association of American Feed Control Officials is made up of the government feed-control officials from each state, plus representatives from the USFDA and others. The AAFCO established a panel of animal nutrition experts to utilize scientific data and set minimum and maximum nutrient standards for animal foods. The AAFCO profile is currently the standard to which commercial pet foods are held. However, pet-food companies can use several methods to document whether or not their foods provide complete and balanced nutrition. Each pet-food label must make some type of AAFCO statement, unless the food comes from a small local company. Pay careful attention to the wording used in this statement. For example, the AAFCO statement may indicate that the diet is not nutritionally complete or is only for intermittent, temporary or supplemental feeding.

If there is no AAFCO statement on a commercially sold pet food, run, don't walk, to another pet-food choice. The lack of this statement on the label means that the company has done no real testing, or rather, to be perfectly accurate, the testing is being done now on their customers' dogs.

AAFCO STATEMENTS

AAFCO statements can vary according to whether the company calculated the formulation on paper or actually tested it with dogs to ensure that the nutrients in the diet are truly available to the dogs that eat it. The gold-standard AAFCO statement will indicate that feeding-trial testing according to AAFCO procedures was used to substantiate that the pet food contains complete nutrition. However, a diet may be formulated to the AAFCO standards, yet may not have been tested in animal trials. A diet that "looks good on paper" doesn't address the variable bioavailability of nutrients in ingredients—that is, a compound may be shown through chemical analysis to be present, but it may not be in a chemical form that can be absorbed and used by a dog.

A word about feeding trials, because some people find this of concern: dogs are not injured or harmed in these feeding trials— they are fed the foods and then analysis is done to see that the nutrients were actually absorbed and utilized by the dogs. The health of the dogs is closely monitored. The feeding dogs are kept in a research kennel setting, which is a concern to some people. But in reality, if you are feeding a diet that has not been tested in a systematic way in a well-designed feeding trial, then animal experimentation is still occurring, only this time it is with your own dog and without the same safeguards in place.

All commercial pet foods have to state that they meet certain minimum nutritional standards established by the AAFCO. A recipe published online or passed from one person to another does not have to meet nutritional standards. Plus, there could be a lot of variety in the nutrients found in the different ingredients, depending on their sources. There are good recipes and diets out there. In fact, some recipes easily meet or exceed the AAFCO standards. However the onus will be on you to distinguish the good from the substandard. In general, I tend to avoid anything backed by proponents who make extreme or emotional claims about their products or feeding methods.

Utilize the same processes for determining veracity with unconventional diets that you do with any other information regarding the health of your pet. Be optimistic, but also be skeptical. Testimonials and photos give good information but do not constitute scientific evidence. It is hard to visually determine that an animal is not getting the nutrients that he needs in optimum amounts.

If you are feeding an unconventional diet, you may consider having your vet consult with an animal nutritionist to evaluate your dog's diet to make sure that you are hitting all the nutritional bases. Resources include the American College of Veterinary Nutrition (www.acvn.org) and the American Academy of Veterinary Nutrition (www.aavn.org).

CHOOSING A DIET

There are many choices. You can feed a high-quality conventional diet made by a reputable pet-food company that utilizes the highest AAFCO testing standards. You can find a high-quality unconventional diet by doing your research and choosing a good recipe. Some people hedge their bets and feed a good-quality commercial diet supplemented with whole foods like nonstarchy vegetables and lean protein sources. I am reminded that my childhood dog Smokey, who lived to be 17 years old, was fed a good-quality adult dog food supplemented with the leftovers from our dinner table, which, when you look at it, amounted to essentially the same thing as a high-quality scavenger's diet.

The best diet for your dog may depend on whether you are considering changing "from" a diet (because you think the one you are feeding might be inadequate) or changing "to" a diet (because you are looking for something better).

To evaluate an existing diet, ask yourself:

- Does my dog do well on it?
- Does he look healthy?
- Does he eat it well?
- Does he have nice, well-formed stools?
- No (or little) gas?
- Is he maintaining a healthy weight?
- Does it meet my dog's nutritional needs?
- Does it meet my needs in terms of cost and convenience?

If the answer to these questions is yes, then there is likely no reason to change. If you answered no to some or all of the questions, consider your options.

To evaluate a potential new diet, ask yourself:

- Who makes it?
- What is that company's reputation?
- Does the company make good-quality foods?
- Does the company know the nutritional needs of dogs? Conduct research? Have good quality assurance programs?
- Does the food meet my dog's nutritional needs?
- Does it contain ingredients that I want or don't want for my dog?
- Is it affordable and convenient?
- Has the nutritional adequacy of the product been suitably tested (e.g., AAFCO animal feeding trials versus AAFCO profile by analysis)?
- If this is an unconventional diet, who recommends it and what are his/their qualifications?
- Has its nutritional content been evaluated or have you checked with a veterinary nutritionist to determine that it meets minimum nutritional standards?
- Do you have the time and energy to prepare the diet as recommended?

There is no one food that is best for all dogs. There are many, many foods to meet the needs of essentially every dog and every owner. There is no easy equation for putting it all together.

HOMEMADE VERSUS COMMERCIAL DIETS

Answering the question of whether homemade or commercial diets are best to feed your dog is frustrating and confusing because there is little unbiased evidence and a lot of belief, hearsay and emotion. Plus time doesn't stand still and the conclusions we draw today may be changed by the evidence of tomorrow.

There is no doubt that a balanced homemade diet made from fresh wholesome foods is an excellent diet for a dog. There is nothing magical about commercial diets that can't be reproduced or even improved by a conscientious, careful pet owner. Fresh ingredients are nutritionally superior. An additional advantage is that you can, if you so desire, control every step of the process.

However, the benefits depend on two important things: the diet you are feeding needs to be nutritionally balanced for the needs of your dog and the diet you are feeding needs to *stay* nutritionally balanced for the needs of your dog.

What can get people in trouble with homemade diets for their pets is that they don't accurately balance the ration they are mixing for their dog and so feed nutritionally deficient diets (and the consequences of these deficiencies may take some time to appear). Dogs do not have the same nutritional requirements that people do, so just going with what we eat is not okay. Therefore you have to start with a formulation that is balanced for dogs. That requires getting your diet formula from someone who knows what they are doing and is not just giving you their belief or opinion. Remember, a testimonial is not particularly good evidence—scientific testing is a lot better.

The second factor that has gotten people in trouble with homemade diets is called ingredient drift. What generally happens is that people start off full of enthusiasm and follow the plan religiously. But as time goes on, they start doing substitutions or leaving out ingredients. Soon a nutritionally complete diet has drifted into one that is nutritionally deficient.

This is important: the quality of your homemade diet will match the quality of your information and your ability to follow the plan.

If you can avoid these two problems and you are dedicated and willing, then you can feed a homemade diet to your dog that is healthy and beneficial. However, a poorly designed or followed homemade diet can be worse than a low-quality commercial dog food, because commercial foods are required to at least meet certain nutritional minimums.

Some other problems inherent in preparing homemade are the expense, time and the variability in your ability to get quality ingredients.

Commercial pet-food companies, particularly the good ones, have the advantage of having trained nutritionists on staff, testing procedures to ensure that the ration provides the necessary nutrients and inspected facilities. In addition, some companies have specialty diets that are available for animals with specific ailments, and there is good evidence-based research demonstrating that these diets are beneficial. Commercial pet food has the advantages of convenience and low cost.

Here, the quality of the food is dependent on the quality of the pet food company's research, compliance with research findings, testing, manufacture and storage of the product.

The problems inherent in the commercial pet-food industry were painfully demonstrated early in 2007 when a pet-food manufacturing plant received a shipment of a contaminated feed ingredient that could be toxic to pets. Manufacturing of pet food, it turns out, can be very centralized and so the contaminated pet food made with that ingredient then went out to many locations under many different labels. Even pet-food companies that did not subcontract with that particular manufacturing plant found that they had purchased the feed ingredient from the same company and the pet-food recall continued to widen. In a highly centralized food supply system, a problem in one small location can easily have widespread consequences. These problems are not restricted to the pet-food industry but are also inherent in the human food supply as well. The same thing has happened in human foods such as with *E. coli* contamination of ground beef and spinach—a problem at one manufacturing plant had consequences in many distant locations. At the same time that manufacturing is very centralized, the sources of ingredients are very widespread. The contaminated feed ingredient in the 2007 incident came clear from China and there was inadequate oversight by the FDA. So food and food ingredients are traveling far and wide, and that makes quality control a dicey proposition.

WHAT TO CHOOSE?

That depends on you. Currently I am adopting a middle road with my pets. I am feeding a commercial diet made by companies that engage in evidence-based research and do their own manufacturing. But, similar to how I feed the rest of my family, I also supplement with homemade foods that I prepare from food ingredients that I get, whenever possible, from regional or local sources (if I can buy from the farmer who grew the food, even better). I figure that this covers all the bases and I can then supplement with ingredients (like colorful non-starchy vegetables and whole eggs) that provide additional antioxidants and high-quality protein that research is suggesting may be beneficial for dogs.

That is what I am doing today. But tomorrow may bring different evidence and I will need to draw a different conclusion. I'm not suggesting pet owners follow my specific example of what I feed my dogs, but I do invite pet owners to follow the process by which I have made my decisions—look for good research-based evidence and be willing to change your conclusions when new evidence appears.

EAT YOUR VEGETABLES!

When I lived in Japan, I learned a saying from the homemakers I met there: in order to be healthy, you should eat something red, something yellow and something green with every meal. It sounded a lot more profound in Japanese, and I should add that there's no word for the color orange in Japanese, so this color is included with red. Instead of following a complicated diet, with a food pyramid or food groups, carbohydrates and the like, the Japanese just have a lot of variety, balance their diets according to color, and they happen to eat one of the healthiest diets on the planet. In order to get those colors into their diets, they don't incorporate artificial coloring agents; instead they eat fruits and vegetables with every meal. Think of how healthy we'd be if we did the same.

Dogs are omnivores, and, if current theories of domestication are to be believed, it is likely that the domestication of dogs took place because they were camp-followers, eating the discarded food of humans. And prior to the cultivation of cereal grains, a majority of our diet consisted of what could be gained by hunting and gathering: game meat plus a wide variety of native plant foods. And the camp-following dogs likely cleaned up after us.

Fruits and vegetables are rich in vitamins, minerals and, importantly, vitamin-like compounds that have antioxidant capabilities. Now we are discovering that these antioxidants play a role in maintaining health and perhaps even slowing the onset of age-related illnesses.

How Antioxidants Work

In order to produce cellular energy, our bodies utilize oxygen. But during the oxygen-breakdown process, by-products in the form of chemicals called free radicals, or reactive oxygen species, are released. While utilizing oxygen is a very beneficial process, producing excess free radicals is not. There is the analogy of the campfire: in order for a campfire to burn, there must be fuel and oxygen. The campfire produces light and heat but also produces undesirable smoke and soot. Like the smoke, free radicals are highly reactive compounds and can cause a lot of cellular damage in their wake.

With increasing age, there is a cumulative effect from a lifetime of free-radical attacks, which can lead to cellular damage and mutations, the beginnings of cancer, autoimmune disease and degenerative diseases. Many researchers now feel that many age-related chronic diseases are associated with cumulative free radical damage.

Of course, bodies naturally have ways of fighting free-radical damage by producing their own antioxidant chemicals—enzymes that are capable of deactivating the free radicals before they wreak havoc. However, under conditions of stress, the natural antioxidant mechanisms may be overwhelmed and unable to produce adequate amounts. In this case, adding dietary antioxidants can be beneficial in preventing disease.

In addition, once oxidative damage has occurred, cells have numerous mechanisms to repair things like DNA. But with increasing age, these cellular repair mechanisms become less efficient. Since the effects of free-radical damage are cumulative, the effects from previous damages will be accruing as your dog ages, and so providing optimal protection from free radicals becomes more important. However, as your dog ages, his energy demands diminish and his food intake may decrease. In consuming less food, he proportionately will be consuming fewer antioxidants, and this is a time when he needs a higher antioxidant intake.

An increasing number of scientific studies have shown that eating a diet rich in colorful fruits and vegetables may decrease the risk of cancer and other diseases in all species. These foods provide not only a wide range of vitamins and minerals but also a pharmacopoeia of phytochemicals, such as antioxidants.

For example, the carotenoid antioxidants are a group of naturally occurring plant pigments that create the brilliant colors seen in vegetables and flowers. In nature, there are hundreds of carotenoids, but only about a half dozen of them are actively absorbed by people and animals. In addition, antioxidants have been shown to work synergistically: eating several of them together will enhance their protective action more than eating one alone.

Some antioxidants are known to you as familiar vitamins, like vitamins C and E, and are an essential part of a healthy diet. Can other antioxidants from plants have an effect on the health of dogs? Recent experiments are offering tantalizing hints that they may. A recent set of experiments involving the effects of aging on learning in older dogs living in a research laboratory setting has shown that dietary enrichment with several mitochondrial cofactors (substances thought to help the mitochondria burn oxygen more efficiently) plus antioxidants was associated with a reduction of age-related learning changes, and it was seen that the earlier this dietary enrichment was initiated, the greater the effect. Because of the synergistic nature of antioxidants, they were given in both purified form and as specific fruit and vegetable preparations added as a small percentage of the diet.

A separate research study on dogs living in homes suggested that, in a breed of dog that shows a high incidence of a particular form of cancer, consumption of vegetables was correlated with a reduction in the incidence of that type of cancer. The study compared the diets of dogs of this breed that had developed this form of cancer with the diets of control dogs of this breed that had not. The dogs that did not get cancer had been fed, as remembered by their owners, more vegetables, particularly of the green leafy variety. This was a retrospective study, not a prospective experimental study—instead of feeding two different diets and comparing the results, the study asked dog owners to recall and describe their feeding styles in the past. So while the variable of owner recollection is a limiting feature in the validity of these results, the highly significant statistical difference seen made this an intriguing finding.

Dog-food companies have been quick to utilize the discoveries of the research laboratories, resulting in the addition of additional antioxidants into foods formulated for older dogs. (If anything, pet-food companies have been more on the ball in utilizing these research findings than have companies that develop processed food for humans). However, as with supplements, it is difficult to determine how bio-available these antioxidants are once they are combined in the food, processed and stored. They may be more about advertising than effectively boosting your dog's free radical-fighting arsenal.

All of which brings us back to the multi-colored diet of the Japanese. Naturally, feeding a high-quality dog diet is highly recommended. But if you want to get high-quality antioxidants into your dog, you might just consider going to the source. In addition to a good dog food, you can feed nonstarchy vegetables to your dog, especially as a treat or snack. We've already mentioned these as nutritional low-calorie options for treats; they also help increase antioxidant intake. Do not offer grapes, raisins, onions or garlic to your dog; while these foods have antioxidant properties, they can be toxic to dogs.

Caveat: if your dog is undergoing cancer treatment, you may be asked to reduce the amount of antioxidants in your dog's diet. Because some anti-cancer agents damage cancerous cells by utilizing an oxidation process, antioxidants could potentially counteract the effectiveness of these types of anti-cancer therapy. If your dog is undergoing cancer treatment, be sure to mention the diet, including treats, that you are feeding and to follow specific dietary instructions.

Getting Your Dog to Eat His Vegetables.

Face it, some dogs are dietary adventurers—almost up to the point of being in the "dietary pirate" category. They will eat almost anything they can get their paws and mouths on. If you have one of these "garbage gut dogs," it is likely that you have spent the majority of your dog's life trying to keep him from eating weird things. On the other hand, some dogs are as fastidious in their eating habits as Felix from *The Odd Couple*. Here are some strategies for getting a dog to eat vegetables.

Make it fun. If you are asking a dog to eat a new food for the first time, up the ante by giving it as a treat or a reward.

Give it frequently, even if it isn't eaten. Some dogs are neophobic—they don't like new things. As a tactic to get our children to try new foods, we used to put it on their plates and ignore whether or not they ate it. If they made a fuss over "the scary little green cabbage" or "the yukky orange goop," we told them that they didn't have to eat it, but they did have to have it on their plates. Sooner or later, the Brussels sprouts and butternut squash stopped looking strange to them and they tried it, often enjoying the new food once they did. Making a big deal about it only delayed acceptance. Similarly, a neophobic dog can be brought around to trying something new by repeated low-key exposure.

Change the form. You might try offering frozen green beans as a crunchy treat. Or give cooked carrots instead of raw.

Combine it with something the dog likes. I still remember the look on Raven's face the first time I gave him a slice of sweet bell pepper to sniff. If dogs could talk, he was saying, "Are you out of your mind? You call this food?" But adding a bit of canned dog food got him to munch on it. In another example, veggie omelets combine vitamin and antioxidant-rich veggies with eggs, a high-quality protein source.

Share the wealth. Increasing the amount of vegetables in our diet is a healthy habit for us as well as for our dogs. There are hundreds of vegetables on the market now, especially with heirloom crops and organic farming being all the rage. While you are fixing your own inventive, colorful salads and vegetables, give the trimmings to your dog. You might find new tastes that he likes more than you do. Who knew Raven would enjoy baby Brussels sprouts?

16 Weight Loss

Balancing the Equation

Always talk to your veterinarian before you start a weight-loss program for your dog. While the following should be regarded as general information to assist you, only your veterinarian knows your pet's current health status and condition. In some disease conditions it would not be advisable to restrict the dog's food intake or increase his activity. So while these recommendations may be beneficial for many pets, they may not be a good fit for yours. Every dog is a unique individual, so trust your veterinarian to help you design a program that is best for your dog.

While weight loss may be healthy for your pet, losing weight too fast or by consuming the wrong nutrients is not. If the diet is too stringent, your dog may also feel uncomfortable and could show anxiety or aggression. Further, studies have shown that dogs on more restrictive diets rebound the fastest. This is why a well-designed and well-monitored weight-loss plan is needed.

Ask your veterinarian if your dog is at the optimal weight for his health. If not, ask the vet for recommendations on how you can help your pet achieve a healthy weight. Most vets will be delighted to double as a doggie diet coach, and you can go for regular weigh-ins on the accurate scales at the vet's clinic. Moral support is helpful for every dieter, even of the doggie variety. In addition, you can learn to score your dog's body condition; this is a systematic way to determine the fat to lean ratio of your dog by looking at specific sites of typical fat deposition. Once your eye is trained in what to look for, you can also monitor the progress of your dog's diet.

Eternal Puppy

You can also have your dog's diet evaluated by a board-certified veterinary nutritionist or veterinarian with advanced training in nutrition. This may be beyond the scope of a pooch who's only a bit overweight, but for real "pound" puppies, dogs who are in fact obese, assistance from a nutritionist may be a sensible life- and pound-saving choice.

RECOGNIZING EXCESS WEIGHT

Is your dog overweight? Probably the biggest problem to overcome in keeping our dogs at a healthy weight is one of perception. Many people with overweight dogs do not recognize that their dogs are overweight. If your dog has gained weight gradually over the course of a year or more, you might not realize how overweight your dog actually is. And since many dogs are overweight, your pudgy pooch doesn't look any different from many other dogs you meet. Plus, many of us are simply in a state of well-meaning, yet detrimental, denial.

You can change your perception by training your eyes and hands to determine your dog's condition. This is possible by using a body-condition scoring system, which is handy to know and easy to learn. Body condition is a way of characterizing how much fat a dog is carrying. You need to start feeding your dog according to his body condition, not just his weight...or his appetite!

Remember that it is not just a matter of your dog's weight—what is important is how much of that weight is fat tissue. Fat tissue accumulates in specific areas on a dog's body, so learning how to look at and feel those areas is an objective way to find out how much fat your dog has and can help you monitor its loss. The gold standard is the body condition scoring method developed and validated by veterinary nutritionist Dr. Dorothy Laflamme. Dr. Laflamme's method is based on a nine-point scale, though other scoring systems based on three, five and seven points exist as well. If your veterinarian gives your dog a body-condition score, be sure you know which system she is using. For example, a body-condition score of four is above the ideal weight on a five-point scale, yet a good score on a nine-point scale. It can lead to miscommunication if you don't identify the system being used.

Nestlé PURINA
BODY CONDITION SYSTEM

TOO THIN

1 Ribs, lumbar vertebrae, pelvic bones and all bony prominences evident from a distance. No discernible body fat. Obvious loss of muscle mass.

2 Ribs, lumbar vertebrae and pelvic bones easily visible. No palpable fat. Some evidence of other bony prominence. Minimal loss of muscle mass.

3 Ribs easily palpated and may be visible with no palpable fat. Tops of lumbar vertebrae visible. Pelvic bones becoming prominent. Obvious waist and abdominal tuck.

IDEAL

4 Ribs easily palpable, with minimal fat covering. Waist easily noted, viewed from above. Abdominal tuck evident.

5 Ribs palpable without excess fat covering. Waist observed behind ribs when viewed from above. Abdomen tucked up when viewed from side.

TOO HEAVY

6 Ribs palpable with slight excess fat covering. Waist is discernible viewed from above but is not prominent. Abdominal tuck apparent.

7 Ribs palpable with difficulty; heavy fat cover. Noticeable fat deposits over lumbar area and base of tail. Waist absent or barely visible. Abdominal tuck may be present.

8 Ribs not palpable under very heavy fat cover, or palpable only with significant pressure. Heavy fat deposits over lumbar area and base of tail. Waist absent. No abdominal tuck. Obvious abdominal distention may be present.

9 Massive fat deposits over thorax, spine and base of tail. Waist and abdominal tuck absent. Fat deposits on neck and limbs. Obvious abdominal distention.

The **BODY CONDITION SYSTEM** was developed at the Nestlé Purina Pet Care Center and has been validated as documented in the following publications:

Mawby D, Bartges JW, Moyers T, et. al. **Comparison of body fat estimates by dual-energy x-ray absorptiometry and deuterium oxide dilution in client owned dogs.** Compendium 2001; 23 (9A): 70

Laflamme DP. **Development and Validation of a Body Condition Score System for Dogs.** Canine Practice July/August 1997; 22:10-15

Kealy, et. al. **Effects of Diet Restriction on Life Span and Age-Related Changes in Dogs.** JAVMA 2002; 220:1315-1320

Call 1-800-222-VETS (8387), weekdays, 8:00 a.m. to 4:30 p.m. CT

Nestlé PURINA

Chart used with permission from Nestle Purina PetCare, St. Louis, MO.

REGULAR WEIGH-INS

Once you have started on a weight-loss program for your dog, make sure that your veterinarian monitors the progress. Regular weigh-ins can not only help monitor your dog's progress but also can alert you to any problems. Diet plans with regular weigh-ins have a higher chance for success.

ENERGY IN

Obesity (there's that awful word again!) in humans or dogs can be viewed as an imbalance in the energy equation. When energy intake is equal to energy used through metabolism and activity, i.e., when energy in equals energy out, body weight remains stable. When intake exceeds energy usage, this results in weight gain. So, logically, when energy use exceeds intake, weight loss should occur. Unfortunately, it can be difficult to achieve this negative balance, but the tips in this chapter should help.

The easiest way to reverse a problem is to address the areas in which you are the most likely to be contributing to it. Let's say, for instance, that you are feeding the right amount of food but giving too much of a high-calorie pet treat. The easiest thing for you to do is to substitute that treat with something your dog likes but isn't high in calories, like baby carrots or green beans. If, on the other hand, you already feed only limited treats but are using a free-choice feeding system, then replacing free-choice feeding with a feeding schedule in which fixed amounts are given at each meal is the easiest way to start your dietary intervention.

Limit Treats

Do you know how many calories your dog is getting from treats in a day? I would hazard a guess that most people don't. But even a rawhide bone can have as many as 100 calories per inch. The amount of treats a dog gets can also vary from day to day. To get a handle on your dog's treat intake, count the calories and don't give more than 10 percent of his daily recommended calorie allotment in the form of treats. Treats aren't meant to be additional calories, so remember to subtract that amount from what you are giving in the food bowl.

One thing you can try is to have a treat bowl. Measure out how many treats the dog can have in a day and put that amount in the treat bowl. Then, for that day, use only what is in the bowl—no refills until the next day! This will keep the amount of calories consistent, and there will be no confusion about how many treats are being offered by the different members of the family. Condition the family to using the bowl; you may have to keep the treat bags hidden or out of reach to keep anyone from giving extra tidbits. Instead of giving your dog a handful of treats at a time, give only one or two so that his treat ration lasts the entire day. And you can try using nonstarchy vegetables as treats—they are usually fairly low in calories while being high in certain nutrients.

Enlist the Whole Family

It does no good if mom is watching the dog's food intake and making appropriate changes while dad and junior are slipping the dog high-calorie treats when mom is not looking. Everyone has to be on the same page and committed to improving the health of this valuable (happy and pudgy) family member. Sit down and have a family council and have everyone agree on the plan. Remember, too, that your dog will know who has the softest heart in the house, and that is the person who will get the full brunt of his soulful brown eyes and half-starved whimpers. (You may be surprised at how well your dog has you trained!) Give that person moral support to help him not give in to temptation. (My husband has a helpful mantra he uses in these cases. He tells the begging dog, "I have a heart of stone." This, of course, is to bolster his own confidence, as the dog still wags her tail in keen anticipation.) It will help if everyone is prepared with healthy alternatives, like crunchy green beans or baby carrots, instead of those high-calorie treats.

For the truly committed (or very forgetful) owner of an obese brown-eyed beggar, it may be helpful to keep a diary posted on the refrigerator. On this form, record all food given to little Oliver. This includes noting that breakfast has been fed (how much?) and when treats are given. Remember your treat bowl! When the day's allotment of treats is gone, no more until the next day.

Thwarting the Beggar

When you change your feeding pattern, your dog will know. Dogs, however, live in the moment. There is no way for our ravenous Rover to understand that weight loss now may give him more comfort and more time over the years. He will only understand that, right now, he is not getting what he wants. His way to get what he needs and wants from life is to turn to you and ask for it…or steal it (which in canine ethics is not nearly as frowned upon as it is in human circles). He will be puzzled and disconcerted when his efforts don't result in the expected food. His response will be to try harder. A hungry hound is a crafty one!

You have two avenues to try to stop the begging: the first is to ignore it. Be forewarned, though, that when you ignore a behavior that previously has resulted in a (yummy) response, your dog will try hard/harder/hardest to get you to respond. A psychologist would call this phenomenon an extinction burst, referring to the "burst" of effort the dog will use to get the expected response. The extinction burst is a normal behavior in canines and most animals, and the only thing a committed owner can do about it is to be firm, sit on the cookie jar and wait it out until failure to get a reward leads the dog to put forth less effort (aka peace and quiet at the dinner table). Remember, if you opt for this approach, that negative attention is still attention and thus seen by the dog as a reward. Ignoring the begging behavior means to ignore it completely—in addition to not giving him food, do not respond, make eye contact or speak to your dog.

The second way to stop the begging is to distract the dog or teach alternative behaviors. Be creative and individualize your plan based on what your dog likes. If your dog has an absolute favorite toy, kidnap it. The next time your dog begs for food, bring out Mr. Chew-My-Head-Off and toss it to the dog a few times. If your dog relishes playtime, reserve a favorite game for these moments: when he starts begging, call him to another room for a cheerful game of hide and seek. Dogs obviously prefer anything to being ignored, so this alternative always gets the dog's vote. His request (for food) is still being recognized, and while fun isn't as good as food, your dog of course will appreciate your attention. For high-energy dogs, substituting treats with some fun interactive activity is even better than liver and cheese. Your loving relationship with your dog is preserved, and your dog is not thinking about food, is getting a little unplanned activity and is saving 100 unneeded calories. It's all good.

In our culture, sharing food is a way of sharing love. Think of our idyllic Thanksgiving feast as depicted in Norman Rockwell's painting *Freedom from Want*. Food equals love, but it is not a loving action to overfeed your dog. There are other ways to share love with your pet (and two-legged charges) that do not involve calories. You can still share love in fun, healthful ways. The most important way to show love to your dog is by giving him your attention, whether in the form of a game, a long walk, a trip to the dog park or a good old-fashioned belly rub.

Calorie-Saving Tips

Here are some calorie-saving tips to help you and your canine dieter:

Reduce the temptation: If your dog's most common begging times are when you are sitting down for a meal, put him in another room while you eat. It also helps to have your dog out of the room when you are preparing meals.

Feed dogs separately: If you have more than one dog, feed each dog by himself to avoid competitive eating. What may appear at first as simply bad manners actually is ingrained in your dog's instincts. In the wild, a wolf wolfs down his food before any of his pack members can steal it. Domestic dogs have the same instincts, particularly the hounds, who were traditionally housed and fed together. (Dogs are not programmed to share!) So, it helps a dog who needs to lose weight to eat in a separate location so he will not be in a race to eat all of his food more quickly than the other dog...and then try to bump his slower housemate from his victuals. Separate feedings (or really close supervision) are the best way to know that your chubby speed eater isn't starving out his slower (slimmer) dinner companion. It also reduces mealtime stress.

Wet food: If you feed a dry dog food, wetting the food with water will increase the volume of the food, which is a no-calorie way of increasing the sensation of feeling full.

Fiber, please: Pet-food companies have come out with weight-reduction kibble formulas, usually through increased fiber content

THE HAZARDS OF FREE WILL

While writing about obesity and weight loss, I felt weighed down by the evidence because I have fought the tendency to be overweight for most of my adult life. I can certainly commiserate with any dog who is experiencing painful joints, feeling out of breath and unable to do things that used to be fun and rewarding. And, unlike dogs, I have the knowledge that tells me that this is doing me long-term harm beyond what I am currently experiencing. I am staring diabetes, arthritis and increased cancer risk in the face and it is a terrifying view. Now I am working hard to lose extra pounds, a difficult but necessary struggle.

In some ways, I envy the overweight dogs who are put on diets by their responsible and loving owners. How much easier it would be to lose weight if I had someone purchasing, selecting and measuring what I could eat in a day and not giving me access to any other choices. How much more effortless life would be if there weren't fast-food restaurants on every other corner or tempting advertisements on TV during every commercial break. How much lovelier if there weren't tasty snacks in my pantry or if I couldn't open the refrigerator door by myself. How wonderful it would be if someone were to distract me with a fun calorie-free game every time the evening munchies came upon me! Imagine if exercise weren't a burden, but a joyful and rewarding sensory experience with someone I love. Imagine if, when dieting, we didn't feel such a drive to express our free will when making food choices. Being a dog— without free will and with a responsible, caring owner—would make dieting a lot easier.

While I have fought the battle of the bulge for some time, I have not owned an overweight dog until recently. I was astonished when I realized that Rosie had gained ten pounds and was no longer in the "fit" category on the body-condition scoring scale. Entering her mature years, she was slipping into the "obese" category.

Helping Rosie to lose weight was a lot easier than it has been for me. It meant cutting back on the amount of food she was getting, substituting veggies, giving her food puzzles, increasing her exercise and barricading her from the cat food when we were out of the house. And we've seen results! I wish it were that easy for me.

Again, don't let your own need for or frustration with weight loss prevent you from taking steps to help your dog. Our trusting, loving dogs should not be made to carry, and be weighed down by, our emotional baggage about weight.

and a decrease in dietary fat. The fiber, which is essentially indigestible carbohydrate, adds bulk to the diet, causes the dog to feel more satisfied and slows the absorption of nutrients from the digestive tract. Lower fat diets have fewer calories and can be a useful aid for weight loss. Check with your veterinarian before switching to one of these.

It's easy being green: The addition of nonstarchy colorful vegetables to your dog's diet can add beneficial micronutrients like antioxidants, fiber for bulk and interesting flavors and textures. Nonstarchy veggies, like green beans, baby carrots, cauliflower and cherry tomatoes, make great treats. Any of those also make terrific frozen treats. Or you might try cooked broccoli, Brussels sprouts, carrots or squash. Experiment to see what your dog likes. Some dogs love crunchy raw veggies, and others prefer soft cooked ones. As with feeding treats, don't let veggies make up more than 10 percent of your dog's total calorie intake for the day.

No free-choice feeding: The common practice of free-choice feeding is totally wrong for an overweight dog, especially one who lives in a multi-canine household (remember the role competition plays). Owners may be tempted to fill a large bowl or container of kibble and just leave it out all day for their dog(s) to consume at will, with the owner just refilling to the top when they see it is empty. This is not a good idea for animals who have limited self-control about food consumption and will lead to eating more than they should. Owners will need to switch their feeding schedule to a twice-daily routine with specific amounts given (in separate bowls for each dog, if there is more than one in the household). Further, if you have multiple dogs who are competitive eaters, you will want to feed them in different locations or at least with some distance between them to avoid their turning eating into a race. Even if you are feeding a lower-calorie food, free-choice feeding generally is not going to work if you want your dog to lose weight. A dog who finishes his food ration by early or midday will constantly remind his owners that his bowl is empty, and it's easy for owners to give in and fill it up again. On the other hand, with a feeding schedule, a dog who finishes his morning meal will still have his evening meal to satisfy him later in the day.

ENERGY OUT

Reducing calories is only half the battle! The other half—the one that burns calories—is exercise. Even today this comes as a surprise to lots of dog owners (and lots of other weight watchers, too). And owners of older dogs must come to realize that they have to take an active role in keeping their dog active. It's ironic that owners love to play with bouncy puppies, who themselves are self-exercising. As those boisterous puppies grow into young dogs, they usually stay self-exercising, tearing around our houses and yards, sometimes with more exuberance than we'd prefer. When our adult dogs finally settle down, we breathe a sigh of relief, knowing that Aunt Joan and the Tiffany lamp are safe from the dogs' high-speed romps. What we often don't recognize is that our adult dogs are no longer getting the exercise they need. We're all too happy to let the dogs become lawn ornaments and couch potatoes. Instead, we need to encourage our older guys and gals to get up and move.

As with weight gain in our dogs, their inadequate exercise is often a result of human factors: our busy lives and sedentary lifestyles have made us less and less active (also to our detriment), and our inactivity can limit access to physical activity opportunities for our dogs. Studies have shown that inactive owners are more likely to have overweight and inactive dogs. Even those pet owners who are themselves interested in physical activities may not be doing activities that are conducive to sharing with their dogs. For example, dogs aren't welcome in gyms and health spas, and they don't do well at rock climbing or kayaking. In addition, some studies have suggested that we may be likely to overestimate how much exercise our dogs get. Our intentions are good: if asked, owners will readily tell how often they walk their dogs. However, if you ask the same owners how often they have walked their dogs this week, you may find that the good intentions often don't translate into actual time spent giving their dogs exercise.

There is an inverse relationship between obesity and activity levels: in a study that used pedometers to measure the activity rates of dogs, it was found that dogs with the highest body-condition scores (indicating more fat) had the lowest activity scores. However, the picture is not clear about the cause and effect of the relationship, as obesity creates a vicious circle with regard to activity: reduced activity contributes to obesity while obesity makes it hard to be active.

If you are going to be helping your dog to maintain a healthy body condition, regular exercise is essential. In fact, if both you and your dog need to lose weight, consider doing it together. When Dr. Robert Kushner, who is a weight-loss expert at the Mayo Clinic, and some veterinarians at Hills Pet Nutrition teamed up for a study, they found that dogs could be beneficial exercise partners for people who need to lose weight. By making dog-walking a routine, you gain an instant exercise buddy who will joyfully remind you and encourage you to stick to your appointed exercise schedule. This is another way that dogs and people can help each other.

It's important to remember to not overdo it with an older dog's exercise and to not introduce an increased amount of activity all at once. Consult with your veterinarian to devise an exercise program that's suitable for your older chubby pal. If needed, get a referral to a veterinary rehabilitation specialist, who can help devise an exercise plan appropriate for a dog with significant movement issues.

JOIN THE SLOW-FOOD MOVEMENT

Food puzzles slow the speed of food consumption and give your dog something to do. How long does it take your dog to empty his food bowl? Thirty seconds? Two minutes? Unless he is one of the rare nibblers out there, your dog now has 23 hours and 58 minutes stretching out for the rest of the day when he doesn't have food to eat. How satisfying is that? Dogs evolved as scavengers and are designed to expend mental and physical energy in finding and consuming food. Fast food leads to frustration, boredom and even a dog who feels hungry when he has had enough to eat.

POISON ALERT

Remember that according to the ASPCA Animal Poison Control Center, food and beverages that dogs should never consume include: alcoholic beverages, chocolate, coffee, fatty foods, macadamia nuts, moldy foods, raisins/grapes, onions, garlic, yeast dough and anything containing the sugar substitute xylitol.

When food is consumed, both nerves and endocrine signals are sent from the digestive tract to the brain to tell the brain to turn off the feeling of hunger. Some of these satiety signals are immediate, like the stretching of the stomach, but others take a while to complete the feedback loop. If the speed of consumption is slowed down, then the sensation of feeling full and satisfied has a chance to develop before over-consumption occurs. (Perhaps this is also one of the reasons why the French can eat Brie and cream sauces and yet are not as overweight as those of us here in this fast-food nation.)

There are numerous toys available now that allow you to put food inside them and the dog can then lick, chew, nudge and paw to get the food out. This slows the speed of consumption and also gives the dog physical activity and rewarding mental stimulation. Some examples of food-puzzle toys are the Kong, Canine Genius and the Buster Cube. Contrary to what your mother told you as a child, for a dog, playing with your food is a good thing.

FOR THE LOVE OF OUR DOGS

Weight loss is not easy, not for us or our dogs. Thousands of years of evolution have given us both the drive to gain more weight than is healthy. But our knowledge can replace that drive and our love for our dogs can give us the strength of will to make the changes necessary to give our dogs healthier, happier lives. If you need motivation to help you make these changes for your dog and stick with them, just remember that you are doing this for love.

THE REVERSE PROBLEM: THE UNDERWEIGHT DOG

While obesity can be a problem for the middle-aged dog, the geriatric dog often has the reverse problem and may start losing weight.

Studies have reported that the average weight in dogs peaks in the middle years, while in dogs 12 years and older, 10 percent in one study and 15 percent in another were categorized as underweight. The weight loss is not proportional, and many will experience a disproportionate loss of muscle mass.

There are many causes of this weight loss, and in some cases a dog owner can have a positive influence. Some causes are consequences of the normal aging process but are nonetheless amenable to quality-of-life adjustments.

One cause of weight loss could be a resultant loss of appetite due to normal age-related loss of taste buds and sense of smell. The geriatric dog has fewer taste buds than he did at one year of age. Because of this, the palatability of his food will be reduced and so he may eat less.

Pain may be a major cause of a dog's not eating enough to maintain a healthy weight. Chronic pain can reduce appetite through neurological pathways, i.e., when in pain, the dog has less desire to eat. In addition, in a dog with painful arthritis or a neck problem, the placement of the food bowl may put the dog into a painful position when he tries to eat. A dog will not eat as much if his teeth hurt and it is painful for him to chew. Osteoarthritis of the jaw can also make chewing painful. The dog in pain may eat only as much as needed to quell the strong pangs of hunger but not enough to maintain weight.

A normal aging change is the reduction of saliva production. Inadequate saliva can make it pretty tough for a dog to eat dry kibble— it would be like trying to swallow a mouthful of bone-dry cookie crumbs.

Dogs also undergo a loss of muscle mass as they age; the muscles affected include the masseter muscles, the powerful muscles that move the jaw. If these muscles are weakened, a dog may grow tired of chewing his food before he has consumed enough to maintain his body mass. This is particularly true of those dogs who like to chew up every morsel, versus the "wolfers" who tend to inhale their food.

Lack of adequate exercise can be a cause of weight loss in older dogs in two ways. The muscle loss seen in older animals has more than one cause; however, muscle is very much a "use it or lose it" tissue. There can be some loss of muscle mass simply from a reduction in exercise and activity. Secondly, a dog who isn't exercised may be mentally "falling asleep at the wheel" with a brain that is shut down from lack of mental stimulation and low-level oxygen deprivation. Exercise releases beta endorphins, oxygenates the body and brain, brings the dog to a more alert state and sharpens the appetite. A ten-minute walk before feeding time may do wonders to improve your old pal's appetite and may even help him maintain a more normal sleep-wake cycle.

There also are nutritional factors to consider. Along with the decrease in saliva production, the nutrient-absorption surfaces of the intestines are reduced in size with increased age, so the dog's gastrointestinal tract may be less efficient at absorbing nutrients. In other words, the need for the nutrient may increase at the same time that the ability to absorb it from the intestines is decreased, so he now might not be getting enough of the needed nutrient in his food. The proper levels of protein in the diets of geriatric animals is a controversial subject among nutritionists; however, there have been reported cases of dogs' losing muscle mass from being on protein-limiting diets. Your veterinarian may suggest a change in diet to one that is more easily digested and assimilated, with a higher quality protein source. Some protein sources are better absorbed by different individuals than others. Again, there is no one diet that is perfect for every geriatric dog.

There are cognitive changes that may affect a dog's ability to eat. One age-related cognitive change is an alteration in sleep-wake cycles. Since eating is associated with these cycles, the dog's body rhythms may be off and not sending the signals to eat during the appropriate times. Knowing that you are hungry and need to seek food is a cognitive process requiring the coordination of a number of different parts of the brain. A dog suffering from age-induced cognitive dysfunction may not be getting the "you need to eat" signals as strongly as he did in his youth. With advanced cognitive decline, a dog may forget where his food bowl is or become distracted in the middle of a meal and forget to finish it.

A behavior concern sometimes seen with increasing age and with cognitive dysfunction in older dogs is an increase in anxiety. The dog could feel insecure about eating in his owner's absence. And a younger dog may be subtly threatening the older dog and preventing him from eating all he needs. Older dogs are less able to tolerate disruption in their environments, and a chaotic eating environment or annoyances may cause the dog to not eat what he should.

Rapid weight loss and changes in body proportions can be early signs of cancer, endocrine disturbances, heart problems and neurological problems, thus rapid weight loss in and of itself should be considered a primary issue of concern, warranting a trip to the veterinarian's office. Realize also that these issues are not mutually exclusive. There could be more than one problem occurring at the same time.

Some things you can do to help your geriatric dog maintain his weight:
- Have your dog seen by a veterinarian to evaluate medical causes of weight loss.
- Switch to canned food, which may be more palatable, more aromatic and easier to swallow.
- Slightly warm your dog's food to increase aroma and palatability.
- Moisten the kibble with warm water or low-sodium chicken, turkey or beef broth.
- With your veterinarian's permission, switch to a more palatable, energy-dense food.
- Give ten minutes of exercise before feeding.
- Stay with your dog while he eats.
- Prevent other dogs (as well as children, cats and other pets) from interfering with your dog during mealtime.
- Make feeding time more comfortable—raise your dog's food bowl if needed, provide a soft cushion for him to stand or lie on, keep his water close by.

Monitor your dog's weight with regular weigh-ins at your veterinary office. If there is a precipitous drop in weight, this is an indication that the presence of some other disease process needs to be investigated.

17 Drugs

Increasing Effectiveness and Safety

Although chewable aspirin is no longer given to young children, I clearly remember the flavor from my childhood. And I have never lived in a house that did not have a bottle of aspirin sitting on a shelf in the medicine cabinet. Low levels of aspirin are recommended for millions of people with high risk for heart attack, and taking an aspirin during a heart attack can improve a person's chance of survival. Yet the same ubiquitous, helpful and seemingly innocuous drug nearly killed my father-in-law, sending him to the emergency room followed by several days in intensive care.

Aspirin—the oldest nonsteroidal anti-inflammatory drug (NSAID) on the market—clearly demonstrates the dichotomy of issues regarding drug therapy: no matter how beneficial a drug can be, there is always risk involved. When administering drugs to our pets, there's the additional matter of their not being able to verbalize how they're feeling. Dogs can't tell their owners if a certain medication makes them feel sick or just "off," so the responsibility falls on pet owners to be aware of potential risks and to be alert to changes in their pets.

Yet conditions such as pain are destructive and debilitating. Inflammation, which can also be moderated by drugs, can cause chronic and irreversible damage. Many diseases, such as hypothyroidism and epilepsy, can be effectively controlled with the appropriate use of drugs. We would not be responsible or humane if we did not treat these conditions with the best means available to pet owners.

So it is a matter of balancing benefit and risk—the fire in your woodstove that keeps your house warm can also burn it down.

SIGNS OF THE SIDE EFFECTS OF NSAIDS

Call your veterinarian immediately if you see any of the following signs:

- Change in behavior, such as lethargy or restlessness
- Hives, facial swelling, red or itchy skin (allergic reaction)
- Decreased appetite
- Seizures
- Vomiting
- Diarrhea or change in stool (if bleeding is in the intestines, you will see bright red blood in the stool; if bleeding is in the stomach, the blood is subjected to the stomach acids and you will see black-colored stool)
- Change in drinking or urination

The challenge is to use these drugs safely. There is no such thing as an effective drug that is also 100 percent safe, although with some drugs there is a rather wide margin of safety. A drug is useful to us because it is a compound that in very small amounts affects the physiology of a living being. It is that ability to affect physiology that is desirable. Given at the right time and in the right amount, a particular drug could be the difference between life and death. But the same powerful effects can also cause harm.

CONCERNS ABOUT NATURAL ALTERNATIVES

The use of medicinal compounds (either from plants or the purified manufactured forms) have been a valuable part of medicine since the prehistoric days, when herbalists scoured the hills for natural ingredients that could be used to help them treat illness. (The "Iceman," discovered in the Alps in 1991 and dating back 5,300 years, carried medicinal plants with him.) Used with respect and knowledge, these natural alternatives can help us still.

However, the risk of unintended harm may be increased with the unmonitored use of nutritional supplements or herbal or "natural" medicinal preparations. These preparations also contain compounds that in small amounts do what conventional drugs do: they affect the physiology of a living being. What increases their risk is that they have not gone through the FDA approval process, and the levels of active compounds can vary according to the quality with which they are manufactured. In addition, these compounds can interact with each other or with other drugs that your dog is being given in unforeseen ways, either rendering the needed drug ineffective or, conversely, increasing the levels of the needed drug in your dog's body, leading to the possibility of overdose. This is not to say that these preparations do not have considerable potential for treatment of medical conditions, and some veterinarians with additional training in alternative medicine are very skilled in their use. However, the lack of oversight, testing and regulation and their easy availability makes their use more challenging.

Whether from a bottle or the leaf of a plant, a drug is a drug and needs to be treated with respect. If you prefer to use these alternative medications, be sure that you are consulting with a veterinarian who has training in the physiological effects of the natural medicinal compounds.

USING OVER-THE-COUNTER DRUGS

Over-the-counter drugs for humans are just that—drugs formulated for use in humans. Humans have a different physiology and metabolize drugs differently than dogs do. Some of these drugs are dangerous to pets at any dosage. Some may be given to dogs but at a vastly different dosage level and frequency than that used by people. Others may be given safely at appropriate doses to dogs but could interact dangerously with a veterinary drug that your dog is receiving at the same time. Younger dogs may be fine with an appropriate dosage of some over-the-counter drugs, though the same drugs would be unsafe for senior dogs because of their reduced kidney and liver function. Don't guess or experiment with your dog's life. Only use over-the-counter drugs if directed by a veterinarian who knows your dog's complete history.

TIPS FOR MEDICINE SAFETY

Our dogs can't use words to report to us how a medication makes them feel, so it is up to us to pay keen attention to our dogs to improve our ability to use these beneficial medicinal compounds safely and effectively. Here are some guidelines for using veterinary drugs as safely as possible:

Maintain good communication with your veterinarian.
Ask questions. Write down the answers. Before you give any drug to
your dog, be sure that you understand what potential side effects may
look like, what to do if you see those side effects and how to seek veterinary advice after hours. Some side effects can be serious and require
immediate attention. Don't adopt a wait-and-see attitude. Ask your
veterinarian also what to do if you accidentally miss a dose. If not
provided, ask your veterinarian for the drug information sheets supplied
by the manufacturer.

Give the drug as instructed. As an example, when the drug
company Novartis did a study on the circumstances surrounding
adverse events involving the NSAID Deramaxx, they found that in 59
percent of the cases involving dogs being treated for osteoarthritis, the
dogs had received doses in excess of the approved dose. (When my
father-in-law suffered his nearly fatal aspirin toxicity, he had also been
taking more than the recommended dosage.)

In our busy household, it is hard sometimes to remember whether
we gave our dog a drug or not, particularly if more than one person has
been giving it. Our solution is to have a calendar with check boxes to
indicate the frequency at which the drug should be given. For example,
if the drug is given twice a day, we will put two little boxes on every day
on the calendar for which the drug should be given. When a person
gives the medicine to the dog, he checks off the appropriate box. This is
a great reminder system as well as useful for reducing confusion.

Stick to the program. Do not give other drugs or supplements unless you have discussed them with your veterinarian. Other
drugs and herbal medications can interact with prescribed drugs,
increasing the potential of adverse reactions. One documented problem
involves pet owners who give an over-the-counter NSAID, such as
aspirin, at the same time as a prescription NSAID, thus magnifying the
effects and possibly causing problems. Further, any herbal remedy
containing willow bark (an NSAID of plant origin) has the potential of
causing an overdose situation if your dog has already been prescribed a
veterinary NSAID.

Visit your veterinarian twice a year. Semi-annual health-
maintenance exams will allow your veterinarian to check for changes in
your dog's condition and how your dog is currently responding to his

ADVERSE EVENT REPORTING

If your dog has an adverse event (side effect) from a medication, you can report it directly to the FDA Center for Veterinary Medicine if your veterinarian does not do so. According to the FDA: "Pre-testing by the manufacturer and review of the data by the government does not guarantee absolute safety and effectiveness of approved veterinary drugs due to the inherent limitations imposed by testing the product on a limited population of animals. Anyone with information to report is also encouraged to contact the manufacturer of the suspect product." In other words, even extensive testing of a drug may not catch something that could be a problem in certain individuals. By making the effort to report any adverse event, should you be so unlucky to have one occur in your pet, you can help protect other pets by sharing the information. To learn more, visit www.fda.gov/cvm/adetoc.htm.

be safe for a six-year-old dog may be unsafe when that dog is nine years old. A dog who develops some other changes due to aging, such as reduced kidney or liver function, may no longer be able to handle the same dosages he could when these organs were functioning optimally. Routine health-maintenance exams, preferably semi-annual exams, will allow the veterinarian to fine-tune the dosages as your dog's condition changes. Laboratory testing can improve the ability of the veterinarian to monitor major body systems that are affected by medications.

Post emergency numbers near your telephones. When I was a new parent, I had emergency numbers posted by every phone: my pediatrician, the local hospital and a nurse hotline. And I remember several times needing to use those numbers in the wee hours of the morning when I was too worried about my sick child to think clearly. In the same way, if there is an emergency with your dog, you can save valuable time by obtaining these numbers before there is an emergency. If your veterinary office is not open for after-hours emergencies, then post the phone number (and address) of the emergency hospital to which your office refers their clients. You could also include the number of the ASPCA Animal Poison Control Hotline: (888) 426-4435. (There may be

WHO SAID NSAIDs?

NSAIDs—that's nonsteroidal anti-inflammatory drugs—are frequently used and very useful drugs. They are often the first line of defense against a number of painful conditions. You probably have more than one type in your medicine cabinet formulated for human use, and there are a number formulated specifically for dogs as well. They work well at relieving pain, often for the older dog who's just started slowing down. Owners are elated when an NSAID can turn back the clock on an older dog, whose newfound pain relief makes the old guy seem nearly puppylike.

NSAIDs function by blocking the conversion of arachodonic acid (an essential fatty acid and constituent of cell membranes) into substances called prostaglandins. There are many kinds of prostaglandins, and they have a wide variety of physiological effects throughout the body. Prostaglandins are involved in pain and inflammation, maintain the protective mucosal lining of the stomach, have an influence on platelet aggregation (the cells that help stop bleeding), affect blood flow to the kidney tubules and regulate bone metabolism, to name just a few functions. When an injury to cells occurs, arachodonic acid is released and a cascade of inflammatory events follows. Because of the potent effects of some prostaglandins on inflammation and pain, NSAIDs, which block their formation, can be effective in managing disease conditions that result in pain and inflammation. But because other forms of prostaglandins are also involved in many maintenance functions in the body, blocking their production can result in some undesirable effects, too, such as stomach ulcers that can cause serious bleeding (from blocking the production of the protective mucosal layer), damage to the kidneys and increased bleeding time.

It was recently discovered that one enzyme system (COX-1) mediated the formation of the mostly beneficial prostaglandins, while another enzyme system (COX-2) mediated the formation of the prostaglandins primarily involved in pain and inflammation. It was then reasoned that if one enzyme system could be influenced over the other, this could be safer because it would be blocking the prostaglandins that cause pain and inflammation while allowing the formation of the prostaglandins with beneficial functions, such as protecting the kidneys and stomach lining. The results have been mixed: the newer formulation is less likely to have side effects, but the risk is not eliminated. And, because the newer NSAIDs were thought to be much safer, perhaps people have let down their guard a bit, being less cautious in admininstering these drugs and looking out for the signs of adverse reactions. Side effects have occurred, even fatal ones, with these as well. There is, after all, no drug that is completely safe.

There are a number of similar NSAID drugs made by competing drug companies, and studies show that not all dogs respond in the same way to each of these drugs. The response is highly individual. So if pain relief is not adequate with one of these drugs, it is sensible to try a similar related one, as your dog might respond better. Realize, too, that NSAIDs are only our first line of defense: there are other drug types that can be used as well, sometimes in combination with NSAIDs.

Giving your dog relief from pain is a very important part of care. Pain is debilitating and destructive. You can reduce the need for and required dosages of these drugs by incorporating other methods of pain management as well: appropriate exercise, maintaining your dog's proper weight, providing a more comfortable home environment (better pillows!) and various forms of physiotherapy. You need to work together with your vet and with your dog to devise the best pain-management scheme possible.

a consultation fee for using this valuable service). Let's hope you will never need to call these numbers, but it is better to have them posted and never need them than to need them and have to frantically find them. In addition, have handy a list of all medications that your dog is being given. This can help the emergency veterinarian quickly determine whether the conditions seen may be due to an adverse event relating to a specific drug your dog may be receiving.

18 Supplements

The Promise and the Problems

Dietary supplements these days have become very popular, many flaunting some very tantalizing claims of health benefits. Now available to consumers, these products are being marketed as dietary supplements for people and for pets. Research shows that in the best cases some of these compounds are showing real promise to improve specific medical problems. As we further our knowledge about their possible benefits, complications and limitations, we are hopeful that these dietary supplements will significantly add to our arsenal of interventions to fight disease and improve health.

Yet, before we embrace these compounds or the industry that markets them, we have to be very conscious of the problems inherent in them as well. The problem with supplements can be twofold: when they don't work and when they do work.

WHEN THEY DON'T WORK

If you bought a car that was supposed to have a 300-horsepower motor in it, and brought it home to find out that it had only a 150-horsepower engine, you would be, shall we say, annoyed? If you didn't know that you had only half the horsepower you had paid for and were counting on the full amount to do a job, such as passing another car, you could be putting yourself in a dangerous position, thinking you were covered when you weren't. Or what if you buy a car that claims to get 50 miles to the gallon, and you find that it doesn't even get 20 miles to the gallon?

Eternal Puppy

No Standards

Because there is no FDA supervision of the supplements industry (a billion-dollar industry, may I add?), this is a situation that can inherently create problems. There is no premarket review for safety, efficacy or quality control for something sold as a supplement. When a prescription drug gets FDA approval, the company marketing it needs to demonstrate that the drug is safe and effective. But if the compound is marked as a nutritional supplement (even if it contains compounds with powerful effects on physiology), the FDA must prove that it is unsafe in order to prevent it from being sold to consumers. Even the claims of safety or "guaranteed analysis" you might read on supplement labels are suspect. Here are some of the problems that have occurred.

There is no standard to determine whether the materials used to produce a dietary supplement were of the best quality or even if the product contains the active compounds that it is supposed to contain. This is a bigger problem than many people suspect. In addition, many compounds are not produced by the company that is selling them—a company just buys the already produced compounds from another company and then places its own label on the bottle and uses its own distribution network.

Various studies indicate how this can be a problem. In one example, the organization called Consumer Labs, which independently tests supplement products, tested a number of supplements purported to contain the joint supplement chondroitin. A number of the compounds that they tested did not contain the amount of chondroitin the label indicated, even though the bottles said guaranteed analysis on their labels. In this particular study, some of the supplements contained as little as 20 percent of what was supposed to be there. Worse yet, they tested two products marketed for pets and found no measurable chondroitin whatsoever. Since that time, Consumer Labs has added testing of pet products to their services (and some products are showing good results when tested). Studies of other substances have found similar results: either the marketed compound did not contain any or a reduced amount of the reported active ingredient or contained other materials that could be harmful. (Fish oils, for instance, have been found to contain unacceptable levels of mercury.)

WHAT IS "NATURAL"?

Many substances are marketed as "natural," a word that is used to imply that they are somehow safer or more beneficial than other products. That something is "natural" in no way guarantees its safety or efficacy. Just think about it: lightning is natural; rattlesnakes are natural; hemlock is natural. And they all can kill you deader than a doornail. The natural world is no Garden of Eden. Nature is neither good nor bad, neither kind nor evil. Nature just is. Some things in nature can help you, and some can hurt you. Even if nature were inherently beneficial, the term "natural" has been so overused in marketing as to render it meaningless.

I have tremendous respect and reverence for nature. I have been awed by its power and magic. But I have seen enough of its facets to know that something that is natural in no way guarantees that it is innocuous. I have too much respect for nature to be fooled by that.

Until the regulation of these products develops, you will need to do your homework and research your selected brand. Only consider those products that have been demonstrated by independent testing to contain active compounds at the levels stated on the products' labels. Another plan is to follow the advice given by the Arthritis Foundation's Guide to Alternative Therapies: "When a supplement has been studied with good results, find out which brand was used in the study and buy that brand."

Lack of Dosing Information and Safety

Another issue of concern is dosing information and safety. If the product has not been studied in dogs, you really don't know the correct dosing amount and frequency interval for optimal results in dogs. Just basing the dosing amount and interval on human metabolism and physiology is sometimes our best guess but is not always appropriate because, while we are very similar, humans are not the same physiologically as dogs. Consider that most people can eat chocolate-covered raisins and macadamia nuts with relatively little

WHO'DA THUNK IT?

I was looking at the label of my recent cholesterol-reducing prescription when I noticed something unusual: "Do not eat grapefruit or drink grapefruit juice while taking this drug." "OK," I thought, "that is odd." We are all familiar with drugs that we shouldn't take on an empty stomach or a full stomach or before driving a car or operating machinery or if we consume alcoholic beverages. But grapefruit? I haven't seen any killer grapefruit lately.

So I called my pharmacist. What I found was that there was a potentially dangerous interaction between this drug and grapefruit due to a chemical in grapefruit that alters the actions of some enzymes in the liver. Those same enzymes metabolize the drug, so if you consume the two together, you could get a dangerous overdose.

"Who'da' thunk it?" as my mother used to say. Most of us never would have guessed that eating something that is healthy while taking a drug that is good for your health could result in a dangerous situation. It defies common sense. But it is no joke.

Many drugs, supplements and even foods can have interactions that we may not anticipate and that defy common sense. One healthy substance plus another healthy substance does not necessarily equal a healthy situation.

Over-the-counter supplements, "natural" compounds, herbal drugs and other medications all have the potential, even if safe by themselves, to interact with each other or with prescription medications that your dog needs to stay healthy. The solution?

Don't assume. Don't give any supplements, especially a smorgasbord of supplements, without first consulting your veterinarian. Further, when your vet asks about any medication your dog is being given, make sure that you include all over-the-counter supplements, natural compounds, herbals or other medicines you are using. Failure to communicate can lead to tragic consequences. You might even want to assume that your veterinarian is not familiar with all over-the-counter products that are being marketed (no one can keep up with everything that is coming down the pike) and take him some literature about the compounds. If your veterinarian does not have training in alternative medicine, it is a good idea for him to contact some resources in alternative veterinary medicine.

Do your homework. Read about the compounds and research them through sources other than the companies who sell them. Go to trusted websites. Talk to your pharmacist.

Our dogs can't choose what they would like to try or tell us that something is making them feel bad. It is up to us to use the brains we were given and do our best to get it right.

indigestion or other problems, while these same foods contain compounds that can be harmful, even toxic, to dogs. Extrapolating a dosage for a dog from the recommended human dosage may not result in therapeutic levels in a dog; conversely, it could be too much for a dog. Although dangerous medical complications in people have occurred with some supplements (Ephedra being the most well known), there is an additional margin of safety with people because we have a greater likelihood of recognizing that something is wrong with us and seeking medical assistance on our own. A dog does not have the same ability to communicate or seek help. A veterinarian trained in alternative medicine techniques would be a good resource for getting advice about appropriate dosages for our dog.

So if we are counting on a compound in a supplement to help our dogs, even one that has shown considerable promise experimentally, we must realize the problems that can occur: the supplement may not contain the compound it is supposed to contain or it may not reach therapeutic blood levels in your dog when administered. In these cases, you are counting on something to help that may not be helping at all. Your dog will not be getting the promising benefits he could be getting.

WHEN THEY DO WORK

The other side of the coin is when supplements do work but produce consequences that are unintended or deleterious. Even though many over-the-counter products will claim to be safe and natural, if they are powerful enough to have a beneficial effect, they are influencing your dog's physiology. Anything powerful enough to alter a being's physiology enough to produce benefits in the right circumstances can also cause harm in the wrong circumstances. Many of the drugs that we now use were first discovered as highly powerful plant compounds capable of affecting physiology. An issue of considerable concern is when an over-the-counter compound interacts with a medication that your dog has been prescribed, causing an overdose, a drug interference or a dangerous side effect.

For example, the supplement white willow bark contains the medicinal chemical compound that we know as the active compound in aspirin. Aspirin, whether it comes from a bottle or bark, is a non-steroidal anti-inflammatory drug (NSAID) that has numerous effects in the body, including reducing inflammation and pain. But too much NSAID can cause dangerous, even fatal, side effects. If your veterinarian has already prescribed an NSAID drug to your dog, he will have based the dosage on your dog's weight and condition. If you give white willow bark on top of that, your dog will be getting too much NSAID in his system and is at higher risk for complications.

Or the reverse can happen: the supplement may render some other prescribed medication ineffective. If your dog needs a medication to stay healthy and the compound interferes with it, your dog is not getting the prescribed medication at the dosage he needs.

Drug interactions are a potential danger, and your veterinarian cannot prevent this danger from occurring if you are giving your dog over-the-counter medications in addition to the prescribed ones without the vet's knowledge. Many dog owners mistakenly think that because something is sold over the counter, it must be innocuous—and that just isn't true. It is the very power of these compounds that makes them of potential benefit. That same power, however, also makes them capable of causing harm if used incorrectly.

CONCLUSION

It is very sad, in fact, that promising supplements, which might prove beneficial in fighting disease, are so poorly regulated that their quality is variable and their benefits are suspect. The lack of reliability compromises safety and also slows the identification and verification of beneficial compounds. This is good for commerce, perhaps in the short term, but ultimately slows scientific progress by making it difficult to determine which compounds most benefit health and under what conditions. Until all supplements are subjected to appropriate testing and oversight, always do your homework when using supplements. Research the supplement, its expected effects and its possible problems, and only buy brands that have been tested independently and shown to contain the ingredients that they claim to contain. Stick with reputable companies, and always keep your veterinarian apprised of what supplements and dosages you are using.

19 Hands-on Therapy

Ancient Wisdom, Modern Medicine

You have to wonder sometimes what it was that dogs, early in the process of domestication, saw in humans. Sure, we had fire and weapons, but wolves had warm fur coats, could run faster than we could and could outhunt us. They certainly didn't need us. Yet something about humans was so attractive that the early dogs decided to eschew their wildness and cast their fate in with our lot. The romantic in me thinks it was the human hand that eventually won dogs over to be our companions. Not only can our human hands make clever devices, but they also can stroke, scratch, rub and massage our dogs in ways that dogs have no ability to do, but have a great desire to receive. My theory is that it was eating the leftovers of our hunt and foraging that attracted early dogs to us, and it was the gift of our sensitive hands that kept them with us.

Medicine is, in a large part, a matter of good observation and having finely tuned hands: hands that can feel inflammation, bones out of place or thorns in the pad of the lion's foot (as in the old Aesop's fable). Trained hands can bring comfort and relief. Both Western and Eastern medicine started with good observation and the application of highly sensitive and experienced hands. Medical science went on to discover much more, but at its core is still the application of sensitive, healing hands.

Physical therapy (called physical rehabilitation when used with animals) in its many forms is the extension of this ancient art and science of trained medical hands, with the addition of an improved understanding of anatomy and disease processes and the application

Eternal Puppy

of modern technological advances, resulting in greater healing potential of this treatment modality. Here are some forms to consider.

MASSAGE

Many ancient civilizations developed their own systems of massage therapy to be used for various medical conditions. The word "massage" comes from the Arabic word *mass*, which means "to press." Massage is a therapy with ancient roots and is still very beneficial today. Recent scientific studies have shown that therapeutic massage can have positive effects on connective tissue, muscles, the lymphatic system and the circulatory system. It can help bring about pain relief as well as reduce distress and anxiety.

As an example, one consequence of pain is for the muscles to respond in a muscle spasm in an attempt at self-protection. Unfortunately, the muscle spasm can go on to produce more pain by reducing circulation and encouraging inflammation and by impinging nerves, all of which causes a self-perpetuating vicious circle of pain and muscle spasm. Massage can help by reducing the tense muscle tone, which reduces the soreness and tenderness, reducing the feedback.

Another example is that following injury or surgery, connective tissue can form adhesions between various tissue layers, which can cause pain and impede function. Massage can help soften adhesions, maintain local flexibility and promote functional recovery.

Therapeutic massage is different from simple stroking and rubbing that all of us do with our dogs (a practice which is rewarding and pleasurable to our dogs as well as to ourselves). Therapeutic massage must be directed towards a specific purpose with the goal of promoting a detectable psychological or physical change. Therapeutic massage should only be performed by a trained practitioner (trained in both massage and the use of massage on animals) under the direct supervision of a veterinarian. While massage therapy is often beneficial, there are conditions under which a dog should not receive massage therapy, and incorrectly performed massage techniques can cause pain and harm. Canine anatomy is different from human anatomy, so the practitioner should have specific training with animals in addition to training in massage techniques. The practitioner should be sensitive to your dog's needs, and the experience should be relaxing and pleasurable to your dog. Once the practitioner is attuned to the needs of your pet and able to assess your skill and sensitivity, they may instruct you in some techniques that you can do at home.

ACUPUNCTURE

Acupuncture is another medical art steeped in ancient wisdom but containing advanced scientific principles. Acupuncture has been practiced in China for at least 4,000 years.

Acupuncture can be used for relief from pain, muscle tension, inflammation, and neurological impairment. It is very beneficial as a therapy that can be used synergistically with other forms of medical treatment, such as drug therapy or surgery, and also can be used in cases in which there are serious risks of side effects from drug therapy or surgery, allowing for reduction or elimination of the need for these forms of treatment. Veterinary acupuncturists tell of cases in which euthanasia was being considered because the animal's level of pain could not be sufficiently resolved with medication or surgery but was alleviated to an acceptable level with the addition of acupuncture.

In arthritic dogs, acupuncture has been shown to improve the ability to move, and this allows for a strengthening of the muscles around the arthritic joint. This allows for more balanced movement and reduction of pain.

Whether acupuncture is used as a primary or secondary treatment really varies according to the individual. The degree to which any pain management regimen, including acupuncture, is beneficial, is highly individual and depends on the patient and his own responsiveness to specific treatments. These individual levels of responsiveness may change over time as well.

Acupuncture consists of inserting tiny needles at specific points on the body. These points are locations at which there is an increased concentration of capillaries and lymphatic vessels or nerves. The acupuncture points are connected in pathways along the body called channels or meridians. Acupuncturists treating animals should be veterinarians with specific training in acupuncture. According to traditional Chinese medicine, energy circulates though the meridians, and blockage of that energy flow can result in disease or dysfunction. The system of stimulating or sedating various points is designed to bring the body back in balance.

It is interesting because, although numerous studies have shown that acupuncture is effective, it is still not known for certain how and why it works. Although there are several theories currently in favor, no single theory explains all the effects seen in acupuncture. This is exciting because it means we have a lot more to learn, which may ultimately result in an increased refinement and more benefits from this science.

PHYSICAL REHABILITATION

Physical therapy for people has been shown experimentally to be of benefit to athletes, to those recovering from injury or surgery and to geriatric patients, so perhaps it should come as no surprise that research is now showing these techniques to be of benefit for pets as well. Physical rehabilitation for dogs offers a wide variety of techniques aimed at reducing pain, improving muscle tone, restoring strength and flexibility to an injured limb and improving overall strength, flexibility and balance. Appropriate physical rehabilitation can greatly improve your dog's well-being and often reduces the need for pain-relieving medication.

A veterinary physical rehabilitator will start in the same way that a human physical therapist does—by doing a complete analysis of your dog's movement and condition, combined with a review of the medical history. Then based on their findings, they will institute a treatment plan designed at strengthening muscles, improving flexibility or relieving pain that is individualized to your dog and his needs.

You may be familiar with some of the techniques used on dogs if you yourself have ever been to a physical therapist. These techniques include range of motion and stretching exercises, therapeutic exercises designed to strengthen specific muscle groups and improve flexibility, therapeutic applications of warmth and cold, electrical stimulation therapy, ultrasound and aquatic therapy.

However, because a dog has different anatomy and can't verbalize discomfort, these techniques should only be applied by someone who has an understanding of the physiology and anatomy of a dog as well as training with the specifics of these techniques. Applied incorrectly, these techniques can cause discomfort or harm. Applied correctly they can be of great benefit for recovery from surgery and osteoarthritis and help maintain muscle tone in a geriatric dog.

AQUATIC THERAPY

Aquatic therapy is a physical rehabilitation treatment that is particularly beneficial for older dogs. The water simultaneously supports the body and provides passive resistance to movement that can build strength and flexibility. Numerous techniques can be applied to a dog while in the water that can build strength in specific muscle groups and improve mobility. In addition to therapy pools, several forms have been developed specifically for dogs, including an underwater treadmill (the treadmill is underwater, not the dog). Preliminary studies have shown that dogs with arthritis have displayed an improvement in mobility with twice-a-week underwater treadmill exercise.

It is important to remember that, even though swimming and other water exercise are wonderful for older dogs, safety concerns must be considered as well. It is always possible for an older dog to drown, especially if it is debilitated or overly tired. Just as with a human toddler, older dogs should never be in the water unattended, and flotation devices are highly recommended.

THE PSYCHOLOGICAL FACTOR—FEAR OF PAIN

A dog who has been in pain for some time or has recently experienced severe pain may be very reluctant to attempt movement that is associated with a bad experience in the past. There could be a lot of fear and learning involved that blocks the dog from using its body to its fullest and to recover. One facet of physical rehabilitation therapy is a recognition that a dog might be experiencing fear of using its body in specific ways, which can sometimes be as big a hurdle to overcome as the actual physical problem itself. But gradual application of physical rehabilitation methods, gently applied with encouragement and rewards, that encourage movement in gentle and protected ways can get a recovering dog over the hump, both mentally as well as physically.

While it is important that physical rehabilitation is performed by a trained professional, once your dog's condition and response to treatment have been evaluated, you may be given exercises that you can work on at home to help your dog's progress. Good communication between you and your dog's health care provider are the cornerstone for success.

20 Home

A Safe and Comfortable Environment

Look around your home and observe how it is arranged for your comfort and safety. Are there handrails installed next to your stairs at the right height for you to grab if you slip? Do you have chairs around your dinner table so you can sit comfortably when you eat? Are the coffee cups and silverware in cupboards and drawers you can easily reach? Do you have a soft comfortable chair for you to relax in while reading or watching TV? Is your mattress the right firmness for your back? Do you have your favorite pillow and blanket on your bed? When it is chilly at night, do you have an extra blanket you can throw on? Are there traction strips in your shower?

Now take a "dog's eye view" and look around your home. Think about what it is like for your older dog to live there. Are there steep, slippery stairs? Does your dog have warm, comfortable places to sleep? Are there places for him to nap in quiet areas? Are you asking your dog to do a bone-jarring jump in and out of the back of your vehicle when he goes places with you? There are a myriad of things you can do to make your home more comfortable and compatible for your older dog.

A HOME FIT FOR A DOG

Consider where your dog sleeps. An older dog is less tolerant of the cold. Not being warm enough can disturb his sleep (and may lead to his disturbing yours). Make sure that where your dog

Eternal Puppy

sleeps is warm and away from drafts. Consider getting a heated dog bed. (For safety reasons, it is not a good idea to use a heating pad designed for people—get something designed for pets with the correct temperature range and safety features.) If your dog is an outdoor dog, now is the time to bring him into the warm, dry indoors. Even if you live in a warmer climate, your senior dog will be more comfortable indoors.

In addition to being warm enough, is your dog's sleeping area cushioned enough? Consider getting orthopedic padding or perhaps a waterbed made for dogs.

Think about mobility issues. If your dog sleeps on your bed or couch, has it become more difficult for him to get there? Is it a big jump up and down? Can you add steps or a ramp to make this easier? Jumping in and out of the car can also be difficult, but there are portable ramps designed for dogs that can make this easier.

Stairs were designed with the human leg in mind, and they can become increasingly difficult for an older dog to negotiate, especially if he is developing arthritis. Look at both the outdoor and indoor stairs. If it is difficult for him to negotiate the stairs leading outdoors to his potty place, this could be a factor if a house-soiling problem develops. Ramps with good traction can be a big help. If stair climbing becomes too difficult (and it is not possible for you to help by carrying or assisting him), keep everything he needs on a single floor of the house.

Traction can be an issue that makes your dog reluctant to move in some locations. If he slips, this can be painful on tender joints. Imagine how comfortable you would be walking on an ice rink all the time. Plus, as he ages, his proprioception sense isn't always what it used to be, making him even less comfortable on slippery surfaces. If you have linoleum or wooden floors, add something such as carpet runners to give him more traction. Add traction strips or carpet to your stairs. Keep your dog's toenails trimmed—by raising the toes, long nails stretch the ligaments in the backs of the legs, making it less comfortable to walk. Walking on nails instead of foot pads also reduces traction. (If you can hear the toenails clicking on the floor, his nails are too long. He should be walking on the pads of his feet, not on his nails.)

Consider where he eats and drinks. If he prefers to eat lying down, you might give him a padded surface such as a carpet remnant on which to lie. If he prefers to eat standing up but has neck pain, he may appreciate a raised pet-food bowl. Are there water bowls at convenient locations?

As the old Beatles song goes: "I get by with a little help from my friends." Give your friend what he needs to get by, get around and get comfortable.

RUNNING INTERFERENCE FOR YOUR OLDER DOG

"Mommmmmmmm! Sammy won't play with us!"

As your dog ages, his interest in doing things with the rest of the family may change. He may want to do everything he did before, so he will try to join in and keep up, but end up lagging behind or hurting himself. These can be signs of medical problems (like arthritis and hypothyroidism) that need attention.

However, he may simply not want to play as he did before. Of course, you should always rule out physical issues that might be sapping his strength and enthusiasm, but he just might not be able to play as he did before and, like any senior citizen, may need his sleep and a more relaxed environment.

That means that it is up to you, his primary caregiver, to run interference for him against those who may not understand his needs, be they other dogs, a playful but irritating kitten or puppy or even your children. Children, particularly, may have a hard time understanding why their playmate doesn't want to play with them anymore. Your old dog may be spending a lot of time worrying about how to avoid a boisterous child who doesn't respect that his joints hurt or that he needs to get more sleep.

This is where you need to step in. You need to explain to your children that Sammy is old and may not want to play. You need to teach your children to respect an old dog's need to sleep undisturbed. In fact, an old dog who is deaf and startled awake may respond in his disorientation by lashing out at a perceived threat, which could be a child. So teaching your children how to behave around your senior dog is an important lesson for everyone's well-being. You may need to have only supervised contact between the dog and children. This is actually a great opportunity for your children to learn the value of kindness and empathy as well as to respect others and showing respect for their elders (the dog may not be older chronologically, but is older physically). These are lessons that will benefit them for their entire lives. Children can also be your best eyes and ears to alert you to changes in your old dog, once you have explained to them that he is aging and needs them to look out for his welfare.

Running interference may also mean that your older dog needs a place to eat away from the younger dog and a place to sleep where other activity in the home won't disturb him. Don't let the younger dog knock the older dog over in his enthusiasm to get to the door.

If the younger dog is not respecting the older dog, let them outside to potty separately. When they are playing, watch to make sure that the younger dog doesn't get too boisterous; step in to calmly intervene, if necessary.

When out and about with your older dog, be on the lookout for things that might compromise his safety. At places such as dog parks, be sure to intervene if another dog is getting too boisterous with your oldster. Remember also that when having fun, playing with you or another dog, your dog will forget about his aches and pains, and overuse will cause a flare-up that results in pain later (particularly if he has arthritis). An older dog also has a higher risk of heat stroke because his cooling system doesn't work as efficiently as it used to. It is up to you to institute rest periods and make sure that he keeps cool and stays hydrated.

Remember that if your older dog gets separated from you, a dog with hearing loss (most older dogs will develop some hearing loss to some degree) will not be able to hear and return to you when you are calling for him. If he is off leash and wanders a little bit away from you, he can become seriously lost. If there is a chance your dog with hearing loss could get out of your sight, put a bell on his collar so that you can find him, because he might have a hard time finding you. He also can't hear traffic and other things that are a danger to him. (So you may not want to let him out of your sight or off leash at any time.) Likewise, a dog with reduced visual ability can run into objects that are left in his regular pathways. Keep objects out of his way. If you must rearrange the furniture, help him to learn the new route. Keep your visually impaired dog away from the pool or garden ponds.

Be careful that running interference for your dog doesn't mean that he gets sequestered and left out of activities. You still want your senior dog to be part of the family and to enjoy the affection and mental stimulation that this brings. For example, you might keep his preferred sleeping location, even if it is in the middle of the living-room floor, but put a safety gate or exercise pen around him, thus keeping children or other animals out of his space. Yet you also want to be attentive to and aware of the needs of your old dog. Maybe he would prefer a new sleeping area that has more peace and quiet. After all, we all need that from time to time. Pay close attention to your senior dog.

21 House-soiling

An Accident Waiting to Happen

From time to time, an older dog may have problems with house-soiling. The first thing to do when this starts happening is to schedule an appointment with your veterinarian. There are a number of disease conditions that can result in house-soiling, including diabetes mellitus, urinary tract infections, bladder stones, intestinal upset, hormonally controlled incontinence and canine cognitive dysfunction, to name just a few. No amount of training or environmental management can correct a problem if it has a medical origin, while appropriate medication usually can.

Before your appointment, take a few moments to consider other factors. Are there other changes you've observed in your dog, like his drinking more water, asking to go out more frequently or attempting to urinate without success? When, where and how do the accidents happen, i.e., is there a pattern? After your veterinarian has ruled out medical causes, you can start looking around your home for potential problems that your dog may be having.

Has there been a change in the household routine? Did you change your work schedule? Have you added a new puppy (or other pet) to your family? Is your Aunt Matilda visiting? Did you injure yourself and take a hiatus from your evening walks with your dog? Did your child just start crawling, walking or running? Changes such as these may change the dog's potty routine, as you may no longer be able to take him out at the times to which he is accustomed. It may also become more difficult for you to pay attention to your dog's requests to be taken out if you are busy with other things or adjusting to a new schedule yourself.

Eternal Puppy

WHAT THE DOG'S NOSE KNOWS

Dogs may live in the same world that we do, but how that world appears to them is quite different from how it appears to us. One reason is because dogs have a much more acute sense of smell than humans do, and dogs use their sense of smell to a much greater extent than we do. The olfactory information that dogs gather from the environment all around them may be beyond our ability to perceive or even imagine. Our visual system allows us to see a diverse and complex landscape, while dogs' scent capability allows them to smell a diverse and complex landscape of scents. Not only is a dog's ability to perceive scents 100,000 times greater than ours, but scents also are a different kind of stimulus because of the way they dissipate with time.

How much a dog's sense of smell changes with age is not known, nor is it known how much other factors may result in a reduced sense of olfaction. Even if an older dog's sense of smell is somewhat diminished, it still will be a major way that he interacts with his environment.

Because we don't use our noses to the degree that our dogs do, we may not realize how much they utilize their sense of smell. Your dog may be using scents as a major way to navigate in your home, especially if his other senses are diminished. He may be finding his feeding area because of the food scents there and the door to the back yard by recognizing the smells on the doormat or in the doorway. So if you clean heavily or rearrange familiar things in the home, your dog may have difficulties in the same way that you might have problems if a familiar landmark were suddenly removed. You would come to rely on new ways to navigate, but initially this change could throw you for a loop.

Scent cues also can be trained; an example is if you add a specific scent to the area where your dog eliminates and praise your dog when he eliminates in that location. Now you have a signal that you can utilize to indicate a proper elimination location. However, you will need to use trial and error to find what scents and at what dilution are attractive to your dog. He will pay more attention to a novel scent, but if the odor is too strong (remember how much more sensitive his nose is than ours) it will act as a repellent.

Many diseases affect a dog's scent capabilities. Diseases such as Cushing's disease and hypothyroidism can greatly reduce your dog's ability to perceive smells, although this is a temporary loss and will resolve when his medical problem is treated. Several canine viruses, such as canine parainfluenza, will render a dog temporarily unable to smell; vaccinated dogs will have a quicker recovery. Often-overlooked conditions such as tartar on the teeth and gingivitis can also interfere with your dog's scenting capability, but studies have shown a rapid return to normal scenting ability after a dental cleaning.

When a dog starts house-soiling, one thing to consider is whether or not he can smell where he should be eliminating. Is he confused due to changes in his environment that may have altered the scent profile in his living space? Has a medical condition affected his ability to smell? If he is relying on scent to tell him the proper place to potty and he can't smell where that is, it would be a lot like you trying to find a restroom with a blindfold on.

Sometimes there can be a bullying issue going on in the household of which you are unaware. Is there a dog, cat or child preventing your older dog from getting to his goal?

Consider access issues with regard to your dog's potty place. Is your dog arthritic, making negotiating the back steps painful? Did a snow storm make it icy outside? Does your new neighbor have a nasty big dog who growls at the fence? Is your dog showing signs of anxiety when outside and wanting your company? Put yourself in your dog's paws and see what you can do to make things easier for him.

Correct whatever problems you find. If your dog is having mobility problems, consider installing a ramp to help him get in and out of the house. If he has sensory problems, better lighting or odor cues (using a prepared scent to indicate a pathway) might help. If your dog has a medium-length or long coat, you may want to trim a "potty path" in the hair to aid in ease and cleanliness.

If the problem still does not improve sufficiently, then review and refresh your dog's house-training (accompany him outside and rein-force desired behavior). Figure out your dog's duration of control and

CAN YOUR DOG ASK TO GO OUTSIDE?

Sometimes the loss of a companion dog can lead to the other dog's house-soiling. While there is no doubt that pets are able to grieve, if a dog starts house-soiling after the loss of a companion, it may be because he doesn't know how to ask to go outside and has been relying on the other dog to do the asking. And this problem could occur even at times when there isn't the loss of a companion.

I didn't believe this when I first heard of it, so I started watching my own dogs. Lo and behold, I discovered that Rosie never asks to go outside or come inside. We routinely let the dogs out in the morning and evening. However, if the dogs go out at any other time, it is always Raven who does the asking. And when I go to the door to let out Raven, up pops Rosie, "Johnnie-on-the-Spot," trotting out after him. And while Raven scratches and eventually barks at the door when he wants to come back inside, Rosie stands behind him, gently waving her plumed tail. Perhaps from her perspective, Raven is some sort of magician—ask and ye shall receive, bark and the door shall be opened. She has never needed to learn the same magical door-opening skills because Raven is always there to do it for her.

Alas, Raven does not need to go out in the middle of the night, but Rosie has a terrible combination of a tender stomach and a desire to eat all kinds of garbage that her stomach won't tolerate. When Rosie has managed to "get into something she shouldn't have," we wake in the morning to find a soggy, smelly mess on the living room floor. "Why didn't she wake me up and ask to go out?" I always wonder, as I clean up the dastardly deed.

Well, now I know…she doesn't know how. When the urge from her dietary indiscretion hits her in the middle of the night, she is stuck. Raven doesn't need to go out, and Rosie has no idea how to ask. Raven asks, Rosie follows, every single time. If Raven were no longer here or Rosie needed to go out at an increased frequency, house-soiling would no doubt be the consequence, simply because she doesn't know how to ask.

the frequency with which he needs to go out and be proactive: take him outside before he has the chance to have an accident. Other solutions may be returning home more frequently for walks, installing a dog door or having a neighbor or dog walker stop by to take the dog out when you are not at home. The basic concept is to revert to a house-training routine similar to that of a puppy; however, it is important that you use no punishment for accidents, not even scolding.

When the dog is at home alone, you may need to keep him in a more restricted area. Use baby gates or ex-pens, not a crate (which is too restrictive for an older dog, especially if he has arthritis), and make sure the area is safe and comfortable. Doggy diapers might not be a bad idea if your dog tolerates them.

Clean up messes promptly using enzymatic and odor-reducing products designed for pet accidents so that the odor doesn't attract your dog to continue using that location. Remember, don't blame your dog. Don't scold your dog. Don't punish your dog. This is not something that he can help. Realize that there can be more than one problem occurring at the same time and that different problems can develop over time. If you continue to see changes in frequency or type of behavior, have your dog checked again for medical causes and then re-examine your home environment.

22 Brain Power

Enrichments for Mental Health

We used to think that a reduction or loss of mental capacity was simply part and parcel of the normal aging process of living beings. And it is true that adolescents and young adults, whatever the species, are in a steep phase of the learning curve. When you think about it, this makes sense from an evolutionary standpoint—this is the time when animals are learning the skills necessary to stay alive and are striking out on their own to raise families. By the time animals reach maturity, this stage of rapid knowledge acquisition has passed, but they can still learn and refine the ability to use what they have learned. It's like making a basket: first you lay in a basic solid structure, then you weave the finer material in between. But what about the aged? Often our picture of the senior's mental skills is one of a basket that is becoming worn and unraveling in places.

Even though we associate increasing age with a reduction of mental capacity, we all know of lively human seniors who stay mentally active and productive well into their geriatric years. They may have some physical challenges to deal with, but it seems that their mental basket stays tightly woven. What this suggests, then, is that a significant reduction of mental ability with age is not a given, so we want to know what can be done to influence mental ability. Are there steps we can take to keep our dogs' mental abilities largely intact as they age? Recent research is offering a tantalizing look into this and revealing that intervention strategies do exist.

THE BENEFITS OF ENRICHMENT

An interesting and ongoing series of experiments is studying the effects of brain aging on learning and memory in old dogs. In this set of experiments, senior Beagles, who had lived their lives in a research colony, were divided into four experimental groups. The dogs in the control group were maintained in the standard manner for dogs at this research facility. The other three groups were experimental groups: one group of dogs was given a diet fortified with several forms of antioxidant vitamins and several nutraceuticals that are mitochondrial cofactors; another group of dogs was given an enriched environment; and another group received both dietary and environmental enrichments. The four groups were tested in controlled settings to assess their learning and memory skills at the start of the experiment. They were then tested a year later, when the three experimental groups had experienced a year of enrichments. The four groups of older dogs were also compared with a group of younger dogs, half of which had also received enrichments for a year.

Not surprisingly, the younger dogs performed better than the older dogs in most tasks that required rapid learning and the ability to apply complex problem-solving. At the start of the experiment, the older dogs all learned at a similar rate and style. However, by the end of the year, the differences between the groups were notable. Each of the groups that had received one form of enrichment, either dietary or environmental, showed an improved ability to learn. It was interesting that these two groups were similar in their level of improvement. However, when the two types of enrichment—dietary and environmental—were combined, the effect appeared to be synergistic, with improvements in learning exceeding that of the dogs who had received only one type of enrichment and approaching the learning ability seen in the younger dogs.

The dogs were continued in these experimental groups; research data was generated for at least an additional three years and the results appear to be holding—the enriched groups continued to apply more flexible learning styles and greater learning abilities than the non-enriched dogs. And now that the study's younger dogs are entering their senior years, those that received long-term enrichments are showing remarkable benefits. And, although the experiments were not designed to look at lifespan, another intriguing observation is that the enriched dogs appear to be living longer.

An experiment done by a different research group in England studied aged dogs living in homes. These dogs showed improvements in the behaviors associated with canine cognitive dysfunction when administered a commercially available dietary nutraceutical supplement with similar characteristics to the formulation used in the Beagle studies (the product used for this experiment is currently not available in the US).

There is a lot that a pet dog owner can take home from these studies. Although we can't stop time and we can't stop the biological aging process, these studies clearly show that even after the age-related changes have started, there are still benefits in environmental and dietary enrichment. These studies suggest that a dog at any age will benefit from enrichment, even when the enrichment is started in the dog's senior years. And because research is showing that enrichments started in younger dogs has ongoing beneficial effects as the dogs enter their senior years, this also suggests that the sooner you start, the better. Starting at any time will have benefits, but keeping your dog mentally active and providing proper nutrition should be the goal for maximum lifelong benefits.

A stunning discovery from the first study mentioned is that the environmental enrichment proved to be as powerful as the dietary enrichment and that the most improvements were seen when a dog received both types of enrichment. And while there are theories about the possible beneficial mechanisms of dietary enrichment, we still don't know how environmental enrichment brings about its positive effects in the brain. But we do know that there is an effect, and this is where we as pet owners may be able to have a big impact. What were the enrichments used in these studies?

Dietary Enrichment

According to the free-radical theory of brain aging, nerve cells in the brain suffer greater oxidative injury with increasing age. As the mitochondria in the cells of aging animals become less efficient at burning fuel, they produce more damaging by-products; further, the aging body has a reduced ability to break down these damaging by-products, called reactive oxygen species or toxic free radicals. So the dietary interventions in these studies were devised to combat both of these problems.

First, alpha-lipoic acid and L-carnitine, compounds that work as mitochondrial cofactors (molecules that help mitochondrial enzymes function), were added to the diet. Second was the addition of nutrients high in antioxidant activity (chemical compounds that break down reactive oxygen species); these were given both as vitamins and as natural sources in small amounts of vegetable and fruit preparations. It is known that antioxidants work synergistically, so the addition of a number of natural sources is likely a superior form of supplementation than just adding several vitamins.

Although these mixtures of nutrients have shown a beneficial protective effect on physiological as well as behavioral aspects in dogs, as well as in other species of animals, the optimal mix of nutrients and the relative contributions of each of these substances are not completely known. This is an area of new and rapidly evolving research in the US, Canada and in Europe.

Environmental Enrichment

Environmental enrichment in growing animals has been shown to play a notable role in the early development of neurological abilities. Experimental studies have shown that animals raised in deficient environments have reduced brain development and lack complexity of neurons and branching between neurons. In the most dramatic of the experimental results, Nobel Prize–winning researchers David Hubel and Torsten Weisel in the late 1950s/early 1960s showed that sensory input to the visual system was necessary in critical periods of early development for the parts of the brain that recognize and process visual images to develop properly. So the effects of early enrichment on brain development have long been known. What made the studies on older Beagles particularly interesting was that enrichment was shown to have a positive effect even when started after the dog was in adulthood.

Some intriguing studies have been done on research mice who have genetic alterations, making them susceptible to neurodegenerative diseases (for example, mice who develop beta-amyloid plaques like those seen in people with Alzheimer's disease and dogs with canine cognitive dysfunction). The studies have shown that an enriched cage environment slowed the progress of these diseases at a cellular level. Studies are now ongoing to determine by what mechanism environmental enrichment produces what appears to be a neuroprotective effect.

An additional finding of the aforementioned Beagle study was that those dogs that were raised in conditions of greater enrichment as puppies (raised in groups and exposed to outdoor runs) had a greater response to the experimental enrichment conditions almost a decade later. The enrichments given to the mature dogs in these studies were toys that were rotated frequently, regular walks outside and participation in the mental challenges of continued positive-reinforcement learning studies. Although little is currently known about what enrichments have what effects, these results clearly suggest that using the brain is a way to help keep mental abilities intact. What these studies further suggest is that not only *can* you teach an old dog new tricks but you also *should* teach an old dog new tricks in addition to practicing what he already knows.

ENVIRONMENTAL ENRICHMENT SUGGESTIONS

There have been no field studies yet looking at the effects of specific environmental enrichments in older dogs in homes, so the best we can do is to extrapolate from the laboratory findings. However, the rapid development and acceptance of dog trainers using humane and mostly positive-reinforcement training methods has given us some clues to what can be utilized in a home setting, hopefully with positive benefits. Any environmental enrichment activities that you do with your dog will need to be designed with a careful consideration of your dog's current condition, preferences and abilities, which will change with age. The bottom line, however, is that these activities need to be within his ability to succeed and they need to be enjoyable to him. If they are frightening, frustrating or too physically demanding, they will not be enriching. Likewise, you want to set the mental activities that you do with your dog at a level of difficulty where he will be challenged, engaged and ultimately rewarded by completing the tasks.

The Great Outdoors

Nature is a source of endless complexity that is much appreciated by our dogs. Nothing in our man-made environment can compare to the scents blowing on a breeze, the changes of texture beneath the feet, the varied pathways and the myriad of "calling cards" left by other dogs. The outdoors is a sensory wonderland for a dog, full of unpredictable variety and things to explore. And just as it is true that "Don't hurry, don't worry and don't forget to stop and smell the roses" is good advice for us, so it is true for your dog. Don't be so goal oriented as to where you are planning on going and how long it will take that you fail to see the enriching activities that may be presenting themselves to your dog along the way. A dog with reduced sight and hearing will still enjoy catching up on the tapestry of scents that he will find while on his walk. Remember, a dog's sensory experiences may be totally outside our perceptual abilities and may not be something we are likely to notice. Just as you may want to stop and listen if you hear a beautiful song, so your dog wants to stop and smell the roses—or whatever he finds so interesting on the fire hydrant.

Toys

Toys are only toys if your dog interacts and plays with them; otherwise, they are just "objects in the environment—" interesting, perhaps, but not giving the value and stimulation of play. Find toys that your dog likes and engage him in play if he does not spontaneously interact with the toys. Food puzzles are rewarding in that they invite interaction by challenging the dog to figure out how to release the treats you put inside. Remember that some toys can be harmful if chewed to bits and swallowed. Be sure to check the toys for signs of wear.

No (Mental) Retirement

Working and competitive dogs are often retired from work or competition when their physical abilities diminish and make them less capable of performing their tasks. But there is a lot of benefit to keeping a dog active at the tasks he is used to, at whatever level he is capable of, if only to keep his mind active. The trick is to let the dog have challenges and successes that are in line with his physical abilities, to prevent him from getting hurt or frustrated.

What do I mean by that? If, for example, your mature dog has done agility but can no longer safely run the courses or compete, consider continuing to let him practice on the easy courses. Lower the jumps, walk instead of run and stay beside your dog to help him balance if he goes on obstacles such as the A-frame (which should be reduced to the least steep setting). But let him go through the course, whatever he can safely do. The purpose here is not to get a fast time but to let your dog continue to do what he loves doing at a pace that he can handle.

Similarly, an older hunting dog may no longer be able to leap into cold water and retrieve ducks, but you can create a hunting scenario for him in a less physically demanding setting. Your senior dog will enjoy the opportunity to do his job, even if it is retrieving decoys in the back yard.

Don't put your dog into situations in which he could get hurt, overextend himself (especially if he has arthritis, as this can cause a painful flare-up) or be frustrated to the point that he gives up because of a challenge that is too difficult for him. It is up to you to manage the difficulty and monitor the ability level of your dog and to give him challenges that are stimulating and ultimately rewarding. Make sure that he gets a chance to "win" sometimes to keep him motivated and interested.

Positive Reinforcement

When properly done, positive-reinforcement training holds the same enjoyment and challenge as solving a puzzle does, but in this case the puzzle for the dog is figuring out what the trainer wants him to do, what earns the reward. An easy way to do positive-rein-forcement training is with clicker training, or the "click-and-treat" method. Click-and-treat positive-reinforcement training best simu-lates the experimental challenges that researchers used with the Beagles in the enrichment studies and allows you to do a number of interesting and varied learned tasks. There are many trainers who can teach you how to clicker train if you haven't done it before; learning how to train this way will be mentally stimulating and enjoyable for you as well. As evidenced by my senior Rosie's first attempt at clicker training, an older dog can learn clicker training later in life provided that it is modified for the dog's needs.

If your dog is going deaf, you will need to check first to make sure that he can hear the clicker. If he cannot, you will need to either find a signal that is in an audible frequency range for the dog or use a different "bridging stimulus" (the scientific word for the click) that he can perceive. It doesn't have to be an auditory stimulus. A competent positive-reinforcement clicker trainer will have a lot of tricks in her bag to individualize training to the needs of a specific dog. When I took gray-muzzled Rosie through her first ever click-and-treat class recently, she had no difficulty picking up on the technique and seemed to enjoy the training sessions a great deal (after all, it involved undivided attention and yummy food; what could be better?). However I observed that after a period of intense learning, she would grow weary and need to take a nap (this seemed to be associated with intense mental activity, rather than physical activity). Be sure to watch your dog for signs that he has had enough and needs to take a break.

Remember that an older dog should never be coerced, threatened or intimidated into performing a task and should never be trained using a choke, pinch, prong or shock collar.

MEDICAL MANAGEMENT

Many diseases first manifest themselves as changes in behavior. If your older dog is showing behavioral or personality changes (disorientation, social-interaction changes, sleep/wake disturbances, anxiety), then a trip to your veterinarian is in order. You need to make sure that some other disease is not adversely impacting your dog's quality of life. If it turns out that your dog is starting to develop canine cognitive dysfunction, there are medical treatments available that can modify the disease course and improve clinical signs in addition to dietary and environmental enrichment. The sooner you start treatment, the more normal brain tissue you can preserve.

If your older dog is showing increasing signs of anxiety, this is cause for concern. Some researchers now suspect that anxiety is a part of canine cognitive dysfunction syndrome and may be an indication that deleterious brain aging (beta-amyloid plaque formation) is occurring.

Other health issues and stressors in the home environment can also be playing a role (i.e., something that has recently changed in your household that may be contributing to anxiety). Sometimes setting up a video camera while we are gone for the day may identify a new stressor of which we were unaware.

Treating the underlying medical issues that may be contributing to anxiety should be your first management strategy; for example, a pain-management protocol for a dog that is experiencing pain, more frequent access to potty locations for a dog with failing kidneys or medication specifically targeted to slow cognitive dysfunction. In addition, with older dogs who are showing anxiety, you should try to keep their environment as consistent and predictable as possible because older dogs are more sensitive to the effects of change (they don't handle change as well). You can teach "settle" and relaxation exercises and have a comfortable "settle" location. (Teaching a dog to settle is a technique where you use gentle, positive training methods to teach a dog to relax.) You can ask your veterinarian for a reference to a behaviorist to help you with these issues and to teach you how not to increase your dog's anxiety. If none of these things helps, then you can discuss anxiety-reducing medication with your veterinarian.

Remember that anxiety is not under conscious control and that the behaviors that an animal may engage in when anxious are not deliberate. Be careful to not fall into the trap of "blaming the victim" when dealing with an anxious older dog, as this will only increase your dog's anxiety.

VARIETY IS THE SPICE OF LIFE

One interesting aspect of mental life is that the more you live it, the more life you have to live. When it comes to keeping the mind healthy, variety really is the spice of life. The "mental basket" that your dog has woven with what he has lived, experienced, learned and can still learn does not need to fall into shabby disrepair. Within this basket he carries the stuff of life: his personality, his emotions, his memories and his ability to adapt and learn. Help him keep it strong by giving him a steady supply of strands to weave into the basket.

23 Food Puzzles

The Fun of Foraging

What if you had no wants; what if all your needs were met? If you had a lovely place to sleep and tasty food was placed before you at regular intervals? No cares, no worries, nothing you have to do. Does that sound like paradise? Well, maybe for a day. Or two. Or even a couple of weeks. But how long before you would get bored and start looking for something to do, some way to make a difference?

The status of "pet" is actually a very new situation for dogs. Although experts disagree about exactly how long ago dogs were domesticated, we know that they have been with us for more than 10,000 years. For most of those years, dogs had something to do all day long, every day. In their role of helpers of humankind, dogs were bred for specialized jobs. Terriers were ferocious hunters of vermin; sporting dogs assisted us in the hunt, some pointing, some retrieving and some baying as they ran through the woods. Our security was dependent on guard dogs who sounded the alarm if strangers approached. Herding dogs used their speed and intelligence to help shepherds care for their flocks. Dogs pulled sleds, followed trails and rescued drowning victims from the grip of icy seas.

Nowadays few dogs have jobs. Although that may seem like a favor we do our dogs, a luxury, it is not. It is actually a matter of your dog's health, both mental and physical, to keep him actively engaged in his environment and with something to do.

Boredom is a health and welfare concern that we often don't consider. Animals have many ways of dealing with boredom. A young

animal that is bored may engage in self-stimulating activities. He may vent his frustration with repetitive behaviors, destructiveness, constant barking—basically bouncing off the walls. Scientists who study animal behavior and welfare report another face of boredom, which is when the animal will decrease his activity and lie around sleeping or dozing, being listless and apathetic.

It is necessary that an old dog get adequate rest, but reduced mental and physical activity from boredom can have serious health-related consequences. Lack of physical activity is a risk factor complicating arthritis and geriatric muscle wasting, both of which can lead to your dog's reduced ability to get around. Lack of mental activity is a risk factor in the development of cognitive dysfunction. One of the worst things you can do for an older dog is to leave him with nothing to do and no challenges to meet.

THE DRAWBACKS OF EASY MEALS

In the 1970s a scientist named Hal Markowitz embarked on a novel experiment at the Portland Zoo in Portland, Oregon. Zoo cages were boring, he observed, and the animals had nothing to do all day and did nothing to earn the food they were eating. This was a shame, he thought, because he knew that in the wild, these animals spent a large part of their day and all their intelligence and cunning getting food from the environment. But in the zoo, food came to them twice a day in stainless bowls on the floors of barren cages. So he set about to improve the way that the animals could interact with their environment and use their intelligence and innate skills to get food.

Dr. Markowitz's designs were simple yet elegant and designed to simulate the skills that animals needed in the wild to get food. For example, gibbons are a small species of ape that spend a majority of their time brachiating in trees. To work for their food in the zoo environment, the gibbons would pull a lever on one side of the cage, then swing on the bars over to the other side of the cage to a second lever and then receive their food.

Some fascinating things were observed when the animals were allowed to work for their food. Food was never withheld from the animals; each day they would be given the same amount of food in a pan as what they were earning from the feeding paradigms. But the animals would leave the food on the cage floor while engaging with the machines to earn the same kind of food. In other words, when given a choice, these animals chose to earn their food.

Other benefits occurred as well. The zoo animals were more active and engaged. Aggression in the small living groups decreased. The animals looked more "alive." When you think of it, this makes sense. There is a joy in doing what you can do well.

How long does it take your dog to eat his food? While some dogs are nibblers, many dogs take about 30 seconds from the time the food bowl is placed on the floor to empty it and lick it clean (OK, that may be an exaggeration—or maybe not!). Now, after all that anticipation of a meal, the day stretches endlessly out for the dog, with hours of boredom waiting for that one minute of gleeful gulping.

And how hard was it for your dog to get his food? Did he have to use his intelligence to work for it? Depending on your feeding ritual, your dog may remind you a few times and dance around when the food bowl approaches, and maybe even sit on command as it is lowered, but that really is about it when it comes to difficulty.

Feeding from a bowl is quick and easy for us to feed and for the dog to eat. But is quick and easy what your dog really needs?

In the 2005 book *Mental Health and Well-being in Animals*, edited by Franklin D. McMillan DVM, Markowitz and his coauthor Katherine Eckert wrote in a section called "Giving Power to Animals":

"In the course of their evolutionary history, animals have become specialized in their abilities to hunt and gather food. When we deprive them of the opportunity to exercise these abilities, we essentially rob them of their natural existence, their source of pride, their sense of well being…How can we expect animals in our charge to be 'mentally healthy' if nothing they do matters?"

Having a stimulating environment is not simply a matter of adding sensory stimulation or asking the dog to do a meaningless task (although these things can help and are part of environmental enrichment). What scientists are now considering is that possibly the best enrichment for an organism is to give it something to do that has meaning, something that accomplishes a task that is valuable to the organism.

FUN WITH "FIND IT!"

Although I had frequently read about hiding food for your pet to search out as a form of environmental enrichment, I had never tried it myself. So I decided to see how this worked on a practical basis at home with my own three dogs, two of which, Raven and Rosie, are seniors.

First I prepared my dogs' morning meal in the usual place in my kitchen/dining room, with my three eagerly anticipating chow hounds at my feet. After preparing the food, I put the dogs out of the room. I hid Raven's bowl, putting it on the floor but beside a chair in a location to which he was unaccustomed. I then let only Raven back in the room. He ran to the counter, where he had seen the food being prepared, and waited. I think he was in momentary disbelief when, instead of putting his bowl down, I walked away from the counter and told him in a cheerful voice to "find it."

I walked slowly around the room once or twice until he followed me, and then I walked on a pathway that took me a few feet from his hidden bowl. It was funny to see Raven's nose catch the scent. It looked as if his nose dragged him into the corner, where he found and ate his food. It took Raven two more days at feeding times to catch on. Then he would take off trotting around the room, searching for his food as soon as I walked away and said "find it."

After Raven was finished eating, I picked up his bowl, put him out of the room and hid Rosie's bowl. I let Rosie into the room to find her bowl. She kept looking at me, even when I walked her near the hidden bowl. It took her about two more days than it took Raven to figure out what I was asking of her; I had to place the bowl closer to her usual eating spot and move it gradually away. She didn't initiate search patterns at first. She needed more hints (such as my going and standing near the bowl but not looking at it). Now that she "gets it," it is clear to see how much she enjoys the game. She trots around the room with her tail wagging in wide delighted sweeps as she searches for her food. Now I can put her food in distant locations, too and she finds it just as quickly as the other two.

My young dog, Spring, had played the "find it" game with tennis balls before, so making the switch to looking for food was easy for him. Interestingly, after all three dogs have been fed and are let back into the room together, Raven makes the rounds sniffing and finds where the other two dogs' bowls had been hidden. He can even find the tougher locations I use for the more experienced dog, Spring. He sniffs around each hiding location, looking for crumbs.

What I've learned from this is that you can't just hide the food and expect the dog to figure out that he is supposed to go looking for it. After all, we spend quite a bit of time trying to teach our dogs not to take food that they can smell in our garbage cans and on our tables. We have taught them that their food comes in bowls in the same location each day. When we start moving the feeding location, it takes a bit of time and help for a dog to shift gears.

You need to lead the dog gradually through what he needs to do. Do not place the food in difficult locations that are hard to find and may cause the dog to give up. If your dog is having trouble catching on, move the bowl to an easier location and give more hints. Always place the bowl where the dog can reach it when he finds it so that he gets an immediate reward for a successful hunt. Do not place the bowl in "forbidden" locations (such as on the table, as we've already taught him not to help himself to food from the table). If you have more than one dog, you will need to let each dog hunt individually; otherwise, the dog who is fastest will get all of the food.

My dogs are very happy when looking for their food. They are active and using their minds and bodies to solve a puzzle. If your dog is not happy to play this game, don't do it with him. Make sure that this is not a burden for him, but a joy. Some dogs may have difficulty moving. Some older dogs are made anxious by changes in routine and may find this challenge distressing. But for those who like it, it is an easy way to provide some entertainment to your family, both the four-legged and two-legged members.

ONE SOLUTION: FOOD PUZZLES

One solution is to use food puzzles at some of the feeding times. You can also leave food puzzles with your dog during the day so that he has something to do when you are at work. In addition to food puzzles, you can play hide-and-seek with your dog's food by placing the food in various locations and letting your dog find it.

Food puzzles help in a great many ways. They are goal-directed mental challenges. Hunger is a great motivator, and succeeding in getting a morsel of food is an instant reward for solving the puzzle. Food puzzles keep the dog active, engaged and interested in what he is doing, providing a self-rewarding mental challenge.

I heard of a Golden Retriever who figured out a novel way of getting the food from his Buster Food Cube, a cube-shaped food puzzle that dispenses kibble as it is rolled around on the floor. This innovative Golden Retriever carries the Buster Cube to the top of the stairs and then lets it go so that the cube bounces down the carpeted stairway, releasing kibble as it rolls. Then he simply walks down the stairs behind it, gobbling up the kibble before carrying it back up the stairs for another run. In addition to showing a novel problem-solving skill, he is getting exercise and is engaged with his environment.

Food puzzles also slow down the eating process. When food is eaten, there are a number of different chemical signals sent from the stomach to the brain, telling the brain to shut off the hunger signals. A signal of satiety tells the animal to stop eating; it has had enough. Some of these signals take a while to engage. So if the food is quickly wolfed down, the animal will still be getting hunger signals and will still feel hungry even after eating adequate amounts of food, because the satiety signals haven't all reached the brain yet. This drive for the animal to eat more even though it has had enough is a major factor behind weight gain (this holds true in humans, too). Slowing down the rate of eating gives the satiety reflex time to work, allowing the dog to feel full, well fed and more satisfied. This is especially important if your dog is overweight and on a weight-loss program with reduced calories. The dog will feel more satisfied by food that he actively acquires and is more slowly eaten.

Using Puzzles Effectively

Food puzzles vary in their difficulty, and some can be adjusted to change the level of difficulty. When introducing a food puzzle to an older dog who might not have used one before, it is essential to start with an easy puzzle and, if adjustable, set it to the easiest level. Some dogs are better at object play than others, both because of their experience and because it comes more easily to some breeds. If your dog is slow at catching on, help him out by engaging him in play and demonstrating that the food does come from the toy. Initially, you can introduce the toy just before regular feeding time when your dog's food motivation is high. But be very careful that your dog is actually learning the technique and getting the food, and not giving up because it is too difficult. Once your dog gets the hang of it, you should vary the food puzzles that you give him so that they stay challenging for your dog to solve. Also, be sure to get food puzzles that are appropriate for the size of your dog. A food puzzle that is too large for a small dog will be frustrating, while a food puzzle that is too small for a large dog can be a choking hazard.

Make sure, if you start using food puzzles, that the amount of food your dog gets every day stays constant. If your dog is already at an ideal weight, you don't want him to gain weight because you are giving him extra food (and thus calories) in the food puzzles, nor do you want him to lose weight because you gave him a portion of his daily food in a puzzle that was too hard for him to solve. Measure out how much food your dog should eat for the day and put a portion of it in the puzzle. At the end of the day, make sure that the food was actually consumed. If you have more than one dog, you will want to use food puzzles when you are around to supervise so that the dog that solves the puzzles faster doesn't get all the goodies. Food puzzles will take you a bit longer than just dumping the food in a bowl and will add a bit of complexity to your job (I consider stuffing the food puzzles as my own form of cognitive enrichment and dexterity training). Some food puzzles can also be messy, but this should not stop you from using them. Instead, use some creative problem solving. For example, you can give the puzzles outside when the weather is acceptable. One recommendation I have heard is to place the puzzle in a large bowl; however, I tried this with Rosie and she problem solved her way out of what she must have considered a restrictive setup, picking up the puzzle and taking it to a different location, on my living room rug. You can put the dog in an ex-pen or crate with his puzzle, but remember that you are trying to stimulate movement, so be careful about limiting the dog's movement too much. Or you can simply choose food puzzles that are less messy (for example, a ball that dispenses kibble rather than a bone that you fill with peanut butter).

Have a variety of puzzles on hand and vary what you put in them. Depending on your dog's personality, he may interact with some better than others. Not only do food puzzles give more mental and physical stimulation for your dog but they also add a level of enrichment to our lives. Choosing which puzzle to use, filling it and then watching your dog solving problems and actively "working" for his food can change a routine task such as feeding into a source of pride and entertainment.

Puzzles to Try

Different food puzzles use different strategies for solutions. Different dogs, based on their breed (or mix) and personality, may prefer some types to others. These are companies that all produce a variety of interactive toys to try, and here are some examples of their food puzzles.

Kong: This company makes great food puzzles as well as other interactive toys. The most popular are the tough rubber toys that are shaped a little like the Michelin man. Kongs are great throwing toys because they bounce in unexpected ways; additionally, the space inside the Kong can be filled with food. To get the food out (depending on what you put in it), the dog needs to nose or paw the toy around or hold it with his paws and lick the inside. You will want to match the size of your Kong to the size of your dog. The Kong company even publishes a brochure with recipes and advice on stuffing the toy with food.

Canine Genius: This company makes a toy called a Leo, which looks a lot like a large rubber bowling pin. Dry food is placed down the narrow neck, and the dog must roll the toy around with his paw or nose to get morsels of food to roll out. If you have more than one of these toys, they can be stuck together to make a more complex food puzzle. The Leo comes in different sizes for different-sized dogs and is also a great throwing toy.

Ourpets: This company distributes both the Buster Food Cube and the Molecuball as well as a number of other innovative interactive dog toys. The Buster Cube is a hard plastic cube that has compartments inside. You fill the toy with dry dog food and, as the dog rolls the cube around with his nose and/or paws, the food rattles around inside until some drops out. The level of difficulty (how easy it is for the food to drop out) can be changed by twisting a dial. There are two sizes of Buster Cubes for small and large dogs. The Molecuball is a hard rubber toy that looks like several balls stacked in a pyramid shape. Dry food is placed inside, and the dog gets the food out by rolling the toy around. The Molecuball comes in mini, small and large sizes.

Premier Pet Products: Premier Pet Products has a line of interactive toys called Busy Buddies. One of the favorites of this line is called the Twist-n-Treat and looks like a purple clamshell or UFO. You can put either kibble or moist food inside and then screw the top and bottom together (more tightly closed means more of a challenge to get the food out).

Premier Pet Products also markets the MannerMinder, which is a training tool invented by veterinarian Sophia Yin. This is not an interactive toy, but rather a remote-controlled kibble dispenser. It can be used similar to click-and-treat training, only the dog goes to the dispenser for the treat rather than coming to you. Although marketed for correcting barking at the door, MannerMinder is a versatile tool for stimulating activity and problem-solving.

24 The Other Dog

The Good, the Bad and the Ugly

Those of us who love dogs rarely have only one in our lifetimes. As often as not, we have more than one dog at a time. What then of the "other dog"? What are the special considerations regarding the other dog in the home of a geriatric dog?

Dogs are social animals and live in family units. When a dog comes into our home, we become his family and so, too, do the other pets in the family. You know the old saying, "You can choose your friends but you can't choose your family"? The same is true for our dog—we choose his family for him.

Just as you don't necessarily get along well with everyone you know, dogs can have personalities that clash with each other. The difference is that you can attempt to avoid contact with people with whom you clash, whereas a dog has to share his home with the canine companions that have been chosen for him, regardless of how well he gets along with them.

In addition, any relationship between dogs can change over time. The relationship between dogs can be good for the entire time they are together, or it can go from good to ugly or from bad to better. However, because an older dog is generally at a physical and sensory disadvantage, and a deteriorating relationship between an older dog and a younger one can result in the injury, even death, of the older dog, we need to be aware that this potential is present so that we can protect against it.

Eternal Puppy

THE PUPPY

A puppy comes to us full of energy, exploration and desire to play and so can be a wonderful enrichment for an older dog, provided the puppy minds his manners. However, puppies do not come fully equipped with good manners any more than human children do. In dog culture, it is up to those dogs around the puppy—first his mother, then his siblings and finally his adult aunts and uncles—to teach him proper manners and communication skills. A dog who doesn't learn these lessons as a puppy is at a serious disadvantage in getting along with other dogs later in life.

Your older dog may regard the introduction of a puppy into the household with everything from maternal glee to something resembling Mr. Wilson's reactions to Dennis the Menace. Part of that will depend on the personality of the older dog; the other part will depend on how astute your puppy is at picking up social cues and how much he has already learned from his mom and siblings. This is why you should purchase a puppy from a knowledgeable breeder who keeps the mother and litter together for the appropriate amount of time, during which the puppy will receive necessary socialization and education.

When a puppy comes into the home of an older dog, it is the older dog who takes over the lion's share of the work of entertaining and teaching canine communication skills and manners to the young upstart. Don't assume this is a good situation for the older dog, even if he appears to enjoy the role. Depending on his health and tolerance level, he may need timeouts from the youngster. In addition, if your older dog is not up to taking on the job of "puppy-etiquette instructor" and lets the puppy get away with bad manners, the lesson that your youngster will be learning is how to be a bully. Regardless, it is important that the older dog be given adequate rest as well as food and attention for which he doesn't have to compete.

If the puppy is pestering the older dog and the older dog growls or vigorously puts him in his place, as long as the puppy is not getting physically hurt, don't rescue the pup. This is how an older dog teaches a younger dog to mind his manners. If you admonish the older dog, the puppy will learn that when his human mommy is around, he can turn the tables on the older dog and will use that to his advantage.

Remember that you are the one in charge. If the puppy is not respecting the older dog, then a timeout for the puppy is in order. If the overzealous puppy is hurting or harassing your older dog, then obviously you need to intervene, separate the two dogs and allow only supervised contact. Not only does this protect your older dog but also teaches your puppy not to be a bully.

THE GOOD

Dogs are social creatures. When their human family is gone for the day, it is nice for dogs to have another of their kind to keep them company. The appropriately respectful younger dog can provide social and physical stimulation, keeping the older dog on his toes in both mind and body. The dogs can play and enjoy life together. They can sleep together and groom each other and be each other's family.

I frequently play the game of "throwing the Border Collie" for Rosie, my older Collie cross. She is not particularly interested in chasing balls herself, but she loves to chase Spring, my five-year-old Border Collie, while he chases balls. So throwing the ball for Spring exercises both dogs, each in his or her preferred way, and gets a lot more activity and play from Rosie than throwing the ball just for her would accomplish. And late in the evening, Rosie likes to hold Spring down with her paw and clean his ears. Rosie needs to remind Spring to "cool his jets" from time to time when he is overzealous and getting in her space, but he generally listens to and respects her.

THE BAD

The bad is a dog that doesn't respect the space of the older dog. This is a dog who is constantly running into or over the older dog and shoving the older dog away from food, toys and opportunities for affection. If the older dog is battling illness or a painful condition such as arthritis, he may start doing his best to avoid his obnoxious housemate because of the pain that these encounters cause him. The younger dog's boorish behavior can be seen as a result of his basic personality, poor socialization, attention-seeking behavior or resource guarding (or a combination of these). The younger dog is probably a bit lacking in confidence, or he may not know gentler modes of play interaction and so will have to be taught how to "play nice."

After getting tired of being battered and bruised, your older dog may withdraw for his own protection. You may see an older dog who plays less, doesn't come to you as often for attention and sleeps in out-of-the way places; he may actually be trying to make himself as small a target as possible. Obviously this is not an acceptable situation for the welfare and enrichment of the older dog. Once we become aware that this is happening, we can make management changes that allow the older dog to have his own space, play and attention, and we can control the interactions of the two dogs (e.g, putting a leash on the younger dog).

THE UGLY

There have been horrifying situations in which a younger dog has savagely turned on a geriatric dog and seriously injured, or even killed, the older dog. "Younger dog" does not necessarily mean a puppy or adolescent; situations like this may happen with dogs who have been living together successfully for years. Why does this happen?

We do not know exactly why, only that it sometimes does. We can only make an educated guess as to what our dogs were thinking. We have to acknowledge that dogs are capable of perceiving things that we are not, so we may never know what would trigger this behavior in the younger dog, only that it might be something outside our perceptions and perhaps outside our realm of understanding.

Although some people like to use dominance theory to explain this (a younger dog usurping the position of the older dominant dog), a lot of what is attributed to dominance theory is based on an incomplete, oversimplified, romanticized or even fictionalized understanding of dominance structure and behavior in wolves. Dominance challenges usually involve wolves of similar age and vigor and may not apply to many of the cases in which aggression against older dogs is seen. Some other explanations are more plausible. Here are a few possible explanations:

The Dynamic Is Different

It has been observed by some behaviorists that when an attack by a younger dog occurred, the older dog often was experiencing some type of a health crisis. In a case presented at a behavior seminar, two dogs had gotten along famously for years and then suddenly one dog, without warning, started attacking the other. It took videotaping the dogs for the explanation to be revealed: just before the attack, the dog who was on the receiving end of the aggression showed a subtle change in behavior that was determined to be a minor seizure. What was surmised was that while in the state of the seizure, the dog suddenly became unrecognizable to his canine companion, who then attacked this stranger who had taken over his friend's body. Controlling the seizures in the one dog eliminated the problem.

What this tale reveals is that dogs are very aware of subtle changes in their companions and can react in unexpected ways. We know that dogs can perceive things that we cannot; there are dogs who work as seizure-alert dogs for people with seizure disorders and dogs that have shown an ability to detect cancerous cells. So it is not inconceivable to suppose that a dog who is ill may not be recognizable, in some way we do not perceive, to the other dog in the home.

Therefore, if a similar situation occurs between your dogs, you may want to consider the possibility that the younger dog is attuned to something that we cannot perceive and have the health of your older dog checked. Of course, a trip to the vet is always warranted if your older dog is injured by the younger one.

Loss of Social Signaling

Dogs communicate with each other through subtle changes in posture and movement. In many cases, these signals are so subtle and rapid that we miss them. A quick turn of the muzzle of one dog toward the other with a momentary direct look, followed by the receiving dog's slightly dropping his head, dipping his ears and taking a step back, was the message "you're crowding me" from the first dog with the response of "sorry, I'll get out of your way"—all of which could have taken place in a second or two. Big movements and dramatic postures are not necessary and are rarely used between dogs who are familiar with each other. They don't need to shout when a whisper will do.

Specific postures have specific meaning to dogs. A fixed direct stare and stiffly held body is a posture indicating aggressive intent. This "frozen" position often precedes an attack; it is a warning that the dog is readying himself to attack.

But, in a case of mistaken identity, an old dog who is stiff from arthritis and perhaps with visual impairment may exhibit the same "I am getting ready to attack you" posture without intent, which can then be misconstrued by another dog. Or the other dog may signal something to the old dog that just isn't received. If the other dog is anxious or has a lack of confidence, he may go on the offensive—attacking before he is attacked, from his perspective. The attacking dog is likely responding out of fear and has no way of understanding that the communication skills of his buddy are impaired by visual and physical disability.

Infirmity Triggering a Predatory Response

A pack of wolves hunting elk may start by driving the entire herd of elk. After the herd starts running, the pack will zero in on one animal to pursue. If you look at the animal they choose, you'll notice that the wolves target the prey showing some sign of infirmity: it may have a slight limp or is not running as fast or as fluidly as the others. For this reason also, researchers who work with wolves that are kept in captive packs often do not let anyone with any form of infirmity enter the wolf enclosures. A sign of illness or weakness is a potential trigger for a predatory attack, even on a well-known caregiver.

Wolves are not dogs, and dogs are not wolves. You can only extrapolate dog behavior to a certain degree from wolf behavior because there have been more than 10,000 years' worth of changes with domestication. Yet the dog evolved from the wolf, and we will never know for sure how much of the ancient behavior patterns are still present. Many dogs are capable of demonstrating predatory behavior, a trait more common in some breeds than in others.

There exists the likelihood that the movement of an infirm geriatric dog could trigger a predatory attack from another dog, even another family dog. However, be aware that it may not be the other dog in the family that reacts in unexpected ways to your geriatric dog. When out on walks or at the dog park, be on your guard for other dogs who might regard your older dog as prey. Be ready to intervene and remove your dog from a situation of potential danger.

With other forms of aggression, the attacking dog may bark or growl prior to attacking; however, predatory aggression happens without sound (the predator would not want to signal to its prey that an attack is imminent). Most documentaries on predatory behavior will dub wolf growls—do a wolf "voice-over"—into what is generally a silent process. Unless you recognize the characteristic posture (stalking and fixed focus on the prey), a predatory attack will occur "without warning." So stay vigilant.

MANAGING PROBLEMS BETWEEN DOGS

Because we don't know for sure which triggers the younger dog is responding to, there is no way to prevent the triggers from occurring. The only safe step to take if a dangerous situation is developing or aggression has occurred is preventing the contact between dogs that can result in aggression incidents.

Although some retraining might be possible in mild cases, the consequences of a training failure are so grim that your primary goal must be protecting your older dog from injury. The objective of management has to be structured in a way that doesn't allow the potential of a fight to occur. This also protects you, because people can get hurt trying to break up a dogfight.

If aggression has occurred, or hostilities and bullying are increasing against the older dog, the dogs should never be left alone together, even in the back yard. Feed them in separate locations out of each other's sight, then pick up the food bowls when they are done. Do not let the younger dog in the same location as the older dog when he is trying to eat. If they are in the same room, they must be supervised, and the younger dog must be kept under physical control at all times. That means the younger dog must be crated, tethered, leashed or muzzled with a basket muzzle when in the presence of the older dog (and even a basket muzzle may not be enough protection if the younger dog is adept at knocking the older one over). Be sure that each dog gets adequate attention when they are by themselves, and try to not increase jealousies when they are together. You may want a consultation with a qualified animal behavior consultant; ask your vet for a recommendation.

Once an injury has occurred, vigilant management of the dogs will be required around the clock for the remaining days of their living together. Although this may seem difficult, it is not fair to the older dog to subject him to even a small risk of attack, nor should your older dog live in terror for what remains of his life.

Conclusion

The first gift we give our dog is our love. This is a shared gift because our dog gives us love, companionship, support and laughter and makes our lives richer in immeasurable ways. It is with great gratitude that we have been allowed the privilege of loving a dog.

The second gift we give our dog is his life. Although his mother gave birth to him, we have been his caregiver from the time he came into our home. We have fed and groomed and played with him, keeping his needs in our minds and his life in our hearts. We have given him a home and a family. Through our love and attention he has thrived and grown old. This book has been about that journey, how we honor our older dogs by giving them the gift of continued life and health when time starts to fray them at the edges. And caring for them as we have done has helped give our lives meaning. By giving care, our lives have been enriched.

With preventative medicine, a full and active life, good nutrition, exercise, mental stimulation, weight control and early intervention for medical problems, our eternal puppies can live a rich life and bring us much joy. But time marches on, and we can't stop the clock altogether.

The third gift we can give our dogs is a good death. This doesn't seem right at first—if we love someone so much, why would giving death be a gift? However, we have to realize that death will come whether we want it to or not. And the death that nature brings can sometimes be neither kind nor painless. Letting nature take its course with our dogs can often be a cruel and difficult pathway to walk. Therefore it becomes a great gift to our beloved dogs that we can bring death in a manner that is kinder and more loving than nature can manage. We can give our dogs a good death. After giving them good lives, giving them a good death is the most loving thing we can do.

This is another gift with shared consequences, because as our dog crosses the threshold of the living world, the way in which we experience that turning point will flavor the memories of his life for us.

GOOD GRIEF

When we are approaching the loss of our pet, it is not uncommon to experience feelings of fear. How we handle that fear can have a bearing on how we care for our dog and ourselves, so it is important to consider. However, at some point in the process, when we come to the realization that we are going to lose our pet soon or have lost him, we then experience grief. Fear comes with the anticipation of loss; grief comes with the realization of loss. Both the fear we feel when approaching that loss and the grief we feel when experiencing loss are important to understand. Ultimately what we are striving for is to reach a state of good grief.

It is hard to think about grief as good—this is one of those emotions that we generally spend our lives trying to avoid. We have a basic need to stay connected with those we love and to feel that connectedness as part of our internal compass. Losing someone we love separates us from that feeling, and we experience the loss with sorrow and a sense of helplessness. We grieve. But while grief is unavoidable and inevitable, what we really want to work towards is good grief.

Why? Because in order to truly grieve for our pets, in order for the human-animal bond to be honored, in order for all of the wonderful memories of our pets to have meaning, we have to have healthy grieving. If our grieving is weighed down with guilt, fear and anger, then the memories of how we lost our pet will overshadow the happy memories of our pet's life with us and how much joy we had together and could forever taint the relationship with our pet that lives on in our hearts. And that would be a double tragedy: to lose our dog and to lose our ability to remember our dog with joy. To truly honor our dog, we have to go through good, healthy grief. Living in a state of fear and sorrow will prevent us from getting to that place in our hearts where we can enjoy the treasured memory of our beloved pet.

Approaching the loss of our dog, who has been one of the family, also touches another basic emotion: fear. Everyone who loves his pet fears losing the animal, and it is particularly frightening when the threat to the pet seems out of our control. But it is important to recognize the influence that fear is having on us and to combat that fear. Fear can hamper our efforts to help our pet, ourselves and our families and can interfere with finding the state of good grief.

THE FIVE FACES OF FEAR

Imagine for a moment that you are walking down a wooded pathway and suddenly find yourself face to face with a grizzly bear. As the bear rises, roaring to his hind legs, you will feel deep fear from the primitive part of your brain, the part that strives to keep you alive. Your heart will pound and your extremities will go cold as blood is routed to your muscles to prepare you for doing what is necessary to save your life. At this point, you will react the same way as any other mammal on the face of this planet would; depending on the situation and your personality, you will respond to the fear in one of five ways:

Fleeing, or running away, is one reaction to fear. When something frightening approaches, running from what we fear is a common reaction. Freezing is another reaction to fear. Frozen into immobility, we become less of a target. Fainting seems counterintuitive as a survival tactic, but since predators often are keyed into movement, perhaps our becoming unconscious means that the predator will go off after something else. Fainting also stops the overwhelming flood of sensations and stimulation. Some people and animals will fight, going immediately on the offensive and striking back at the threat. Or the fight may come after fleeing is no longer a feasible option. Fiddling also seems initially counterintuitive. Instead of directly confronting the object of his fear, the animal or person may throw up a web of distracting behaviors. A dog confronted by an aggressive dog ready to attack may suddenly find something interesting to sniff in the bush. A student confronted with a test question that he can't answer may whistle, tap his pencil on the desk or bite his fingernails.

When confronted with the fear of losing our pet, we might engage in psychological versions of these behaviors. When confronted by something that scares us, we may refuse to face the situation (flee), be unable to make a decision (freeze), feel completely overwhelmed (faint), get angry and argue or snap at everyone around you (fight) or let other things distract us from the matter at hand (fiddle). All of these are perfectly normal human behaviors and all are results of our fear when we are faced with a serious health crisis or risk of losing someone we love. We need to know that these potential reactions are present and learn to recognize them in ourselves. When we react out of fear, we may not be capable of making the best decisions for ourselves and for our dogs.

Eternal Puppy

It is perfectly normal to experience fear when we consider serious illness or the loss of our dog. We fear the unknown, we fear sorrow, and we fear the feeling of isolation and loss that we see in our future without our eternal puppy. Like any other fear reaction, this fear can make our hearts pound and our hands go cold. But to do the best for our dogs, who depend on us, we have to acknowledge the fear's presence and then go on. There will come a time when your dog will have taken all he needs of this life and is ready to move on. The most loving thing that we can do at that point is to not let our fears hold our dogs in lives that are filled with pain and misery. Our love for our dogs must be more powerful than our fear of their deaths. In this way we can let go at the time that is the best for them. This is the last gift that we can give them—gentle deaths.

Dogs live in the here and now and with the memories of their past. They do not project into the abstractions of the future as we do. They don't imagine what death is like or dwell on what their existence will be like when they leave you. They have no dread or fear of death; they only desire an avoidance of pain. They face death, this great immensity, with innocence and acceptance.

The decision to euthanize is difficult, and deciding when to euthanize can be even harder. Our challenge then is to find that time, based on our understanding of our dog and advice from our veterinarian, when life can no longer be enjoyable for your dog and the future for them will only be worse. But, if we wait for that moment in time, we have waited too long and let them experience that unhappiness. Without a crystal ball, we can only do our best. Sometimes the decision will be taken from our hands or the signs that this is the right time are crystal clear. Other times the "best time" is hard to determine, but if we keep the needs of our dogs and the needs of our families firmly in mind, whatever decision we make will be the best that can be made.

Because they live in their memories and the here and now, they are aware of their feelings of pain, and most dogs will be aware of our fear and sorrow of our impending loss. They, who should be comforted and gently supported through this transition, may instead be reflecting the fear and sorrow that we are projecting. And as tuned as they are to our needs and emotions, they may be experiencing a desire to comfort us. They may be struggling to say to us "I can tell you are sad—what can I do to help?" while having no idea what it is that is causing our sorrow. Or they may be already reaching for that unknown where all their pains are relieved.

INCLUDING THE CHILDREN

Another gift that our dog gives us is the ability to allow our children to develop an understanding of death and to learn healthy grieving patterns. This is a gift that will give our children preparation for their future, which will always, at some point, have some loss and sorrow in it. No matter how much we desire to protect our children, they will experience the death of a friend, a family member and eventually us, their parents. What they learn from us at this time will be lessons that they will hold with them for the rest of their lives.

Unfortunately, in our desire to protect our children from all things that may cause them pain or sorrow, some parents will try to shield their children from the reality of a pet's death. Sadly, such attempts can sometimes backfire to make the situation worse for them. As examples, consider the child whose mother, wanting to save her from the trauma associated with the loss of her pet, takes the dog to be euthanized while the child is in school, without telling her in advance or letting her say goodbye. The mother later finds out that her child is now doing poorly in school because she is always worrying about who else she is going to lose while she is at school. Or the example of the child who was told that the family's dog was put to sleep because he was sick, and now starts to fear that if he becomes sick, his parents will get rid of him, too.

Realize also that some day it will be our old age and death that our children will be experiencing. Isn't it better that they learn the lessons of patience, kindness, consideration, letting go and grieving now, rather then when we are no longer around to help them?

How best to handle the death of the dog depends on the age of your children, their personalities, their relationships with the dog and the communication patterns you have established in your family. Don't be afraid to let them see that you are sad. Allow them to honestly express their feelings without judgment, and honestly share yours with them. If needed, enlist the help of a grief counselor who has experience with children.

GRIEF IS A JOURNEY

Grief is often described as involving five stages: denial, anger, bargaining, depression and acceptance, based on a model developed by Dr. Elisabeth Kubler-Ross 40 years ago when she studied people receiving catastrophic news. But this model is now thought by some to be too simplistic—some people don't go through predictable stages or experience the stages in a predictable order, and the model leaves out other common expressions of grief, like shock and disorganization. Grief is a process as much as anything. It is the way we experience loss and sorrow and then recover from that sorrow. It is a multi-dimensional and complicated process, and the way that any individual experiences this will be unique to that person. Grief can have a physical as well as emotional component.

Now, although grief is very individual, it is also not uncharted territory—there are many resources to which we can turn for help, for ourselves, for our children or for other family members. There are many good books and resources available to help people understand the process they are going through and the effect that grief will have on them. Many people will go through the process quickly. Or a person may think that he has reached a stable healed state, only to have something trigger his memory and bring up unexplained tears months or even years after losing his dog. The important point is not to get stuck. Grief is a journey, and you need to keep walking up the trail until you reach the place where peace comes to your heart. There may be rest stops along the way, places where anger and guilt and sorrow may reside. We will visit these places because they are part of the journey, but don't move in and live there. Get back on the path and continue moving toward peace. If we are having trouble letting go of anger or sorrow, we don't have to go it alone. There are guides who can help us get back on the path if we have become lost. There is no shame in asking for help or directions if we are lost or spinning in circles. It does not honor the life of our dog if the grieving becomes unhealthy for us.

FROM ETERNAL TO ETERNAL

When we come to the place of peace, we will find the last gift that our dog has to share with us. Now our dog will never leave us. He will be in our hearts for the rest of our lives. He will have gone from being our eternal puppy in life to being our eternal puppy always in our hearts. And what greater gift can we give each other than that?

Index

Index